Advanced Web Applications and Progressing E-Learning 2.0 Technologies in Higher Education

Jean-Éric Pelet
ESCE International Business School, France

A volume in the Advances in
Higher Education and Professional
Development (AHEPD) Book Series

Published in the United States of America by
    IGI Global
    Information Science Reference (an imprint of IGI Global)
    701 E. Chocolate Avenue
    Hershey PA, USA 17033
    Tel: 717-533-8845
    Fax: 717-533-8661
    E-mail: cust@igi-global.com
    Web site: http://www.igi-global.com

Library of Congress Cataloging-in-Publication Data

Names: Pelet, Jean-Eric, 1976- editor.
Title: Advanced web applications and progressing e-learning 2.0 technologies
  in higher education / Jean-Eric Pelet, editor.
Description: Hershey PA : Information Science Reference, [2019] | Includes
  bibliographical references.
Identifiers: LCCN 2018049692| ISBN 9781522574354 (hardcover) | ISBN
  9781522574361 (ebook)
Subjects: LCSH: Education, Higher--Computer-assisted instruction. |
  Education, Higher--Effect of technological innovations on. | Education,
  Higher--Computer network resources. | Internet in higher education.
Classification: LCC LB2395.7 .A37 2019 | DDC 378.1/7344678--dc23 LC record available at
https://lccn.loc.gov/2018049692

This book is published in the IGI Global book series Advances in Higher Education and Professional Development (AHEPD) (ISSN: 2327-6983; eISSN: 2327-6991)

British Cataloguing in Publication Data
A Cataloguing in Publication record for this book is available from the British Library.

All work contributed to this book is new, previously-unpublished material.
The views expressed in this book are those of the authors, but not necessarily of the publisher.

For electronic access to this publication, please contact: eresources@igi-global.com.

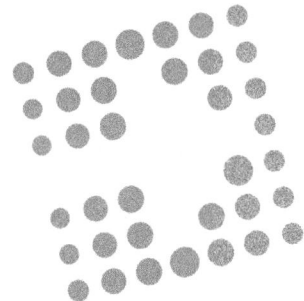

Advances in Higher Education and Professional Development (AHEPD) Book Series

ISSN:2327-6983
EISSN:2327-6991

Editor-in-Chief: Jared Keengwe, University of North Dakota, USA

MISSION

As world economies continue to shift and change in response to global financial situations, job markets have begun to demand a more highly-skilled workforce. In many industries a college degree is the minimum requirement and further educational development is expected to advance. With these current trends in mind, the **Advances in Higher Education & Professional Development (AHEPD) Book Series** provides an outlet for researchers and academics to publish their research in these areas and to distribute these works to practitioners and other researchers.

AHEPD encompasses all research dealing with higher education pedagogy, development, and curriculum design, as well as all areas of professional development, regardless of focus.

COVERAGE

- Adult Education
- Assessment in Higher Education
- Career Training
- Coaching and Mentoring
- Continuing Professional Development
- Governance in Higher Education
- Higher Education Policy
- Pedagogy of Teaching Higher Education
- Vocational Education

IGI Global is currently accepting manuscripts for publication within this series. To submit a proposal for a volume in this series, please contact our Acquisition Editors at Acquisitions@igi-global.com or visit: http://www.igi-global.com/publish/.

Titles in this Series

701 East Chocolate Avenue, Hershey, PA 17033, USA
Tel: 717-533-8845 x100 • Fax: 717-533-8661
E-Mail: cust@igi-global.com • www.igi-global.com

Table of Contents

Detailed Table of Contents

Chapter 1

Liliana Mata, "Vasile Alecsandri" University of Bacău, Romania

The aim of the chapter is to analyze the most recent studies on attitudes towards the internet in higher education. In recent years, there have been studies that focus on investigating the attitudes of students and teachers towards the use of internet in higher education. Thematic content analysis was used to investigate the studies conducted in the period 1998-2018 to measure the attitudes towards the internet. The thematic content analysis of the studies determined establishing the following three categories: 1) studies focused on investigating attitudes towards the implications of internet use; 2) studies based on identifying the relationship between attitudes towards the Internet and different variables; 3) studies centered on exploring attitudes of different members of higher education. The analysis of studies over the last 20 years contributes to determine the action directions for initiating new studies in this field.

Chapter 2

Francois Acquatella, Telecom Paristech, France
Valerie Fernandez, Telecom Paristech, France
Thomas Houy, Telecom Paristech, France

This chapter aims to suggest a new conceptual framework by presenting a view of the main disruptive strategic trajectory implemented by a particular model of training platforms. It aims to participate in the understanding of the dynamics of training platforms strategy through the analysis of the Cousera case. The iterations of this platform with a market under construction can be read as a strategy to bring out new proposals and value networks. Finally, the authors discuss the "drivers" of future changes in the MOOC market.

Chapter 3

Miguel A. Sánchez-Acevedo, Universidad de la Cañada, Mexico

When new educational games are developed for teaching languages, a set of ideas or intuitions about how students can gain more knowledge are used; however, few of them are based on a solid theory or substantiated with linguistic research. This chapter presents a brief review about second language acquisition theories; describes the importance of recovering, maintaining, and transmitting indigenous languages; and analyzes efforts made for enhancing bilingual education. Serious games are presented as an alternative for learning indigenous languages, and guidelines to develop serious games implementing second language acquisition theories are proposed. Finally, a discussion about challenges and future trends in recovering, maintaining, and transmitting indigenous languages is presented.

Chapter 4

Xavier Inghilterra, Université de Lorraine, France

This chapter is based on a research that has been focusing on social sharing device effects and on students' practices of collaboration, communication, and mediation. The author has analyzed the recurring temporal split between academic environment and students' sphere in a context of distance learning. The goal is to understand the origin of the collaborative process of collective apprentice which is illustrated in the communities of apprenticeship outside the academic institution. A netnographic observation was conducted with Bachelor and Master's degrees in a private training center. The author assumes the information and communication socio-technical devices participate in the horizontalization of student practices. The author has highlighted the paradox of these learning communities, which are, unwittingly, in a process of social domination by having choosing a priori a decentralized structure. In light of the social criticism of the time, the observation reveals that digital technologies cause a temporal acceleration.

Chapter 5

Anna Liza Daunert, University of Mainz, Germany
Linda Price, University of Bedfordshire, UK

As digital technologies become an integrated part of our everyday lives, we need to consider how to harness their educational potential in higher education. However, despite considerable research into the use of technology in higher education, there still remains a gap between what teachers might perceive as valuable digital curriculum design and what students perceive as valuable digital learning experiences. One key component is how ubiquitous technologies can be harnessed to support students' learning experiences. In this chapter, the authors examine the implications of students' preferences and usage of u-technologies for designing teaching and learning curricula that positively exploit technology. This chapter builds on the research conducted by Daunert and Harteis that investigated pre-service teachers' preferences and experiences of u-technologies. The results of this cross-sectional survey are considered in relation to designing curricula in digital environments.

Chapter 6

Pedro Isaias, The University of Queensland, Australia
Paula Miranda, Polytechnic Institute of Setubal, Portugal
Sara Pífano, Information Society Research Lab, Portugal

The abundance of evidence of Web 2.0's value in educational settings has provided both educators and researchers with prized information about the application of a panoply of technologies. The experience that this evidence portrays can be used to meaningfully direct teachers in their own ventures of Web 2.0 implementation. In online learning environments, any collaboration between the students must occur with the support of technology, so it is fundamental that technology functions as an enabler, maximizing the opportunities that online settings offer, and that students can tap into those technologies to enhance their learning experience. This chapter focuses on the implementation of Web 2.0 within higher education from the viewpoint of e-learning experts. It reports on the findings of on online questionnaire that examined both the barriers and the best practices of implementation and that was applied internationally among researchers and teachers in the higher education sector.

Chapter 7

Liliana Mata, Vasile Alecsandri University of Bacau, Romania
Georgeta Panisoara, University of Bucharest, Romania
Silvia Fat, University of Bucharest, Romania
Ion-Ovidiu Panisoara, University of Bucharest, Romania
Iulia Lazar, University of Bucharest, Romania & InfoCons Association
  Bucharest, Romania

Optimal public policies, including education, have been applied for the sustainable economic growth of the European Union. In European countries, the use of Web 2.0 tools for increasing the education quality is constantly expanding, even if it is divided into two categories. One category consists of developed countries, Organization for Economic Cooperation and Development (OECD) members where there are the strongest of computing tools companies. Another category consists of OECD partner countries which hopes to fulfill the OECD requirements. The main study aim is the exploration of Web 2.0 tools adoptions for e-learning in one OECD candidate. A case study details how behavioral perceptions have been applied. Thus, a survey containing questions about socio-demographic characteristics alongside respondents' perceptions related to Web 2.0 tools for e-learning in higher education was applied. The research outcomes confirm the students' limited knowledge of Web 2.0. Authorities must indicate what measures are necessary for large-scale adoption of all Web 2.0 tools useful for education.

With the coming of the digital age over a period of the last three decades, the letter "e" is used to refer to the electronic world. Formerly known as computer-based training, e-learning has also come of age and is increasingly oriented to real-time learning, that is, activities facilitating simultaneous interaction between learners and instructors. Further, the knowledge explosion makes it more a necessity than a luxury even for emerging economies to consider the e-learning platforms and adopt e-learning strategies. The objectives of this chapter are to understand the essentials of effective e-learning strategies and identify the barriers and facilitators in embedding e-learning for emerging economies so as to align well in this knowledge era. The methodology adopted is in depth literature review and grounded theory approach. Contextual analysis and is restricted to effectiveness of e-learning from an emerging economy point of view.

The chapter concerns the implementation of novel and advanced HCI (human-computer interaction) methods in the design of educational systems aimed at people with disabilities. E-learning applications can significantly improve the quality of life for handicapped students by increasing their self-reliance and adjusting the learning time frame. The structure and methods used to design the interaction applied in this kind of educational system varies significantly depending on the type of the user's disability. There are examples of the interaction developed with the needs of disabled students in mind discussed in the chapter. The main advantages of different solutions were identified and examined. The authors also try to recognize possible threats and suggest some solutions to avoid them.

Preface

Education is strongly impacted by digitalization, regardless of the level of education, the age of the learner, and the type of education: distant or in classroom. Everyone, from young students aged 6-8 or older students in an MBA program at 50 years old, must maintain a connection with the course's content whether the class is online or offline. Indeed, there is a paradox here because students, even when they are present in a physical classroom, can have some digital content to take into consideration. For example, a professor taking attendance at the beginning of a lecture can sometimes be performed using an online platform. This enables professors, administrators, and more importantly parents, to know that their child is attending the lecture.

At the same time, all of us as professors, can see the importance given to social media once the lectures of the semester start. For example, students often create a Facebook page for the group of students in the classroom, which enables them to discuss the professor. These Facebook pages also serve as a diary or written record of the lecture, so that the students are able to track of what was said and what has to be done prior to the next lecture.

Some courses are now performed using digital assets such as apps, websites, social media, and instant messengers (Facebook Messenger, Whatsapp, or Slack) for groups. Digital tools like these enable our students to share links and rich media content (sounds, images, and video). Students also tend to collaborate on projects electronically using simple web-applications such as Google Sheets and Google docs. More elaborate platforms are also becoming more accessible for teachers. For instance, Content Management System (CMS) can assist teachers and professors with managing their MOOCs (Massive Open Online Courses). CMSs allow the teachers and professors to interact with their students via online forums and "1 to 1" conversation systems such as messengers or chat systems.

According to Huet and Simon (2018), digital learning is a valuable tool that helps businesses to boost their digital transformation and reach their targets. Digital learning boosts understanding, as well as beliefs and feedback to assist learners in harnessing this tool as a manager/stakeholder. Students may be pondering the 'how' or the 'why' of the lecture they assist as a digital learning, struggling to understand, or dragging their feet. Whatever the case, it is Huet and Simon's aim to shed light on the background of digital learning development and its strengths. The role and attitude of managers looking to fully exploit digital learning in support of lifelong learning, is also interesting to consider.

Digital learning offers access to educational resources via digital tools and channels. These tools are available as online or in-person (led by a trainer in a classroom), group or individual, synchronous[1] or asynchronous training sessions.

E-learning is a primary asynchronous method which is devised and produced ahead of time and is delivered on a Learning Management System (LMS) platform. Will it be a norm? I am not sure, considering the spread of handheld devices on the planet.

With e-learning, participants are responsible for training themselves and often receives little guidance (Huet & Simon, 2018). Motivational techniques and efficiency assessments are sometimes lacking and the learner may feel very isolated. Digital learning is different because it offers a comprehensive training environment with virtual classes, mentoring, and workshop. It draws on a variety of formats, inspired by the Internet, films, etc. It uses participants' digital devices and encourages them to make use of online resources. The participant moves from a consumer role to a producer role as a community contributor, blogger, *instagramer*, *snapchatter*, etc.

Digital learning does not distinguish between in-person and remote sessions and suggests the most suitable approach based on the participants' circumstances. Face to face (in person or classroom training) becomes valuable and may also be digitized or phygitised (an amalgamation of "physical" and "digital") for a stronger and more intense learner experience.

These aspects made digital learning a real opportunity to boost the impact of the training.

If we mention an example of a European country, e-learning modules are in the lead with 37% of trained French employees having followed one (Huet & Simon, 2018). When e-learning modules are integrated into a course to prepare for or enhance the learning process, they can help the training stand the test of time. When offered as a stand-alone module, without prior information on the training challenges, e-learning may seem unappealing, especially if its design or ease of use are outdated. This is the reason why it is important to consider ease of use as well as aesthetic variables when conceiving an e-learning platform (Pelet, Pratt, & Fauvy, 2017; Pelet & Papadopoulou, 2010).

As pointed out by Huet and Simon (2018), videos and virtual classes are close behind with 35% and 33% penetration. Up by 17 points, these methods are the big winners of the digital learning roll-out in organizations, according to Huet and Simon (2018). The educational video presents training micro-moments geared towards learning 'on the move' and easy to slot into busy work days. The virtual class mimics the synchronous classroom learning style and brings together geographically distant employees by cutting out transport obstacles. The better managed the video conferencing tools and the more professional the synchronous distance learning developers and leaders, the greater the educational value.

In order to understand this ever-evolving world, this book brings up to date content, issued from academic works mainly conducted by professors and PhD students. In their chapter, recent information on MOOCS are given, thanks to the contribution Acquatella, Fernandez, and Thomas made.

The target audience of this book will be composed of professionals and researchers working in the field of marketing, information systems, IT-enabled change, ergonomics, cognitive psychology and change management in various disciplines, including library, information and communication sciences, administrative sciences and management, education, adult education, sociology, computer science, and information technology.

Mata analyzes the most recent studies on attitudes towards the Internet in higher education in her chapter. In recent years, there have been studies that focus on investigating the attitudes of students and teachers towards the use of Internet in higher education. There was used thematic content analysis to investigate the studies conducted in the period 1998-2018 to measure the attitudes towards the Internet. The thematic content analysis of the studies determined establishing the following three categories: a) studies focused on investigating attitudes towards the implications of Internet use; b) studies based on identifying the relationship between attitudes towards the Internet and different variables; c) studies centered on exploring attitudes of different members of higher education. The analysis of studies over the last twenty years contribute to determine the action directions for initiating new studies in this field.

In their chapter, Acquatella, Fernandez, and Thomas suggest a new conceptual framework by presenting a view of the main disruptive strategic trajectory implemented by a particular model of training platforms. These authors try to participate to the understanding of the dynamics of training platforms strategy through the analysis of the Cousera case. The iterations of this platform with a market under construction can be read as a strategy to bring out new proposals and value networks. Finally, they discuss the "drivers" of future changes in the MOOC market.

In his chapter, Sánchez-Acevedo explains that when new educational games are developed for teaching languages, a set of ideas or intuitions about how students can gain more knowledge are used; however, only few of them are based on a solid theory or substantiated with linguistic research. His chapter presents a brief review about second language acquisition theories; describes the importance of recovering, maintaining and transmitting indigenous languages, and analyze efforts made for enhancing bilingual education. Serious games are presented as an alternative for learning indigenous languages and guidelines to develop serious games implementing second language acquisition theories are proposed.

Inghilterra writes a chapter which is based on a research which has been focusing on social sharing devices effects and on students' practices of collaboration, communication and mediation. We have analyzed the recurring temporal split between academic environment and students' sphere in a context of distance learning. The goal is to understand the origin of the collaborative process of collective learning which is illustrated in the communities of apprenticeship outside the academic institution. A netnographic observation was conducted with Bachelor and Master's degrees in a private training center. Author's observation reveals that digital technologies cause a temporal acceleration.

Daunert and Price examine the implications of students' preferences and usage of u-technologies for designing teaching and learning curricula that positively exploit technology. This chapter builds on the research conducted by Daunert and Harteis (2014) that investigated pre-service teachers' preferences and experiences of u-technologies. The results of this cross-sectional survey are considered in relation to designing curricula in digital environments.

According to Isaias, Miranda, and Pífano, in online learning environments, any collaboration between the students must occur with the support of technology, so it is fundamental that technology functions as an enabler, maximizing the opportunities that online settings offer, and that students can tap into those technologies to enhance their learning experience. Their chapter focuses on the implementation of Web 2.0 within higher education from the viewpoint of e-learning experts. It reports on the findings of on online questionnaire that examined both the barriers and the best practices of implementation and that was applied internationally among researchers and teachers in the higher education sector.

Mata, Panisoara, Fat, Panisoara, and Lazar bring a study where their main study is the exploration of Web 2.0 tools adoptions for e-learning in one OECD (Organization for Economic Cooperation and Development) candidate. A case study details how behavioral perceptions have been applied. Thus, a survey containing questions about socio-demographic characteristics alongside respondent's perceptions related to Web 2.0 tools for e-learning in higher education was applied. The research outcomes confirm the students' limited knowledge of Web 2.0. Authorities must indicate what measures are necessary for large-scale adoption of all Web 2.0 tools useful for education.

Baporikar gives as objectives of her chapter to make the reader understand the essentials of effective e-learning Strategies and identify the barriers and facilitators in embedding e-learning for emerging economies so as to align well in this knowledge era we are crossing. The methodology adopted is in depth literature review and grounded theory approach with contextual analysis and is restricted to effectiveness of e-learning from emerging economy point of view.

Zukowska and Sroczyński's chapter concerns the implementation of novel and advanced HCI (Human-Computer Interaction) methods in the design of educational systems aimed at people with disabilities. E learning applications can significantly improve the quality of life for handicapped students by increasing their self-reliance and adjusting the learning time frame. The structure and methods used to design the interaction applied in this kind of educational systems varies significantly depending on the type of the user's disability. There are examples of the interaction developed with the needs of disabled students in mind discussed in the chapter. The main advantages of different solutions were identified and examined. We also try to recognize possible threats and suggest some solutions to avoid them.

Thanks to the great diversity of topic and chapters related to e-learning systems, or practices, with or without the use of social media, this book aims at providing relevant theoretical frameworks and the latest empirical research findings in the area. It has been written for professionals and academics who want to improve their understanding of the strategic role of e-learning at different levels of the information and knowledge society. People working in management, business and economist students, people working on a continuing education base and professionals in general can be interested in the potential of this book, which is fresh, up-to-date and very well written.

REFERENCES

Huet, J.-M., & Simon, A. (2018). The new digital horizons: What are the digital revolution trends? In *Coll. Management in action* (p. 119). Pearson.

Pelet, J.-É., Pratt, M.A., & Fauvy, S. (2017). MOOCs: curating the web and using social media to enhance e-learning. In Mobile Platforms, Design, and Apps for Social Commerce. IGI Global.

Pelet, J.-É., & Papadopoulou, P. (2010). *Investigating the effect of color on memorization and trust in e-learning. In Impact of E-Business Technologies on Public and Private Organizations: Industry Comparisons and Perspectives* (pp. 52–78). IGI Global. doi:10.4018/978-1-60960-501-8.ch004

ENDNOTE

[1]   Synchronous: participants meet at the same time and interact live.

Chapter 1
Current Studies Based on the Investigation of the Attitudes Towards the Internet in Higher Education

Liliana Mata
"Vasile Alecsandri" University of Bacău, Romania

ABSTRACT

The aim of the chapter is to analyze the most recent studies on attitudes towards the internet in higher education. In recent years, there have been studies that focus on investigating the attitudes of students and teachers towards the use of internet in higher education. Thematic content analysis was used to investigate the studies conducted in the period 1998-2018 to measure the attitudes towards the internet. The thematic content analysis of the studies determined establishing the following three categories: 1) studies focused on investigating attitudes towards the implications of internet use; 2) studies based on identifying the relationship between attitudes towards the Internet and different variables; 3) studies centered on exploring attitudes of different members of higher education. The analysis of studies over the last 20 years contributes to determine the action directions for initiating new studies in this field.

DOI: 10.4018/978-1-5225-7435-4.ch001

INTRODUCTION

The Internet has an important contribution to modernizing the process of learning and teaching in higher education. The Internet provides students and teachers with independence and utility in academic activities, which has positive effects on attitudes towards the Internet-based learning environment (Lee et al, 2005).

Improving students' abilities in using the Internet has become a current requirement in the academic environment. The students appreciate the usefulness of the information and communication technologies. They have positive feelings while using the Internet and feel confident in the independent control of Internet use (Peng et al., 2006). The Internet is a means of gaining access to different types of online knowledge and sharing them as well as collaborating with group colleagues (Zhang et al., 2014). The Internet is used in the educational environment to support the process of learning and teaching, both in face-to-face and distance learning (Cocorada, 2016). With the help of the Internet, students can easily and quickly access learning materials. Also, using the Internet offers students the opportunity to take responsibility for informing and creating learning experiences in the academic environment or in their community. Students will learn how to communicate with others about their subjects and research projects. Together with the benefits it presents, the use of the Internet can also lead to a number of negative effects. The use of the Internet in academic activities has encouraged the tendency to deceive during presentations and exams. Easy access to information and relevant materials leads students to study content briefly, leading to superficiality in knowledge (Shneiderman, 1998). Research on Internet attitudes has shown that users who use it less often have little confidence in their ability to use and progress in technology (Cazan et al., 2016). Otherwise, the confidence in information technologies and their positive influence on people's and society's well-being reduces the anxiety towards Internet. The use of the Internet for educational purposes should become commonplace in all universities, as it offers opportunities for students to adapt to new technologies, which leads to a favourable attitude towards the Internet. Israel (2013) identified the main advantages of educational usage of the internet: flexibility and variety, ease and low cost of access, ease and low cost of setting information online, ease of updating information, information resources.

The use of the Internet in educational activities has the potential to motivate both students and university professors by increasing participation and interaction in classes, by involving participants more actively in learning and facilitating an integrated curricular approach. Internet-based teaching strategies create specific challenges for both the instructor and the student (Stoney & Wild, 1998). Educators who advocate technology integration in the learning process believe it will improve learning and better prepare students to effectively participate in the 21st-century workplace (Hopson et al., 2002). For university professors, the Internet becomes a convenient tool to teach different courses. Internet use in teaching can bring many advantages such as (Madden et al., 2005): flexibility of use, high speed in creating new programs compared to video and CD-ROM systems, changing the teacher's style from teaching to guiding and monitoring, obtaining study materials at any time and in any location, and gaining the views of scientists and scholars in various fields. Anderson & Reed (1998) highlights the role of professor as facilitator when teaching with the help of the Internet. A key role is represented by the professional development of teachers in how to use the Internet, due to the decisive impact on the formation of positive attitudes towards the integration of new technologies in higher education.

CURRENT CONTEXT OF INVESTIGATING THE ATTITUDES TOWARDS INTERNET USE IN HIGHER EDUCATION

The Importance of Conducting Studies on Internet Attitudes

The optimal use of the Internet in higher education as a means of learning requires favourable attitudes towards it. Rapid changes to new technologies have favoured the emergence of positive attitudes of students and teachers towards the Internet to improve teaching and learning activities. The frequent use of computers in universities influences the attitudes of both students and teachers. The study of Internet attitudes has grown over the past twenty years as a result of the valorisation of information technologies in academia, at work and at home (Powell, 2013). Teaching and learning activities based on Internet are increasingly common in the university environment, which highlights the need to investigate students' and teachers' attitudes towards new technologies.

Adapting the definition of computer attitudes elaborated by Deniz (1995), the attitudes towards the Internet refer to a person's tendency to use the Internet and the effects on thoughts and feelings about the user and society. Attitudes toward Internet usage represents according to Smith et al. (2000) "a person's general evaluation or feeling towards ICT and specific computer and Internet related activities". According to the model developed by Abedalaziz et al. (2013), attitudes towards the Internet include different components: perceived usefulness, emotional response and perceived control. Tsai et al. (2001) consider that the attitudes towards the Internet are a multidimensional factor.

Kirkwood and Price (2005) notes that it is important to know students' attitudes towards using the Internet as an important educational tool in their student life. Woodrow (1991) claimed that students' attitudes towards computers were critical issues in computer courses and computer-based curricula. Students' attitudes towards the Internet may influence their motivation and interests towards learning to use the Internet, or vice versa (Coffin & MacIntyre, 1999). Also, students' Internet attitudes may impact their future involvement in Internet-related careers or activities (Tsai et al., 2001). Student attitudes to the Internet affect self-efficacy on the Internet (Peng et al, 2006). The attitudes can be improved by stimulating to participate in training on how to use the Internet.

Alongside students' attitudes toward Internet use in universities, it is important to know the attitudes of teachers, because they affect the successful use of computers in the classroom (Huang & Liaw, 2005). The teachers' attitude towards Internet use influence the integration of modern technologies in the teaching activity from the academic environment. The success of technology implementation depends largely on the attitudes of faculty members and their interest in integrating it into teaching activities. Improving university teachers' attitudes towards the use of Internet would be possible by developing teachers' technical abilities and increasing their interest in investing in training and learning the use of technology in education.

Research on the Investigation of Attitudes Towards Internet Use in Higher Education

In recent years, there have been studies that focus on investigating the attitudes of university students and teachers towards the use of information and communication technologies.

Some of the studies are focused on exploring the *attitudes towards the implications of Internet use*. The aim of the study achieved by Ali (2014) is to explore the perceptions of Pakistani university students regarding the positive and negative aspects of using the Internet in their studies. In the students' perceptions, the Internet determines positive changes in academic activities because it provides study materials for research as well as information about educational institutions and the possibility of preparing for examinations. Regarding the negative aspects, the students consider that the Internet affects the studies and the results. In another study conducted by Aydin (2007), the results show that students feel the Internet is an interesting way to get information and intensify the exchange of cultures. Along with these positive aspects, students also identify a number of negative effects, such as the fact that the Internet detaches the user from real life, creates addiction and forces people to be alone. The results of the study conducted by Jain et al. (2011) indicated both positive aspects of students' attitudes towards the Internet as a way of building trust and negative aspects of the decline in verbal communication capacity. Angadi (2012) obtained positive results in terms of students' attitudes, as they have expressed their confidence and satisfaction with the use of the Internet.

Almarabeh et al. (2016) achieved a case study at the University of Jordan to determine the attitudes of university students in terms of the factors underlying their use of the Internet in educational activities. In a survey on Internet use by university students, Bashir et al. (2008) have found that the main reasons are ease of work and time saving features. Anafi et al. (2015) examined the attitudes of engineering students regarding the effect of Internet use on the learning process. According to the study results, the students consider that Internet integration has positive effects on the increase of learning outcomes. The results obtained by Sepahpanah et al. (2015) show that students use the Internet for research, educational activities and communication. The educational use of Internet in higher education has positive effects on different aspects of learning, so more and more educators and students are interested in capitalizing of new technologies. Selwyn et al. (2000) explored the factors underlying the educational use of the Internet by university students in their activities: the ways in which students were introduced to using the Internet, operational problems encountered when using the Internet as an information resource, treatment of information retrieved from the Internet, the social element of learning in on-line environments. The results of the study achieved by Usun (2003) show that students appreciate that the Internet is a practical and enjoyable research tool, equally important to any other research tools. In the study conducted by Reddy & Karthik (2013), the results show that in the students' perception the Internet provides extensive information on the tasks requested and covers many dimensions that respond to educational needs.

Abedalaziz et al. (2013) assessed the students' attitudes towards various aspects of Internet use, such as perceived usefulness, emotional response and perceived control. Research results demonstrate that participants have high-level perceptions about Internet usefulness and Internet control and a moderate level of emotional response when using the Internet. Anderson (2001) investigated the impact of using the Internet on the social relationships and the levels of academic achievement. The results of the study revealed that the use of the Internet for several hours a day has a negative impact on students' academic outcomes and leads to feelings of isolation from the social point of view. Petare & Mohite (2016) examined another aspect of attitudes of students towards the Internet, like enjoyment, efficacy, usefulness, and anxiety. According to the study results, students considered the Internet to be an indispensable tool in everyday life and to keep up-to-date with current information. Other researchers (Eduljee & Kumar, 2017; Luan et al., 2005) measured the attitudes towards the Internet in relation to usefulness, perceived control, and affection.

There are very few studies that are based on exploring teachers' perceptions about the solutions of using Internet in teaching. Ghalem (2017) was interested in studying how teachers use the Internet-assisted language learning to solve English language problems at medical students from higher education. Palesh et al. (2004) analysed the ethical aspect of Internet use.

Another category of studies is aimed at capturing the relationship between attitudes towards the Internet and different variables (gender, experience, computer anxiety, computer or Internet self-efficacy). There are many studies in this area that consider the gender's influence on attitudes towards the Internet. Most studies reveal positive attitudes among male students towards Internet use (Aydin, 2007; Durndell & Haag, 2002; Sam et al., 2005; Wu & Tsai, 2006), but there are studies showing a positive attitude of female students (Ali, 2014). In other studies, gender differences related to the attitudes towards Internet are not obtained (Abedalaziz & Muaidi, 2012; Al Mahmud, 2011; Hong et al., 2003; Joyce & Kirakowski, 2013; Sharma et al., 2014; Tuncer et al., 2013). Some researchers were interested in capturing the influence of experience in using the Internet for attitudes. The results obtained by Liaw & Huang (2006) demonstrate that the students with many years of computer experience have a more positive view of the social and personal effects of using the Internet. Also, the results of other studies (Cocorada, 2016; Wu & Tsai, 2006) show that students who have more experience in using the Internet tend to have positive attitudes towards the less experienced. According to the results obtained by other researchers (Luan et al., 2005; Eduljee & Kumar, 2017; Noor ul Amin, 2017) Internet users have a favourable trend of the dimensions of attitude towards the Internet (Tuncer et al., 2013), students with a high level of experience in using Internet have had more positive attitudes than less experienced students.

Cazan et al. (2016) investigated the correlation between computer anxiety and attitudes towards the computer and the Internet at university students. In other studies (Cocoradă, 2016; Morse et al., 2011; Peng et al., 2006; Sam et al., 2005; Wu & Tsai, 2006), there was determined the correlation between attitudes towards the Internet and computers or Internet self-efficacy. Demirdag (2016) determined the Internet attitudes of substitute teachers and their self-confidence towards Information and Communications Technology (ICT). The results of the study showed that the confidence in ICT had a positive impact on their attitudes towards the Internet.

Referring to the Internet use for educational purposes, the results obtained by Duggan et al. (2001) indicate that the students who have a favourable attitude often use the Internet for different educational activities. Another variable that has been correlated with the attitude towards the Internet is the level of parental education (Isman & Dabaj, 2004). The research results indicate significant differences between students' attitudes towards the Internet and the mother's education level.

Some researchers (Maican & Cocoradă, 2017) have investigated the influence of specialization on the attitudes towards Internet: they have found that students in the Sciences have more favourable attitudes than those in the Humanities. Also, according to the results of the study achieved by Hong et al. (2003), students with the specialization of Engineering and Technological Sciences have positive attitudes compared to those in the field of Human Development. The results of another study (Dahiya & Verma, 2014) highlight that the students in Sciences have predominantly positive attitudes towards the Internet than students in Arts. Regarding the age, research has shown that the use of the Internet is most widespread among young people. According to the results obtained by Aydin (2007), younger students feel more enthusiastic about obtaining information about the Internet. Some studies are focused on investigating the influence of culture on Internet attitudes. According to the results of the study conducted by Li and Kirkup (2007), both Chinese and British students have positive attitudes towards Internet use.

Al Otaibi (2012) investigated the relationship between the attitude towards the use of the Internet and its cognitive, emotional and behavioural components. Regarding the students' impressions about the Internet, most of them have appreciated that the Internet is a quick way to get information, a good source of information and a good tool for continuous self-learning. In terms of feelings about the Internet, a large number of subjects agreed to prefer to use the Internet to improve their communication and debate skills and abilities. Students' behaviour in using the Internet is in line with their ideas and feelings that are generally positive.

Most studies are focused on investigating the attitudes of university students (Abedalaziz et al., 2013; Al Mahmud, 2011; Al Otaibi, 2012; Ali, 2014; Aydin, 2007; Cazan et al., 2016; Cocorada, 2016; Duggan, 2001; Durndell & Haag, 2002; Isman & Dabaj, 2004; Israel, 2013; Jain et al., 2011; Joyce & Kirakowski, 2013; Li & Kirkup, 2007; Liaw & Huang, 2006; Luan et al., 2005; Maican & Cocoradă, 2017; Peng et al., 2006; Reddy & Karthik, 2013; Sam et al., 2005; Petare & Mohite, 2016; Selwyn et al., 2000; Sepahpanah et al., 2015; Wu & Tsai, 2006), while very few studies are centred on identifying the attitudes of university teachers towards Internet use (Abedalaziz & Muaidi, 2012; Demirdag, 2016; Ghalem, 2017).

Aim of Study

The objective of the present study consists in the analysis of studies focused on measuring attitudes towards the Internet in the academic environment. The objectives that support the aim are the following: a) analysing the main themes occurring in the studies based on identifying the attitudes towards the Internet in higher education and; b) establishing the thematic categories corresponding to each category.

METHODOLOGY

A qualitative methodology employing the content analysis was used "to describe the characteristics of the document's content by examining who says what, to whom, and with what effect" (Bloor & Wood, 2006). This approach is useful for a systematic analysis of studies centred on investigating attitudes towards the Internet over the past twenty years.

Method

Thematic analysis as an independent qualitative descriptive approach is described as "a method for identifying, analysing and reporting patterns (themes) within data" (Braun & Clarke, 2006, p. 79). The method presents several advantages, because it is a flexible and useful research tool, provides a purely qualitative, rich and detailed, complex, and nuanced account of the data. By using content analysis, it is possible to analyse data qualitatively and at the same time quantify the data (Gbrich, 2007). The main stages of the content thematic analysis were (Gall et al., 2007): establishing the categories, analysing them, identifying the unit analysis, standardizing the coding procedure, coding the entire material, quantifying the unit analysis, producing the results, interpreting and explaining the results. The use of the method requires a rigorous and complex data analysis. Nowell et al. (2017) consider that "the lack of focus on rigorous and relevant thematic analysis has implications in terms of the credibility of the research process".

The Procedure

The content analysis of the research was achieved in the period June – August 2018. There were selected and analysed specific studies focused on the investigation of university students and teachers' attitudes towards Internet use in the last twenty years (1998-2018). 52 studies have been identified in journals indexed in international databases, of which 40 were selected for the thematic analysis and 12 were eliminated because they were not carried out in higher education.

RESULTS

The thematic content analysis of the studies based on identifying attitudes towards the Internet in higher education determined establishing the following three categories: a) studies focused on investigating attitudes towards the implications of Internet use; b) studies based on identifying the relationship between attitudes towards the Internet and different variables; c) studies centred on exploring attitudes of different members of higher education.

Studies Focused on Investigating Attitudes Towards the Implications of Internet Use

There was established types of studies centred on:

- The positive and negative aspects of Internet use (Ali, 2014; Angadi, 2012; Aydin, 2007; Israel, 2013; Jain et al., 2011);
- The factors underlying the Internet use in educational activities (Almarabeh et al., 2016; Bashir et al., 2008; Reddy & Karthik, 2013; Selwyn et al., 2000; Usun, 2003);
- The effect of Internet use on the learning process (Anafi et al., 2015; Sepahpanah et al., 2015);
- The components of Internet use (affective, perceived usefulness, perceived control, and behavioural intention - Abedalaziz et al., 2013; enjoyment, efficacy, usefulness, and anxiety - Petare & Mohite, 2016; perceived usefulness, perceived control, affection - Eduljee & Kumar, 2017; Luan et al., 2005);
- The impact of using the Internet on the social relationships and the levels of the academic achievement (Anderson, 2001);
- The solutions of using Internet in teaching (Ghalem, 2017);
- The ethical aspect of Internet use (Palesh et al., 2004).

Studies Based on Identifying the Relationship Between Attitudes Towards the Internet and Different Variables

At the level of this category of studies, there was included various types of correlation between attitudes towards the Internet and different variables:

- Gender (positive attitudes at men - Aydin, 2007; Durndell & Haag, 2002; Sam et al., 2005; Wu & Tsai, 2006; positive attitudes at women - Ali, 2014; positive attitudes at both women and men - Abedalaziz & Muaidi, 2012; Abedalaziz et al., 2013; Al Mahmud, 2011; Hong et al., 2003; Joyce & Kirakowski, 2013; Sharma et al., 2014; Tuncer et al., 2013);
- Experience (Cocoradă, 2016; Eduljee & Kumar, 2017; Liaw & Huang, 2006; Luan et al., 2005; Noor ul Amin, 2017; Tuncer et al., 2013; Wu & Tsai, 2006);

- Personality traits (computer or Internet self-efficacy - Durndell & Haag, 2002; Cocoradă, 2016; Morse et al., 2011; Peng et al., 2006; Sam et al., 2005; Wu & Tsai, 2006; self-confidence towards ICT - Demirdag, 2016; computer anxiety - Durndell & Haag, 2002; Cazan et al., 2016, Sam et al., 2005);
- Internet use for educational purposes (Duggan et al., 2001; Sepahpanah et al., 2015).
- The level of parental education (Isman & Dabaj, 2004);
- Specialization (Dahiya & Verma, 2014; Hong et al., 2003; Maican & Cocoradă, 2017);
- Age (Aydin, 2007).
- Ethnicity and cultural context (Abedalaziz et al., 2013; Li & Kirkup, 2007);
- Cognitive, emotional and behavioural components (Al Otaibi, 2012).

Studies Centred on Exploring Attitudes of Different Members of Higher Education

The main representatives of the academic environment who participated in these studies are: students (Abedalaziz et al., 2013; Al Mahmud, 2011; Al Otaibi, 2012; Ali, 2014; Aydin, 2007; Cazan et al., 2016; Cocorada, 2016; Duggan, 2001; Durndell & Haag, 2002; Isman & Dabaj, 2004; Israel, 2013; Jain et al., 2011; Joyce & Kirakowski, 2013; Li & Kirkup, 2007; Liaw & Huang, 2006; Luan et al., 2005; Maican & Cocoradă, 2017; Peng et al., 2006; Petare & Mohite, 2016; Reddy & Karthik, 2013; Sam et al., 2005; Selwyn et al., 2000; Sepahpanah et al., 2015; Wu & Tsai, 2006); and teachers (Abedalaziz & Muaidi, 2012; Demirdag, 2016; Ghalem, 2017).

The frequencies of the specifications for the main three categories and specific themes derived from studies based on identifying the attitudes towards the Internet in higher education are presented in Table 1.

DISCUSSIONS

The analysis of the obtained results is made by reference to the three categories of studies. Regarding the studies focused on investigating attitudes towards the implications of Internet use, there are established different directions: the positive and negative aspects of Internet use (Ali, 2014; Angadi, 2012; Aydin, 2007; Israel, 2013; Jain et al., 2011), the factors underlying their use of the Internet in educational activities (Almarabeh et al., 2016; Bashir et al., 2008; Reddy & Karthik, 2013; Selwyn et al., 2000; Usun, 2003), the effect of Internet use on the learning process (Anafi et al., 2015; Sepahpanah et al., 2015), the components of Internet use (Abedalaziz et

Table 1. Categories and specific themes derived from studies based on identifying the attitudes towards the Internet in higher education

Categories and specific themes		The frequency of the specifications		Total
		1998-2008	2009-2018	
a. attitudes towards the implications of Internet use	a.1. the positive and negative aspects of Internet use	1	4	5
	a.2. the factors underlying their use of the Internet in educational activities	3	2	5
	a.3. the effect of Internet use on the learning process		2	2
	a.4. the components of Internet use	1	3	4
	a.5. the impact of using the Internet on the social relationships and the levels of academic achievement	1		1
	a.6. the solutions of using Internet in teaching		1	1
	a.7. the ethical aspect of Internet use	1		1
	Total	*7*	*12*	*19*
b. the relationship between attitudes towards the Internet and different variables	b.1. gender 　b.1.1. positive attitudes at male 　b.1.2. positive attitudes at female 　b.1.3. positive attitudes at both male and female	 4 1	 1 6	 12
	b.2. experience	3	4	7
	b.3. personality traits (Internet self-efficacy, self-confidence towards ICT, computer anxiety)	4	4	8
	b.4. Internet use for educational purposes	1	1	2
	b.5. level of parental education	1		1
	b.6. specialization	1	2	3
	b.7. age	1		1
	b.8. ethnicity and cultural context	1	1	2
	b.9. cognitive, emotional and behavioural components		1	1
	Total	*17*	*20*	*37*
c. attitudes of different members	c.1. students	17	20	37
	c.2. teachers		3	3
	Total	*17*	*23*	*40*

al., 2013; Eduljee & Kumar, 2017; Luan et al., 2005; Petare & Mohite, 2016), the impact of using the Internet on the social relationships and the levels of academic achievement (Anderson, 2001), the solutions of using the Internet in teaching (Ghalem, 2017) and the ethical aspect of Internet use (Palesh et al., 2004).

From the perspective of the studies based on identifying the relationship between attitudes towards the Internet and different variables, the research results indicates increased concerns over the investigation of the influence of gender (Abedalaziz & Muaidi, 2012; Abedalaziz et al., 2013; Al Mahmud, 2011; Ali, 2014; Aydin, 2007; Durndell & Haag, 2002; Hong et al., 2003; Joyce & Kirakowski, 2013; Sam et al., 2005; Sharma et al., 2014; Tuncer et al., 2013; Wu & Tsai, 2006), personality traits (Cazan et al., 2016, Cocoradă, 2016; Demirdag, 2016; Durndell & Haag, 2002; Morse et al., 2011; Peng et al., 2006; Sam et al., 2005; Wu & Tsai, 2006), as well as the experience (Cocoradă, 2016; Eduljee & Kumar, 2017; Liaw & Huang, 2006; Luan et al., 2005; Noor ul Amin, 2017; Tuncer et al., 2013; Wu & Tsai, 2006). An interesting result of the analysis of research that focused on identifying gender influence on attitudes towards the Internet is that the ones made during 1998-2008 revealed the favourable attitude of the male subjects, as opposed to the studies carried out during 2009-2018, showing that there are no significant gender differences. Cocoradă (2016) explains that gender differences have been reduced over the last decade as a result of increasing opportunities to learn to use the Internet. Abedalaziz and Muaidi (2012) find that previous studies are inconsistent and even contradictory regarding the influence of different factors on attitude towards the Internet. Powell (2013) mentions that the results of studies based on identifying attitudes towards the Internet are divergent and depend on the context in which the research was achieved or the research instruments.

In terms of analysing the studies according to the target group they are targeting, the analysis reveals a lack of relevant research to explore the attitudes of university teachers (academic staff) towards the use of the Internet. There are no studies on the attitude of university managers and administrators towards the use of the Internet.

CONCLUSION AND RECOMMENDATIONS

It is very important to measure the students' attitudes regarding the role of the Internet as a tool increasingly used in higher education institutions. Attitudes towards the Internet are an essential element of successfully introducing and implementing web-based learning in academic environment. The positive attitude of university professors and students is conducive to teaching and learning because of the influence on efficiency, motivation and application of knowledge.

The results of qualitative approaches based on content analysis of the studies achieved in the last twenty years in the field of the investigation of attitudes towards the Internet in the academic environment allowed the shaping of three categories of research: studies focused on investigating attitudes towards the implications of Internet use; studies based on identifying the relationship between attitudes towards the Internet and different variables; studies centred on exploring attitudes of different members of higher education.

Research results are important to the academic context, as they can provide useful information for making decisions about Internet-based teaching and learning strategies. Based on the analysis of research results in the field of Internet attitudes in higher education, it is recommended that more studies be conducted in the future to determine the attitude of the academic staff and to measure the influence of other factors on attitudes towards Internet use. Teachers and decision makers from the academic environment need to pay more attention to planning, developing and implementing information technologies to trigger positive attitudes in using the Internet.

ACKNOWLEDGMENT

This work was supported by a grant of Ministery of Research and Innovation, CNCS - UEFISCDI, project number PN-III-P1-1.1-TE-2016-0773, within PNCDI III.

REFERENCES

Abedalaziz, N., Jamaluddin, S., & Leng, C. H. (2013). Measuring attitudes toward computer and internet usage among postgraduate students in Malaysia. *TOJET: The Turkish Online Journal of Educational Technology*, *12*(2), 200–216.

Abedalaziz, N., & Muaidi, H. (2012). Attitudes towards Internet-Based Distance Education Among Academic Staff of Malaysian Universities. *OIDA International Journal of Sustainable Development*, *5*(1), 81–90.

Al Mahmud, A. (2011). Students' Attitudes towards Internet: A study on Private Universities of Bangladesh. *European Journal of Business and Management*, *3*(6), 9–19.

Al Otaibi, K. N. (2012). Attitudes towards the use of the internet. *Psychological Research*, *2*(3), 151–159.

Ali, Z. S. (2014). Pakistani Students' Perceptions about Use of the Internet in their Academic Activities. *E-Learning and Digital Media*, *11*(3), 222–230. doi:10.2304/elea.2014.11.3.222

Almarabeh, T., Majdalawi, Y. Kh., & Mohammad, H. (2016). Internet Usage, Challenges, and Attitudes among University Students: Case Study of the University of Jordan. *Journal of Software Engineering and Applications*, *9*(12), 577–587. doi:10.4236/jsea.2016.912039

Anafi, F. O., Obada, D. O., & Samotu, I. A. (2015). Integrating Internet into Engineering Education: A Case Study of Students' Usage and Attitudes in Faculty of Engineering, Ahmadu Bello University. *Bulgarian Journal of Science and Education Policy*, *9*(1), 129–147.

Anderson, A. (2001). Internet use among college students: An exploratory study. *Journal of American College Health*, *50*(1), 21–26. doi:10.1080/07448480109595707 PMID:11534747

Anderson, D. K., & Reed, W. M. (1998). The effects of Internet instruction, prior computer experience, and learning style on teachers' Internet attitudes and knowledge. *Journal of Educational Computing Research*, *19*(3), 227–246. doi:10.2190/8WX1-5Q3J-P3BW-JD61

Angadi, G. R. (2012). Post graduate students attitude towards the use of the internet. *International Journal of Education and Psychological Research*, *1*(1), 30–37.

Aydin, S. (2007). Attitudes of EFL Learners towards the Internet. *The Turkish Online Journal of Educational Technology*, *6*(3), 18-26.

Bashir, S., Mahmood, K., & Shafiq, F. (2008). Internet Use among University Students: A Survey in University of the Punjab, Lahore. *Pakistan Journal of Library & Information Science, 9*, 49–65.

Bloor, M., & Wood, F. (2006). *Keywords in Qualitative Methods:A Vocabulary of Research Concepts* (1st ed.). London: SAGE Publications. doi:10.4135/9781849209403

Braun, V., & Clarke, V. (2006). Using thematic analysis in psychology. *Qualitative Research in Psychology, 3*(2), 77–101. doi:10.1191/1478088706qp063oa

Cazan, A. M., Cocorada, E., & Maican, C. I. (2016). Computer anxiety and attitudes towards the computer and the internet with Romanian high-school and university students. *Computers in Human Behavior, 55*, 258–267. doi:10.1016/j.chb.2015.09.001

Cocorada, E. (2016). The internet attitude with socio-humanities high-school and university students. *Romanian Journal of Experimental Applied Psychology, 6*(1), 21–30.

Coffin, R. J., & MacIntyre, P. D. (1999). Motivational influences on computer-related affective states. *Computers in Human Behavior, 15*(5), 549–569. doi:10.1016/S0747-5632(99)00036-9

Dahiya, S., & Verma, C. (2014). Analysis of student's attitude regarding internet in relation to study level and stream. *International Journal of Science and Research*, 447-452.

Demirdag, S. (2016). Examining the Computer Attitudes and Internet Attitudes of Substitute Teachers: Self-Confidence towards ICT. *International Journal of Psycho-Educational Sciences, 5*(2), 89–100.

Duggan, A., Hess, B., Morgan, D., Kim, S., & Wilson, K. (2001). Measuring Students' Attitudes toward Educational Use of The Internet. *Journal of Educational Computing Research, 25*(3), 267–281. doi:10.2190/GTFB-4D6U-YCAX-UV91

Durndell, A., & Haag, Z. (2002). Computer self efficacy, computer anxiety, attitudes towards the Internet and reported experience with the Internet, by gender, in an East European sample. *Computers in Human Behavior, 18*(5), 521–535. doi:10.1016/S0747-5632(02)00006-7

Eduljee, N. B., & Kumar, S. S. (2017). Exploring Attitudes Towards the Internet: A Study of Indian College Students. *International Research Journal of Multidisciplinary Studies, 3*(1), 1–12.

Gall, M. D., Gall, J. P., & Borg, W. R. (2007). *Educational Research: an Introduction*. Boston: Pearson Education, Inc.

Gbrich, C. (2007). *Qualitative Data Analysis: An Introduction* (1st ed.). London: Sage Publications.

Ghalem, A. (2017). Teachers' Perceptions of the Use of The Internet-Assisted Language Learning in Solving Medical Students' English Language Problems. *Asian Journal of Educational Research, 5*(4), 30–42.

Hong, K. S., Ridzuan, A. A., & Kuek, M. K. (2003). Students' attitudes towards the use of the Internet for learning: A study at a university in Malaysia. *Journal of Educational Technology & Society, 6*(2), 45–49.

Hopson, M. H., Simms, R. L., & Knezek, G. A. (2002). Using a technologically enriched environment to improve higher-order thinking skills. *Journal of Research on Technology in Education, 34*(2), 109–119. doi:10.1080/15391523.2001.10782338

Huang, H. M., & Liaw, S. S. (2005). Exploring user's attitudes and intentions toward the web as a survey tool. *Computers in Human Behavior, 21*(5), 729–743. doi:10.1016/j.chb.2004.02.020

Isman, A., & Dabaj, F. (2004). Attitudes of Students Towards Internet. *Turkish Online Journal of Distance Education, 5*(4). Retrieved from https://pdfs.semanticscholar.org/a5c7/3921b2e7b656deeb6116088bb484e730915c.pdf

Israel, O. (2013). Attitude of undergraduates towards educational usage of the Internet: A case of library schools in Delta and Edo States of Nigeria. *International Journal of Science and Technology Educational Research, 4*(4), 57–62.

Jain, N., Patidar, P. C., & Malviya, R. (2011). Internet as learning tool: Indian engineering student's perception. *Indian Journal of Computer Science and Engineering, 2*(2), 244–247.

Joyce, M., & Kirakowski, J. (2013). Development of a general internet attitude scale. In *Design, User Experience, and Usability. Design Philosophy, Methods, and Tools* (pp. 250-260). Academic Press. 10.1007/978-3-642-39229-0_33

Kirkwood, A., & Price, L. (2005). Learners and Learning in the Twenty-first Century: What do we know about students' attitudes towards and experiences of information and communication technologies that will help us design courses? *Studies in Higher Education, 30*(3), 257–274. doi:10.1080/03075070500095689

Lee, M. K. O., Cheung, C. M. K., & Chen, Z. (2005). Acceptance of Internet-based Learning Medium: The role of extrinsic and intrinsic motivation. *Information & Management, 42*(8), 1095–1104. doi:10.1016/j.im.2003.10.007

Li, N., & Kirkup, G. (2007). Gender and cultural differences in Internet use: A study of China and the UK. *Computers & Education, 48*(12), 301–317. doi:10.1016/j.compedu.2005.01.007

Liaw, S. S., & Huang, H. M. (2006). Information retrieval from the World Wide Web: A user-focused approach based on individual experience with search engines. *Computers in Human Behavior, 22*(3), 501–517. doi:10.1016/j.chb.2004.10.007

Luan, W. S., Fung, N. G., Nawawi, M., & Hong, T. S. (2005). Experienced and inexperienced Internet users among pre-service teachers: Their use and attitudes toward the Internet. *Journal of Educational Technology & Society, 8*(1), 90–103.

Madden, A., Ford, N., Miller, D., & Levy, P. (2005). Using the internet in teaching:the views of practitioners –asurvey of the views of secondary school teacher in Sheffield, UK. *British Journal of Educational Technology, 36*(2), 255–280. doi:10.1111/j.1467-8535.2005.00456.x

Maican, C. I., & Cocoradă, E. (2017). Computers, Internet and Smartphone Attitudes Among Romanian University Students. *European Journal of Multidisciplinary Studies, 5*(1), 85–92. doi:10.26417/ejms.v5i1.p85-92

Morse, B. J., Gullekson, N. L., Morris, S. A., & Popovich, P. M. (2011). The development of a general Internet attitudes scale. *Computers in Human Behavior, 27*(1), 480–489. doi:10.1016/j.chb.2010.09.016

Noor ul Amin, S. (2017). Internet-users and Internet Non-users Attitude towards Research: A Comparative Study on Post-Graduate Students. *Journal of Education and Practice, 8*(1), 1-9.

Nowell, L. S., Norris, J. M., White, D. E., & Moules, N. J. (2017). Thematic Analysis: Striving to Meet the Trustworthiness Criteria. *International Journal of Qualitative Methods, 16*(1), 1–13. doi:10.1177/1609406917733847

Palesh, O., Saltzman, K., & Koopman, C. (2004). Internet use and attitudes towards illicit internet use behavior in a sample of Russian college students. *Cyberpsychology & Behavior, 7*(5), 553–558. doi:10.1089/cpb.2004.7.553 PMID:15667050

Peng, H., Tsai, C.-C., & Wu, Y.-T. (2006). University Students' Self-efficacy and their Attitudes toward the Internet: The role of students' perceptions of the Internet. *Educational Studies, 32*(1), 73–86. doi:10.1080/03055690500416025

Petare, P. A., & Mohite, P. V. (2016). An empirical study on measuring attitude towards enjoyment and usefulness of internet among management students. *Imperial Journal of Interdisciplinary Studies, 2*(6), 250–252.

Powell, A. L. (2013). Computer anxiety: Comparison of research from the 1990s and 2000s. *Computers in Human Behavior*, *29*(6), 2337–2381. doi:10.1016/j.chb.2013.05.012

Reddy, P. R., & Karthik, E. K. (2013). A study on students attitudes towards internet. *International Journal of Electronic Marketing and Retailing*, *3*(1), 1–9.

Sam, H. K., Othman, A. E. A., & Nordin, Z. S. (2005). Computer Self-Efficacy, Computer Anxiety, and Attitudes toward the Internet: A Study among Undergraduates in Unimas. *Journal of Educational Technology & Society*, *8*(4), 205–219.

Selwyn, N., Marriott, N., & Marriott, P. (2000). Net gains or net pains? Business students' use of the Internet. *Higher Education Quarterly*, *54*(2), 166–186. doi:10.1111/1468-2273.00153

Sepahpanah, M., Movahedi, R., & Farani, A. Y. (2015). The Study of Students' Attitudes towards the Use of Internet in Education (Case Study: Kermanshah Azad University). *Magazine of E-learning Distribution in Academy*, *6*(3), 40-50.

Sharma, A. K., Pyase, R., & Jain, S. (2014). A study & survey of B. Ed students' attitudes towards using internet. *International Journal of Science and Research*, *4*(12), 1155–1158.

Shneiderman, B. (1998). *Designing the User Interface: strategies for effective human–computer interaction* (3rd ed.). Boston, MA: Addison-Wesley Longman.

Smith, B., Caputi, P., & Rawstone, L. (2000). Differentiating computer experience and attitude towards computers: An empirical investigation. *Computers in Human Behavior*, *16*(1), 59–81. doi:10.1016/S0747-5632(99)00052-7

Stoney, S., & Wild, M. (1998). Motivation and interface design: Maximizing learning opportunities. *Journal of Computer Assisted Learning*, *14*(1), 40–50. doi:10.1046/j.1365-2729.1998.1410040.x

Tsai, C.-C., Lin, S., & Tsai, M.-J. (2001). Developing an Internet Attitude Scale for high school students. *Computers & Education*, *37*(1), 41–51. doi:10.1016/S0360-1315(01)00033-1

Tuncer, M., Dogan, Y., & Tanaş, R. (2013). Vocational School Students' Attitudes Towards Internet. *Procedia: Social and Behavioral Sciences*, *103*, 1303–1308. doi:10.1016/j.sbspro.2013.10.460

Usun, S. (2003). Undergraduate Students Attitudes towards Educational Uses of Internet. *Interactive Educational Multimedia*, *7*, 46–62.

Woodrow, J. J. (1991). A comparison of four computer attitudes scales. *Journal of Educational Computing Research*, *7*(2), 165–187. doi:10.2190/WLAM-P42V-12A3-4LLQ

Wu, Y. T., & Tsai, C. C. (2006). University Students' Internet Attitudes and Internet Self-Efficacy: A Study at Three Universities in Taiwan. *Cyberpsychology & Behavior*, *9*(4), 441–450. doi:10.1089/cpb.2006.9.441 PMID:16901248

Zhang, X., de Pablos, P. O., & Xu, Q. (2014). Culture effects on the knowledge sharing in multi-national virtual classes: A mixed method. *Computers in Human Behavior*, *31*, 491–498. doi:10.1016/j.chb.2013.04.021

Chapter 2

The Coursera Case as the Prefiguration of the Ongoing Changes on the MOOC Platforms

Francois Acquatella
Telecom Paristech, France

Valerie Fernandez
Telecom Paristech, France

Thomas Houy
Telecom Paristech, France

ABSTRACT

This chapter aims to suggest a new conceptual framework by presenting a view of the main disruptive strategic trajectory implemented by a particular model of training platforms. It aims to participate in the understanding of the dynamics of training platforms strategy through the analysis of the Cousera case. The iterations of this platform with a market under construction can be read as a strategy to bring out new proposals and value networks. Finally, the authors discuss the "drivers" of future changes in the MOOC market.

DOI: 10.4018/978-1-5225-7435-4.ch002

INTRODUCTION

The analysis of evolution of Coursera strategy allows understanding the different sequences of strategic decision of this type of platform. This analysis case allows us to make assumptions about the dynamic form of its strategy (Teece, 2010). It also presents the interest of enriching our reflection on a kind of "intentionality" of strategic groping: through the analysis of internal and external contingencies and constraints to which this platform is subject. Finally, the case of Coursera allows us to question the "drivers" of upcoming changes in the online training market.

The authors base their analysis on the "disruption" concept (Christensen, 1997). This conceptual approach covers several types of innovation producing differentiated effects in different markets (Markides, 2006). Platforms are symbols and catalysts of diverse forms of disruption. Authors are mobilizing the different notions induced by "disruption" concept to distinguish a particular platform case, through a review of the main disruptive strategy observed.

COORDINATION PLATFORMS: A STRATEGY BASED ON THE DISRUPTION OF THE CREATION VALUE MODEL

The levers of this disruptive strategy are based on the creation of a new value proposition by mobilizing under exploited assets (house, cars etc.). Because they are valued in a new way, these assets create and coordinate a market by building a new demand (Kim & Mauborgne, 2005). This strategic platform approach consists in changing the rules of the competitive game of a sector (Lehmann-Ortega & Roy, 2009). This disruption of value creation modes occurs by allowing asset owners to take advantage of their "property" in a new way. The platform is then a vector of new modes of consumption through an unprecedented form of intermediation. Coordination platforms reinvent business models by changing the way users consume and the type of service / good they consume.

Coursera platform illustrates this phenomenon becoming the disruption emblem of traditional way of educational training. Coursera, which offers free intermediation between individuals and academic institutions, is now platform number one worldwide.

One of the main ambitions of the coordination platforms lies in their ability to create new value networks (Caron-Fasan & Chanal, 2008): amplify and change the scope of the platform by exploiting new assets, support the development dynamics of this type of platform.

The iterations of these platforms with the market can be read as an approach aiming at continuously testing different value propositions. This kind of strategy is part of an "effectual approach" (Sarasvathy, 2003): successive experiments to explore new offers. Experiments between the platform and the market allow testing the adhesion to new value propositions. The partnerships operated by the platform aim to discover new sources of value. The platform will use, in a reflexive way, the data of its various satellite actors to reflect on the strategic possibilities.

ANALYSIS OF THE "COORDINATION PLATFORM": COURSERA

The coordination platforms' strategic trajectory framing makes it possible to exhaustively describe the evolution of Coursera's strategy. In particular: to draw lessons on the strategy of this type of platforms – to understand the impact of MOOC's strategic innovation on "high / low customers"; i.e. segmentation by type of customer likely to use the product MOOC.

Coursera's initiatives to make profit and develop its business model represent both a form of strategic intent in the sense of Hamel & Prahalad (1989), but also a form of strategic groping. This case analysis provides more general lessons on the issues and consequences of the strategic groping of coordination platforms with unstable economic models.

Coursera emblematic case is an opportunity to describe, question and formalize the strategic groping of online training platforms. Our analysis is also part of a prospective approach. Given the upcoming developments on MOOCs, the strategic reversals will still be many and sources of new lessons.

Authors point out the evolution of the economic model of this platform over a period that may seem relatively short (5 years), but which in the digital sphere is long enough to draw lessons on the strategic trajectory of this platform.

Framework of the Analyzed Case

The Coursera platform positions itself as one of the ambassadors of a paradigm shift in the world of education, with the mission of creating a technological environment conducive to a new type of learning. Coursera coordinates an entire ecosystem composed of different actors "sides" (Hagiu & Wright, 2015) characterized mainly by academic institutions on one side and users of the other one (learners).

Through an elitist partnership strategy based on an "academic excellence" positioning (the most famous universities, very relevant and specific content), the platform has developed a form of "virality" around its value proposition, in order to acquire a large free audience. Coursera quickly took advantage of the new mechanics of the digital economy: relying on network effects based on free courses. Coursera then focused on monetizing its user base.

By offering a free service meeting a newly identified and unsatisfied need in the online training market, Coursera platform has managed to develop a massive use among low-end customers. The attractiveness of general public for Coursera's value proposition has led to new teaching and learning habits leading to the creation of a "detached market" or "new detached market" on e-learning.

Articulation of the Value Network of the Platform

- The freemium model is a paradigm of platform development based on a disruptive value proposition
- Interest of the platform for one side depends on the number of agents on the other side (network effects)
- Aggregated sides contribute significantly to value creation for the platform
- Platform creates value for each side
- Platform combines divergent interests between sides

The Keystone: A Governance Issue

Coursera organizes the platform by bringing together universities and users in an ecosystem based on network effects. The keystone is positioned as an intermediary between the aggregated sides. The keystone manages and animates the sharing of the value between the sides.

Academic Institutions: An Issue of Positive Visibility

Academic institutions are thus referenced on the platform among several prestigious universities (Stanford, HEC...). In a large number of cases, the platform increases the positive visibility of the partner institutions. Establishments whose reputation is not internationally anchored thus have access to an installed base of "global" users, enabling them to develop their visibility / reputation internationally.

Users (Learners): Develop Knowledge / Skills

Users have free access to quality education provided by renowned academic institutions. They communicate, share and learn collectively through a new socio-technological artifact.

An Unstable Economic Model

To date, the platform's revenues are mainly based on the purchase of a "signature track" certificate, representing a monthly income of about $ 1 million dollars, showing relative success. This income does not cover all costs of the company, or those of its partners (Depover, 2014). Concretely, certification is based on the possibility given to learners to buy a certificate at the end of their apprenticeship. If the MOOCs display a great number of registrations (regardless of the type of platform), Completions remain relatively low (around 6%). The vast majority of registered learners drops out and do not complete the training. Witch reduces the number of learners likely to contract certificate.

The platform does not develop the content (i.e., the courses). The production of these resources (contents) is done by partner academic institutions. Even if they do not seem inclined to think their teaching in commercial approach, the question of profitability and production costs of a MOOC seems to become in the short and medium term a compelling need of profitability for academic partners. Recall that the costs of producing a MOOC about $ 50,000, and the revenue-sharing benefits (6-15% per share) operated by Coursera are generally far from amortizing these production costs.

The Coursera platforms finance its structural costs by successive rounds of fundraising ($ 146 million to date, including $ 65 in venture capital). For now, the platform economy is based mainly on a regular and synchronous growth of its two sides (Users and academic institutions). This approach relies on one of the most observed digital strategies among pure players. This consists of acquiring a massive audience with a high potential in terms of exploitation and valuation of associated data.

The evolution of the number of learners (and providers of courses content) encourages different external economic agents to invest directly (funding) or participate indirectly (sponsorship) in the development of the platform.

Articulation of the Economic Model of the Platform

- Conversion of value into revenue is fundamental for the sustainability of the platform
- Creation and distribution of resources (training contents) generate the economic model of the platform (certification)
- Value proposition of the platform concerns an offer of a form of "quality control" of the proposed certifications (quality training, prestigious institutions)
- Creation of resources depends on variables of each side
- The economic model of the platform is constrained by co-opting actors with diverging and related interests, mainly expressed by the desire to have a return on investment
- Robustness of the platform's economic model influences the variables (possible return on investment) and influences the updating of third-party funding offers, for the creation of new resources (content for academic institutions, Interface and functionalities for Coursera)
- Revenue growth is essentially based on the monetization of users

The propensity to "pay" of users depends mainly on:

- Recognition and enhancement of apprenticeship and certification in the labor market
- The user experience of the technical device (optimization of the learning experience by the "gamification" of the interface)
- The quality of the proposed content, mainly the media, but also complementary resources, exams...
  - The keystone (Coursera): an issue of sustainability of the economic model

Coursera as a "keystone" ecosystem manage and operate all the resources (or assets) of the platform; Coursera ensures the quality control of the contents via a policy of selection of the partner university establishments (the certification is valorized). The Keystone grant a revenue development opportunity by deploying a "freemium" model via a specialization offer based on a "win / win" approach (shared rewards for specialization). The keystone leverage user-generated data to enhance interaction design (maximizing the user experience). Coursera wishes to reassure its investors about the economic viability of the platform in the short/ medium term in order to continue to finance itself by raising funds.

Academic Institutions: A Return on Investment Challenge.

The partner institutions want the platform to generate a stable and sustainable economy in order to amortize their costs of producing training contents.

Users: An Issue of Socio-Professional Gratification

Users subscribe to a certificate to promote their new skills within their company or on the job market

Strategic Experimentation of the Platform

The strategy deployed by Coursera is analyzed as continual iterations with the market: a progressive enlargement and enlistment of new segments market, an enlargement of the courses' catalog, and the addition of new features to the platform.

The incentive effects of this disruptive value proposition, relayed by a free-of-charge model, favored a network externality dynamic that facilitated the penetration of several "multiple market encroachment" markets. Coursera has been able to build and test a range of specific offers (freemium, specialization, business) for each target market and type of specific needs expressed by different categories of consumers.

The Coursera strategic groping is viewed as a series of experiments inconclusive to monetize his audience. The iterations of the platform with the market can be envisaged in several ways. On the one hand, they are seen as participating in a relevant method to test the market adherence to different value propositions. On the other hand, they can also be seen as permanent strategic adjustments in front of a situation that forces them to combine competing interests of different actors in "coopetition".

In addition, some academic institutions are more and more tempted to develop their own platform thus creating "multi-homing" phenomena (Fun, Edx...). The multiplicity of media offering the same training contributes to the instability of demand by exacerbating a form of "hacking" behavior of the trainings. In this case, strategic experiments (defined as market learning by «trial-and-error») become less intentional; it is also undergone and constitutive of the economic instability of the platform. In this perspective, Coursera is therefore in a position to continually perform strategic adjustments to try to federate its ecosystem.

Articulation of the Strategic Experimentation of the Platform

- The platform develops new opportunities for exploitation (commercialization) of exploitable resources (contents, data)

- The platform provides access to new markets at zero or low costs. The contents and interface (interaction design) are reassigned without causing any major technical changes
- Strategic expansion experiment is fed by iterations between the keystone and users and partners (Content / data / interaction design)
- Revenue development is based on experiments of new market (Coursera for Business/government)
- Propensity to "pay" from these actors depends mainly on: richness and quality of the content offer (creation of targeted learning programs); user experience (optimization of the learning experience through "gamification"); tariff proposal (possibility of achieving economies of scale)
  - Coursera wants to multiply paying partners in order to develop its sources of revenue. For that purpose, Keystone mobilizes its resources to test new offers.
  - Organizations / governments: an issue of capacity development for actors and the organization.

Organizations access a wide range of content through a packaged pricing offer. They wish to adopt a device allowing them to achieve economies of scale (to train a large number of staff at reduced costs).

PROSPECTIVE DISCUSSION ON THE COURSERA CASE

Discussion on Coursera Platform Ambitions

The Schumpeterian perspective seems illustrative of this continual ambition of value creation and especially by this fundamental impulse to innovation in markets characterized by instability.

The Coursera coordination platform through its strategy shows a productive apparatus which vocation seems focused on the fundamental idea of bringing out new needs among consumers.

MOOCs are training products that, like any product, require many adjustments, to be able to establish themselves as a market standard. Coursera by its proposal of breaking value chain based on a marketing strength, idealistic speeches, social interdependencies, allowed it to stabilize its basic offer in the training market.

Nevertheless, the difficulty of finding a sustainable business model illustrates the problem of positioning the platform as a digital social entrepreneur.

Raises the question regarding the collaborative ideal carried by MOOC platforms: is the platform innovation at the service of the society or is it serving private interests?

To sustain its business model, the Coursera coordination platform strives to perpetuate a model where needs are not always that would preside over innovation, but above all a motivation to create new markets in order to extend its competitive perimeter and thus develop new economic perspectives and incomes.

The strategic groping of Coursera's platform through its continuities, its experiences, the resistances observed, and its adaptations, reveals a paradigm of economic development that tends to the omnipresence of the postmodern principles of productivity and profitability in all the domains that govern life of individuals.

The underlying questions posed by our strategic analysis are as follows: Is the objective of coordination platforms such as Coursera to contribute to the "instrumentalization" and commodification of a growing share of education? And possibly to introduce a form of industrialization of education that has spread to other service sectors?

Drivers for Upcoming Changes

Three Dimensions of the Current Quality of MOOCs Can Be Questioned

Let's first examine the intrinsic quality of the MOOC product. The rate of average completion of the MOOCs, previously discussed in the article (7%), reveals a gap between the intention of online courses users and the effective use of the platform.

Which demonstrates the inability of platforms to retain Internet users from end-to-end. This reality is not likely to invalidate the promise of MOOC, but characterizes a form of diversion of the product. The learners rarely enroll in an online course to validate it.

Learners instrumentalize it to learn differently, or to meet peripheral needs (Acquatella, 2017):

- To satisfy a curiosity
- To draw on notions taught in different courses - to build their own knowledge
- To access specific academic information

To date, this MOOC platform can't be too deterministic in its offer because of so many different uses. The perceived quality of online courses by Internet users also raises questions. Often satisfied with the general experience offered in an online course, learners frequently report that they have not acquired the skills they originally imagined (Cross, 2013; Hennis, Skrypnyk & De Vries, 2015).

They discover and acquire new knowledge, along the way. But they rarely access the mastery of skills that motivated their registration. This observation reflects the difficulty of MOOCs to become complete educational "vehicles". Qualification upstream of all knowledge developed in the course is a necessary condition for being able to think about the overall learning of online learners. Without certainty about skills acquired in each course, it becomes impossible to register MOOCs in an overall educational perspective. The lack of interoperability MOOCs between them therefore significantly impacts their modularity and constrains the ambitious uses that could be made of it.

Finally, there is a real difficulty in assessing the quality of a MOOC. Actually, the rate of Completion is an imperfect indicator. It varies too much depending on the level of requirement of the MOOC holders and the design of the course. It makes this metric irrelevant to characterize the quality of a MOOC. The qualitative and quantitative surveys of learners appear to be questionable methods because of the difficulty of accessing representative panels of Internet users on the platforms. As a result, initiatives to advance the quality of MOOCs are complex because they do not benefit from a clear indicator allowing establishing this progression. Any form of innovation in online courses is subjective judgment, which makes it impossible to identify with certainty the relevance of new developments (Vitiello & Al. 2018).

In summary, MOOCs seem not to meet the specific needs of learners. The user experience offered by the platforms is considered pleasant. Nevertheless, the MOOC distributors are not succeeding in imposing themselves as powerful educational innovations to develop strong and organized learners' skills.

In the short term, MOOCs are also likely to change drastically due to the emergence of several disruptive technologies. The potential of Artificial Intelligence could significantly improve the quality and volume of interactions between teachers and learners. The "chabots" could quickly become a way to make MOOCs more interactive.

The Machine Learning and the use of large databases are tools that could improve the personalization of the offered courses online. Virtual Reality and all immersive devices could also participate in advancing the user experience of learners on the MOOC platforms. The development of these news technologies will not only affect online courses, but the way they are distributed. Customer acquisition and retention on the Internet platform will probably be rethought in the short term.

Current changes in the environment in which online courses are written also invite MOOCs to transform themselves. Internet is a changing space that gives rise to many learnings. This form of learning already engaged by Internet users could be retained, but in that case it would be opposed to the legitimate wishes of the platforms to lock up knowledge on a proprietary basis. One of the drivers of the upcoming changes will probably be the ability of MOOCs to support the natural serendipity that Internet users already experience when they are learning on the web (Hong & AL, 2017).

Some Possible Futures

Until now, MOOCs have always been considered as products belonging to the academic world. They are almost always designed and produced by the academic world. This property of online courses could be questioned because of the reflections to be made on the shape of the product itself.

MOOCs can be defined as products whose main function is to transmit, remotely, educational content. Other products already exist and are successfully pursuing the same intentions. TedX conferences are viewed by tens of millions of Internet users. The 52-minute documentaries of specialty television stations win remarkable audiences. Popular programs devoted to complex scientific phenomena multiply and find their audience.

All these products are intended to educate their audiences however; they are not from the academic world. They come from the audiovisual world or are pure products of Internet. These formats are interesting because all of them have already made success. They have demonstrated the interest of a wide public who recognizes them for their quality.

To improve their level of quality, MOOCs will certainly have to move closer to the audiovisual world and the Internet (Peraya, 2017).

They could then benefit from the good practices used by professionals in these industries to improve end-to-end Internet users on a given content.

This rapprochement between the academic world and the world of audio-visual and the internet will not fail to impact significantly both universes. Teachers will have to rethink their profession and learn how to write scripts -either by written or by video- to effectively convey the key concepts they want to teach.

Producers and directors, responsible for staging videos, will have to imagine attractive formats, without degrading the relevance of the arguments developed in the courses.

The creation of this new generation of MOOC could create new rents, coveted by all contributors. Producers could legitimately claim the paternity of innovation. They could indeed activate the right associated with the protection of the new created images (intellectual property, right of publicity between others.). Teachers could from their side, desire to remain the exclusive owners of the content because of the copyright and their status of writers of the created videos. Since the contributions are interdependent, the new annuities will be disputed and will have to be distributed equitably.

These possible evolutions of the product could also defeat the economic model of the universities which act today as sponsors of the MOOCs in order to promote their brands, their notoriety and, sometimes, increase their incomes.

When learners will look at these new online courses, will they value the university that supports it or the one of the teacher? By analogy with the "long-trail" phenomena in the music market, some teachers, accompanied by production companies, could become brands and attract learners on their own names.

Will learners watch a MOOC tomorrow because they have been supported by a prominent university or will they look at it because it is given by the star teacher in the field?

According to the scenarios, teachers could become potential disruptors for universities and platforms currently distributing online courses. The transformations of the world of education could be of great magnitude. Through the Coursera case, authors show how platforms today seek to be the instigators of these upheavals to come.

CONCLUSION

In its specific character, the Coursera platform is an agile organizational model in its capacity to develop and manage new offers that percolate in different market segments - to found new partnerships based on groping strategy.

The management of its ecosystem reveals a strategic trend clearly oriented from "low end to high end customers". The platform agilely explores opportunities in different market segments through a trial-and-error strategy. Coursera opts for a strategic rationality combining a short-term effectual posture, completed by a causal posture in the medium and long term. As an agile organization, it gropes in the short term while building a disruptive competitive advantage and over the medium and long term by a technological improvement of its interfaces. Thus, by maintaining control of its architecture, the platform deploys a range of offers and creates a self-referential reputation framework in terms of skills and ability to develop new educational features.

REFERENCES

Acquatella, F. (2017). MOOC as an organizational learning process. *Question(s) de management, (2),* 21-34.

Caron-Fasan, M.L, Channal V. (2008). Scenarios for exploring business models. *Expansion Management Review, 128.*

Christensen, C. M. (1997). *The Innovator's Dilemma: When New Technologies Cause Great Firms to Fail.* Boston Harvard Business School Press.

Cross, S. (2013). *Evaluation of the OLDS MOOC curriculum design course: participant perspectives, expectations and experiences.* Milton Keynes, UK: OLDS MOOC Project.

Depover, C. (2014). Economic and pedagogical models for MOOCs? *Distance and Mediation of Knowledge, 2*(5).

Hagiu, A., & Wright, J. (2015). Multi-sided platforms. *International Journal of Industrial Organization, 43,* 162–174. doi:10.1016/j.ijindorg.2015.03.003

Hamel, G. P., & Prahalad, C. K. (1989). Strategic intent. *Harvard Business Review,* 3. PMID:10303477

Hong, J. C., Tai, K. H., Hwang, M. Y., Kuo, Y. C., & Chen, J. S. (2017). Internet cognitive failure relevant to users' satisfaction with content and interface design to reflect continuance intention to use a government e-learning system. *Computers in Human Behavior, 66,* 353–362. doi:10.1016/j.chb.2016.08.044

Kim, W. C., & Mauborgne, R. (2005). Blue ocean strategy: From theory to practice. *California Management Review, 47*(3), 105–121. doi:10.1177/000812560504700301

Lehmann-Ortega, L., & Roy, P. (2009). Disruptive strategies. *Revue française de gestion,* (7), 113-126.

Markides, C. (2006). Disruptive Innovation; In need of Better Theory. *Journal of Product Innovation Management, 23*(1), 19–25. doi:10.1111/j.1540-5885.2005.00177.x

Peraya, D. (2017). Au centre des Mooc, les capsules vidéo: un renouveau de la télévision éducative? *Distance and Mediation of Knowledge,* (17).

Sarasvathy, S. D., Dew, N., Velamuri, S. R., & Venkataraman, S. (2003). Three views of entrepreneurial opportunity. Handbook of entrepreneurship research, 141-160.

Teece, D. J. (2010). Business models, business strategy and innovation. *Long Range Planning*, *43*(2), 172–194. doi:10.1016/j.lrp.2009.07.003

Vitiello, M., Walk, S., Helic, D., Chang, V., & Guetl, C. (2018). User Behavioral Patterns and Early Dropouts Detection: Improved Users Profiling through Analysis of Successive Offering of MOOC. *Journal of Universal Computer Science*, *24*(8), 1131–1150.

KEY TERMS AND DEFINITIONS

Keystone: The keystone manages the interactions between the different sides of its ecosystem. This type of organization controls moving flows (courses, resources, and data).

Chapter 3
Indigenous Languages Learning Through Serious Games Based on Second Language Acquisition Theories

Miguel A. Sánchez-Acevedo
Universidad de la Cañada, Mexico

ABSTRACT

When new educational games are developed for teaching languages, a set of ideas or intuitions about how students can gain more knowledge are used; however, few of them are based on a solid theory or substantiated with linguistic research. This chapter presents a brief review about second language acquisition theories; describes the importance of recovering, maintaining, and transmitting indigenous languages; and analyzes efforts made for enhancing bilingual education. Serious games are presented as an alternative for learning indigenous languages, and guidelines to develop serious games implementing second language acquisition theories are proposed. Finally, a discussion about challenges and future trends in recovering, maintaining, and transmitting indigenous languages is presented.

DOI: 10.4018/978-1-5225-7435-4.ch003

INTRODUCTION

When educational games are developed for teaching languages, ideas or intuitions about how students can gain more knowledge are used, but only few are substantiated with linguistic research or based on a solid theory. Several studies have demonstrated that learning a second language doesn't consist only of phonetic and grammar; there are factors involved such as cognitivism, psycholinguistics, culture and sociology (Song, 2018). Acculturation, behaviorism, connectionism, comprehension hypothesis, interaction hypothesis, output hypothesis, sociocultural theory, and universal grammar hypothesis are found among the most relevant theories for second language acquisition (Menezes, 2013). Those theories provide the basis to increase the knowledge acquired by learners of a second language. There is a gap among theories and learning practice. Serious games are an approach that can close this gap. Indigenous languages have an opportunity of being recovered, maintained and transmitted through serious games.

The UNESCO (2015) has reported that around 199 languages in the world have less than ten speakers; estimations predict that a half of the languages spoken today will be lost in 2050. The disuse of indigenous languages generates a loss of cultural value since various customs, maintained by indigenous groups, are transmitted through their native language. This situation has attracted the interest of the scientific community for recovering, maintaining, and transmitting indigenous languages. When education is introduced in indigenous groups through the adoption of an official language, the use of native language is reduced (Furniss, 2014). Bilingual education has been adopted as strategy for transmitting knowledge without reducing the use of native language (Correa Ferreira et al., 2018). It is important to strength bilingual education through educative technology to avoid the reduction on the use of indigenous languages while enhancing the acquisition of a second language.

Nowadays, children are living in a technological world, where almost at all schools they have access at least to a cellphone or a computer at the classroom. A software which is present in those computing devices are games. The development of the first video game is remounted to 1962 at the MIT, where Steve Russell created the game Space War, which ran in a vacuum tube computer (Rabin, 2010). Due to the fast evolution of technology, video games were widespread over the world; according to a report published in Statista (2018), in 2016 there were 2515 million of video game players in the world. Considering that majority of children can access a computer, tablet or smart phone where a video game can be played, an opportunity of inducing learning through video games arises. Serious games are the approach for developing video games directed to enhance learning over a wide variety of topics.

The term Serious Game was introduced by Abt (1987); he stated that "serious games combine the analytic and questioning concentration of the scientific viewpoint with the intuitive freedom and rewards of imaginative, artistic acts". Nowadays, there is a tendency to increase learning through serious games (Wilkinson, 2016); however, there is not a consensus about rules for developing and evaluating whether the process of learning was improved through the game. In this chapter a set of guidelines to develop serious games focused in learning indigenous languages based on theories of second language acquisition are proposed, and recommendations for evaluating the acquired knowledge are presented.

The chapter is organized in four sections; the first section illustrates how the learning of a second language has been improved through serious games; next, a brief review about second language acquisition theories is presented; then, third section describes the importance of recovering, maintaining and transmitting indigenous languages, and analyze efforts made for enhancing bilingual education; guidelines to develop serious games implementing second language acquisition theories are proposed in the fourth section; finally, challenges and future trends in recovering, maintaining, and transmitting indigenous languages are discussed.

SERIOUS GAMES FOR SECOND LANGUAGE LEARNING

Teaching a second language at schools has presented issues with respect to the number of learners per teacher, a wide curriculum to be covered in a limited time, and the resources required for improving the learning process (Vetter, 2014). Although most students learn a foreign language through an organized process, there are persons who learn through a non-formal or informal environment. Formal learning is intentional, organized and structured, non-formal learning doesn't have a defined structure but has some organization, and in the informal learning there isn't structure not organization. (Eaton, 2010). Technology has made possible the acquisition of a second language through an informal learning process. Chat services and video conference applications allow learners to start a conversation with people who speak a different language, and through this conversation, they acquire basic communication skills; translation applications are also useful for learning new words which meaning is unknown. Albeit a second language can be acquired through informal learning technologies, the learning process is slow, and the knowledge acquired is limited to specific situations where the language is used. Serious games emerge as a technology through formality can be introduced in an informal learning process.

Since their inception, serious games have been used in military, training, health care, and education (De Gloria, Bellotti, and Berta, 2014; Wattanasoontorn, García-Hernández, and Sbert, 2012). In the militia, there are tactical operations where the use of foreign languages is required for better communication with native speakers, like in rescue operations. The Tactical Language and Culture Training System (TLTS) is a robust game for teaching Levantine Arabic, Iraqi Arabic and Pastho, based on technologies for speech recognition, interactive animated simulations, intelligent agents, pedagogical software agents, and natural language technology (Valente, Johnson and Vilhjálmsson, 2006). Another area where a foreign language is required is at work; there are companies where workers from different regions collaborate and require communication skills to maintain the productivity. SiLang (Tsalapatas, Heidmann, Alimisi, and Houstis, 2013) is a serious game developed to enhance the communication skills on a foreign language at the workplace. In Europe, researchers of different universities, teachers and students, have established the Serious Games Network (SEGAN) with the aim of spread and contribute to the adoption of serious games in the learning process. Aljaz and Genc (2016) presented evidence that serious games are useful for both young and adult people.

As mentioned before, acquiring a second language is not only related with grammar; there are factors that improve the learning process like sociocultural and specific situations where language is used. I-FLEG (Amoia, Bretaudiere, Denis, Gardent, and Perez-Beltrachini, 2012) is a game developed over Second Life, a virtual environment where specific situations can be generated; furthermore, the user can obtain feedback of its performance. Although multiplayer is not supported in the proposed game, Second Life is a multiplayer platform through which more realistic scenarios that improve the learning process can be developed. In Taiwan there exist specific places known as English Village where English language is taught by following the sociocultural theory; in those places, students can learn the English language through real life activities; Lan (2015) proposed a 3D virtual environment over Second Life to imitate English Villages and motivate students to acquire a second language through sociocultural activities in the game. Other technology which has been used in the learning process of a second language is augmented reality.

Augmented reality has emerged as an attractive technology due to its portability and the interaction it provides with the environment. This technology makes use of tags and markers attached to real objects; when the markers are detected by a cellphone, an animation, sound or additional information is displayed about the object observed through the device. Teachers of second languages have used those resources to make the learning process of a second language more interactive while students perform different activities to reinforce their knowledge. Some projects have created smart environments by allocating markers in several objects and places into the classroom; those environments generate a learning sequence through stories or cultural virtual tours (Godwin-Jones, 2016).

SECOND LANGUAGE ACQUISITION THEORIES

Acculturation was one of the first models proposed to predict the degree of learning acquired by students through integration with groups speaking a second language (Schumann, 1986). This theory states that the degree of learning is controlled by the degree of acculturation of the learner; however, this variable only starts the chain of causality where other factors are involved. The acculturation theory is based on a learning environment generated by immigration, where there exists a need for communication; moreover, a lack of instructors is common. There are several factors influencing the acquisition of a second language: social, affective, personality, cognitive, biological, aptitude, personal, input, and instructional factors. Acculturation is a variable which join social and affective factors. (Schumann, 1986).

Behaviorist theory emerges as a theory to model how mother tongue is acquired. The theory is based on the idea of obtaining small habits which contribute to increase the knowledge of a language. The good habits in the acquisition process are rewarded, while incorrect habits are punished with the intention to eliminate them; this way, habits can be acquired by repetition and training (Demirezen, 1988). Audiolingual Method (ALM) is a teaching method which is based on the stimulus-response concept (Alemi and Tavakoli, 2016). Learning a new language with this methodology consists of listening, speaking, reading and writing, acquiring habits through repetition exercises, indicating when an error is produced to avoid it later, using dialogues to practice languages skills, avoiding the use of mother tongue in the classroom, and encouraging the use of specific words (language lab) to conduct the learning process (Budiman, 2017).

The connectionism theory has employed artificial neural networks to predict how efficient a second language could be acquired. By following this theory Elman (1991) demonstrated that it is easier to learn data presented incrementally and the ability to learn decrease over time. Although, there is not a direct application of the theory over the learning process, their fundamentals allow researchers to evaluate how this process can be improved. Although connectionism lost popularity for a long time, in recent years a new generation of researchers is using the principles established in connectionism to find new insights about how complex structures on language can be easily learned. Among the models available, it is possible to find those related to reading and past tense, syntactic and semantic processing, and sentence processing (Joanisse and McClelland, 2015).

Comprehension hypothesis claims that a language is learned when the input is comprehensible, which means that the message transmitted has been understand (Krashen, 2018). This hypothesis also states that reading allows to acquire skills for writing and extends the vocabulary. Sugiharto (2010) mentions that also light reading, like comic books, are good for enhancing the skills obtained for communicating in a foreign language. Critics of the comprehension hypothesis mentions that the hypothesis is only part of a complete strategy, resulting in the development of new theories to provide a more inclusive methodology. This theory was further complemented with the interaction hypothesis supporting the relevance of interaction, and the output hypothesis which states that input, interaction, and negotiation are important to acquiring a second language (Paiva, 2014).

Sociocultural theory proposed by Vygotsky suggests that learning can be improved through social and cultural interaction among learners. This theory has been adopted in second language acquisition by using the notion of self-regulation and Zone of Proximal Development (Pathan, Memon, Memon, Khoso, and Bux, 2018). The Universal Grammar hypothesis proposed by Chomsky, states that there is a biologically structure in the brain with the capacity to provide skills needed to acquire a language quickly (Hulin and Na, 2014). Sociocultural theory is focused in how learners acquire the linguistic knowledge while Universal Grammar is focused in discover the linguistic competence (Dongyu, Fanyu, and Wanyi, 2013).

There are several differences among learning a second language and learning an indigenous language: first of those is the absence of a grammar structure and second, the lack of a curriculum learning. Even though second language acquisition theories are a good approach, the knowledge of indigenous people must be included. Chou (2016) proposed a 12 principles for teaching indigenous languages to children: content related to the official curriculum, understandable input and output, second language improvement through first language, easy and understandable teaching process, scaffold of language, correction of errors, use of body language, use of teaching materials, tell stories, use of games and songs, friendly environment for communicating in the target language, and cooperation with parents and community.

INDIGENOUS LANGUAGES LEARNING

Indigenous groups maintain around 4000 languages in the world (United Nations, 2018). African continent harbors a great diversity of native languages; however, schools don't have enough resources to provide an inclusive education. Almost 70% of the indigenous people of the world live in Asia; in this region there exists several conflicts among indigenous groups. Those conflicts generate massive movements of people, loss of identity and obstacles for the preservation of native language; despite the situation, there exists groups that have achieved the renaissance of indigenous education. The European continent is formed by a great number of minority groups, which have been constituted due to migration phenomena; although most of those groups suffer of discrimination, they have created communities to maintain their traditions and language heritage. Latin America poses a richness of culture originated in their native people, although they are part of the poverty population, many of them are self-sufficient allowing the maintenance of their traditions and native languages; problems arise when members of those groups leave their communities for being part of the cities, consequently resulting in the reduction of the use of their language. Canada and United States have created schools dedicated to the maintenance of native languages, although contents need to be improved to be more inclusive. Oceania has taken a step forward by proposing their own theory for native language education, allowing students learn by their own perspective (Jacob, Cheng and Porter, 2015).

Among the native languages which have been recovered to a level where they can be taught in language schools are: Nahuatl, Navajo, Macedonian, Bauan, and Swahili. Their study has established grammar rules and learning techniques to transfer the knowledge to students; also, second language acquisition theories can be employed. On the other hand, there are native languages where the number of speakers is minimum and there aren't established grammar rules; moreover, the language is only spoken but not written. To recover those languages, some governments have been proposed guidelines for the implementation of indigenous languages in schools. In Australia the adopted phases are: maintenance, the community and the students speak the language; bilingual, the community speak the language and the students speak two languages; revitalization, there is a generation of old people who speak the language and the students know some words; renewal, only a group of old people speak the language and the students don't understand the language; reclamation, the community doesn't speak the language and the students don't understand the language (Northern Territory Government of Australia, 2017).

Language at indigenous groups are transferred through generations; old people transmit their knowledge through language and traditions. Young generations learn an official language at school. The curricula of courses in schools is always related with a general culture of the world, homogenizing diverse regions of the country.

This situation starts the process of losing the identity of minorities through education. An inclusive education is required, where traditions, customs, and daily activities of communities are introduced in the education process; whether a fully grammaticized language is not available, words in native language, used to describe an action or an object, must be included gradually in the learning process until a 50:50 use of native language and official language is reached.

According to King and Schielmann (2004), an intercultural bilingual or multilingual education includes: the recognition and inclusion of several cultural systems, teaching and learning on native, official, and international languages, and activities for promoting exchange, reciprocity and solidarity of different cultures. Ozfidan and Aydin (2017) state that the better way of reducing discrimination is starting the formal education of children using their native language in a bilingual education model. Globalization has caused a mix of several cultures resulting in a loss of identity; it is required to take advantage of the cultural interchange to strengthen indigenous cultures through basic education, eliminating racism and discrimination, and preserving ancient knowledge through the native languages.

SERIOUS GAMES FOR INDIGENOUS LANGUAGE LEARNING

After reviewing the benefits provided by serious games in the learning of a second language, a need to establish guidelines for including second language acquisition theories in the game development process arise. It is important to maintain a balance between fun and knowledge acquisition for keeping user engagement. Acculturation, behaviorist theory, connectionism, comprehension hypothesis, and sociocultural hypothesis discussed before have elements which can be incorporated naturally in the game. A great advantage of games is the possibility to design scenarios which behaves as real-world environments, bringing the possibility to design games where the scenes represents real situations where the target language will be employed. Indigenous languages are strongly related with culture of communities; scenarios representing communities where indigenous language is spoken has a special relevance at the design process. In the next section, the proposed development phases of a serious game designed for indigenous language learning are described; it illustrates how second language acquisition theories can be implemented into the game. Those guidelines are an approach to include learning theories in the process of game development and not represent the only possibility, the objective is to provide a general process which can be adapted to the game goal.

Development Stages

Developing a game is a challenging process because it involves art, music, programming, acting and the integration of all those aspects to obtain a good quality game (Ramadan and Widyani, 2013). The game development life cycle (GDLC) is constituted mainly by three phases: pre-production, production and post-production (Aleem, Capretz and Ahmed, 2016). In the pre-production phase activities related to game requirements establishment, game design and assets creation are performed; production phase is related to the production of the story board, programming, and integration of the game; post-production phase involves activities of testing and quality assurance (Figure 1).

When developing serious games for indigenous language learning, the pre-production phase is the most demanding activity; it is required to design scenarios where the language is used frequently and highlighting those aspects which give relevance to the language, like traditions, customs, ceremonies, or real-life games played by the indigenous group, which can maintain the interest of learners. In the production stage the story board production needs special attention for provide a good sequence of the elements obtained in the pre-production phase. Finally, in the post-production stage, final users, teachers, and people belonging to the communities could reveal problems on the game or activities which require refinements.

Theory Inclusion

Acculturation can be integrated in a serious game through the inclusion of exploration in the game, through the design of scenes where the main character must interact with an indigenous group speaking the language to be learned; new words can be introduced to find specific elements in the scene; as the level increases, words can

Figure 1. Game development life cycle

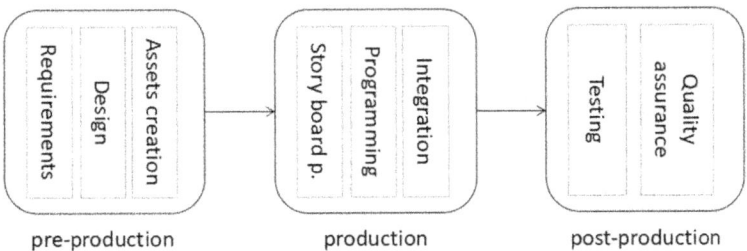

be transformed in phrases. Exploration is great to discover characteristics of the communities, allowing to players the acquisition of knowledge about the culture of the indigenous group. Exploration should be no limited only to walk in the community looking for objects, but to require the interaction with characters representing people of the community to reinforce the learned words or phrases. 3D environments are the most attractive to players, but also a good 2D design can be addictive. The design of a game is a challenge activity, it is required that new tools be developed for helping teachers to create their own games or modify existing ones. Acculturation is a theory which allows the learning of common phrases which are part of daily communication. Increasing the complexity of conversations among levels could be a good metric of the acculturation of player. Don't forget to include social, affective, personality, cognitive, biological, aptitude, personal, input, and instructional factors.

To include behaviorist theory in the game, the establishment of a set of repetitive activities, which provide points to players, is ideal to maintain the user performing a reinforcement learning until a specific communication skill is acquired. A good source of inspiration are the social games which are designed to maintain the players performing activities every day; with this philosophy, users come back to the game continuously to perform the pending activities. Including activities related to a traditional day of the community, where the player is involved, helps to known not only words or phrases but also when and where to use them (Figure 3).

Figure 2. Including acculturation in the game

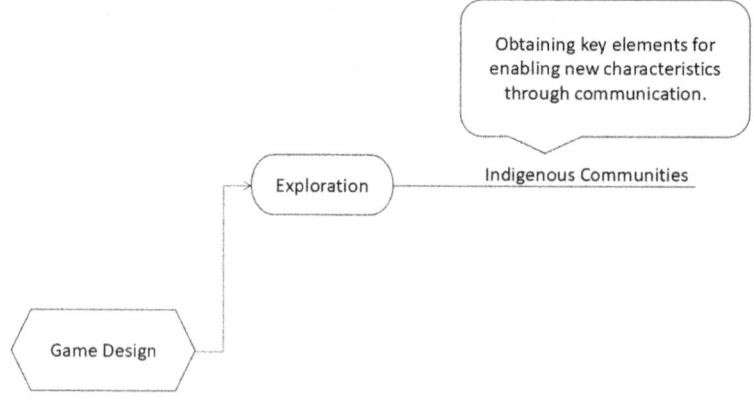

Figure 3. Including behaviorist theory in the game

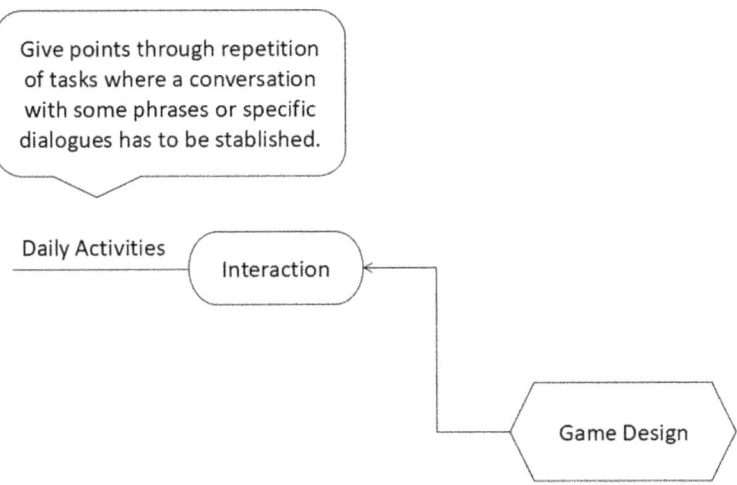

The connectionism theory is strongly related with the Artificial Intelligence (AI), and can be integrated to the game by virtual agents (representing friends of the player) which learn the behavior of player and could predict what activities will improve the learning process. This way, agents could generate spontaneous activities into the game helping to improve the knowledge and skills acquired by the player to reach the learning objective. Also, activities of player can be tracked by an agent to generate scenarios that challenge their skills (Figure 4). Maintaining a registry of activities performed by the player not only help to the AI, but also allows to teacher for identifying the weaknesses of the user. Games should be designed for allowing modifications according to user's skills, since users learn in different ways.

Comprehension hypothesis recommends providing comprehensible input. This can be done through the game design by integrating elements familiar to players and reinforcing previous knowledge through new learning activities. This hypothesis could be integrated to the game by including scenarios representing characteristics of communities and adding reading activities about historic or relevant events to maintain the interest in the game (Figure 5). Reading can be improved through brief introductions to activities explained in the indigenous language. When passing to a new level, it is necessary to include activities where the user has obtained good performance; making the user feel comfortable and ready to overcome the new challenges. Additional resources as a dictionary can help users through the game to remember or acquire new vocabulary.

Figure 4. Including connectionism theory in the game

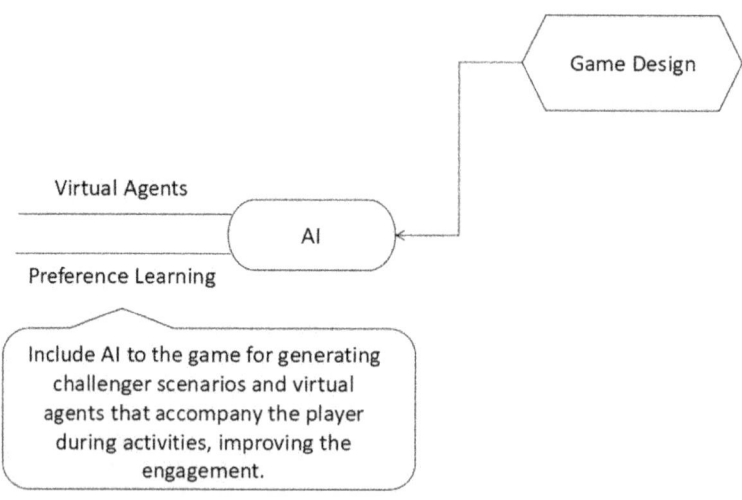

Figure 5. Including comprehension hypothesis in the game

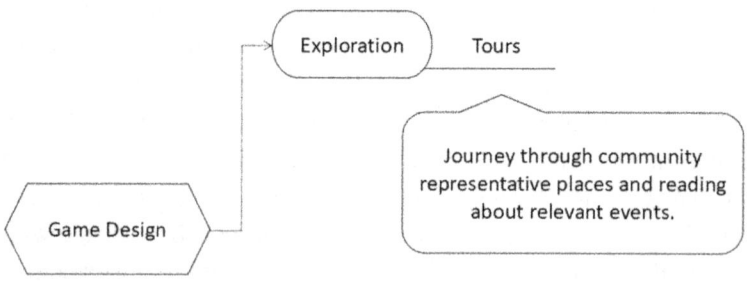

Sociocultural theory states that interaction among learners improves the learning acquisition. The inclusion of multiplayer capabilities allows the interaction among players to complete tasks where the employment of communication skills in the indigenous language are required (Figure 6). The game should have sections designed for one player and sections designed for multiplayer. Designing activities which require the participation of a group of students are a good complement to the personal learning and puts the knowledge acquired to the test. To reach the Zone of Proximal Development proposed by Vygotsky, there should be activities that need the guidance of more advanced users or the teacher; this brings the possibility of including the teacher as part of the game in a multiplayer scenario. Writing skills can be developed by requiring communication through chat among players. Speech also can be improved through a multiplayer scenario; allowing not only conversations through chat, but also voice communication among users.

Figure 6. Including sociocultural theory in the game

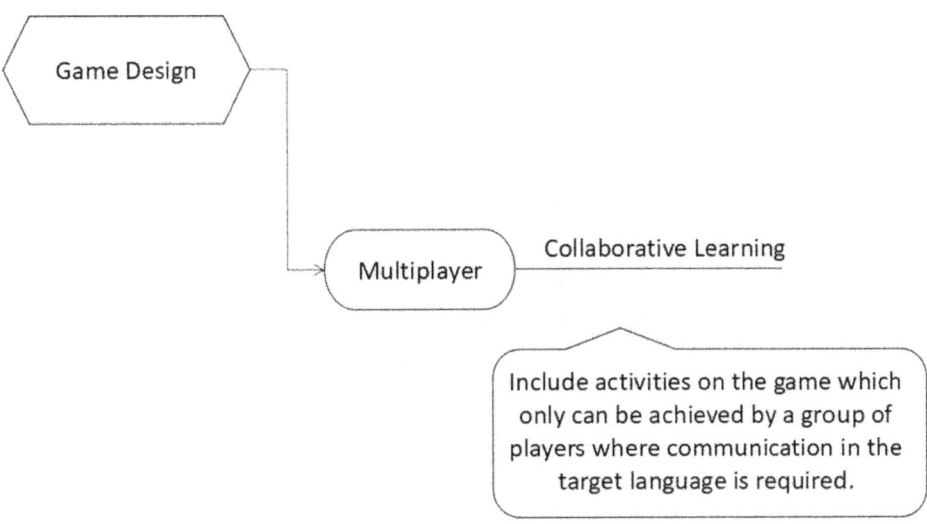

A game designed with repetition of daily activities, exploration of indigenous communities, tours over relevant places, virtual agents which collaborate with the player to achieve specific task, agents learning from the player preferences to improve the game experience, multiplayer capabilities for allowing collaborative learning, and challenging activities which require help of advanced users to reach the zone of proximal development, will produce a well-structured tool for an indigenous language acquisition, where learning can be evaluated not only by teachers, but also by classmates or the own student (Figure 7).

Figure 7. Elements of serious game for indigenous language learning based on SLA theories

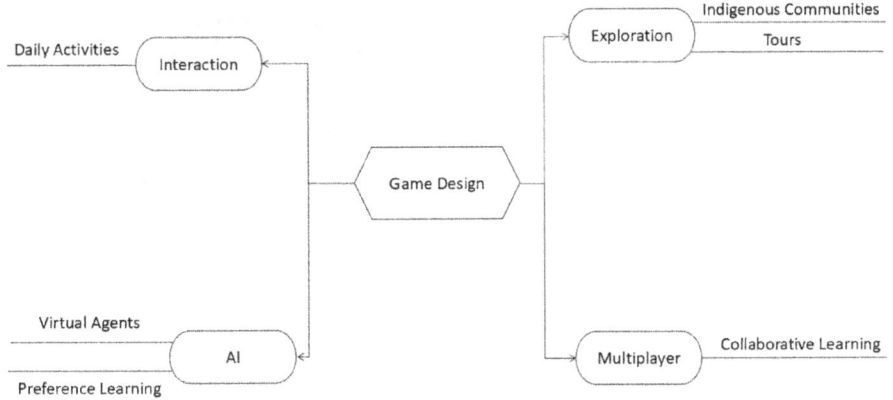

Learning Evaluation

A serious game cannot reach their goal if an evaluation of learning is missing. To identify the level of advance acquired by the user, there are additional tools which should be included in the design of the game; those tools should help to teachers in the control of the game to reinforce the learning acquired with activities in the classroom. Some of them are proposed below:

- Include brief quizzes after every level completion.
- Record the time and attempts required to complete a task.
- Design a dashboard where acquired and missing skills are illustrated.
- Allow users to generate their own scenarios by providing a set of game resources related with learning objectives.
- Allow scenario adjustment and activity elections by teachers.

CHALLENGES AND FUTURE TRENDS

Developing games which maintain users engaged, while indigenous language learning is increased, is a challenge which requires the development of new tools for producing quality games while the development complexity is reduced. Through the provision of tools for the development of serious games to teachers focused on indigenous language learning, second language acquisition theories can be included easily. There is a gap between serious games developers and second language teachers which should be reduced through video game development tools. Nowadays there are several tools for the development of serious games; however, it is necessary to improve the story, quality of scenes, user interaction, and user experience to keep students interested in playing the game until the learning objectives are reached.

Including new technologies like artificial intelligence, virtual reality, augmented reality, natural language processing, voice recognition, among others will generate more attractive games; however, it is required to design tools with a low complexity for the inclusion of those technologies, such that teachers can use them to design their games. Serious games should be developed and designed by teachers since their known better the requirements of learning of their groups. To reach that, new frameworks for serious games development must be proposed.

Recovering, maintaining, and transmitting indigenous language is a big challenge, and doing these through serious games is only a proposal of many activities need to be done. Serious games for indigenous language learning should not only be used with groups interested to learn an indigenous language, but also adopted as a tool to learn about culture of indigenous communities. The knowledge about cultures will reduce the racism and generate a better integration of different cultures and ideologies. Children are in the most permeable stage of learning and must be taught to respect, value, and preserve languages, traditions, and customs of indigenous communities for generating a more tolerant world.

CONCLUSION

Through the chapter a set of guidelines to develop serious games oriented to indigenous language learning was proposed. Indigenous languages are prone to disappear whether no interest of people is present. Serious games are a good approach to recover those language while persons are entertained. Second language acquisition theories are fundamental to guarantee a good learning process. The guidelines for the design of a serious game, can be used as a first approach to other learning activities and adjust it according to the learning content, and learning goals. Evaluation of learning is required in order that both teachers and students could measure the acquired skills. Serious games are a great complement to education when are well designed; students are less prone to do homework, but more enthusiasts of playing video games after schools. Including serious games in those leisure times, will increase the skills of students. There are many topics to be covered yet to produce mature games which can be designed by teachers, and after those games could be designed easily, it is required to evaluate their performance to maintain a right balance between learning and entertainment.

REFERENCES

Abt, C. C. (1987). *Serious Games*. University Press of America.

Aleem, S., Capretz, L. F., & Ahmed, F. (2016). Game development software engineering process life cycle: A systematic review. *Journal of Software Engineering Research and Development*, *4*(6), 1–30.

Alemi, M., & Tavakoli, E. (2016). Audio lingual method. *3rd International Conference on Applied Research in Language Studies*, Tehran, Iran.

Amoia, M., Bretaudiere, T., Denis, A., Gardent, C., & Perez-Beltrachini, L. (2012). A serious game for second language acquisition in a virtual environment. *Systemics. Cybernetics and Informatics*, *10*(1), 24–34.

Ayaz, Y., & Genc, Z. S. (2016). Digital game-based language learning in foreign language teacher education. *Turkish Online Journal of Distance Education*, *17*(4), 130–146.

Budiman, A. (2017). Behaviorism in foreign language teaching methodology. *English Franca*, *1*(2), 101–114.

Chou, H.-C. (2016). Strategies for teaching indigenous languages to preschoolers in Taiwan: A case of language immersion. *International Journal of Humanities and Social Science Invention*, *5*(9), 57–62.

Correa Ferreira, G., Ortiz Torres, E. M., Vargas Garcia, M., Lemos Vasconcellos, S. J., Schopf Frizzo, N., & Julio Costa, M. (2018). The effect of bilingualism on cognitive and auditory abilities in normal hearing adults. *Revista CEFAC*, *20*(1), 21–28. doi:10.1590/1982-0216201820112417

De Gloria, A., Bellotti, F., & Berta, R. (2014). Serious games for education and training. *International Journal of Serious Games*, *1*(1), 1–15. doi:10.17083/ijsg. v1i1.11

Demirezen, M. (1988). Behaviorist theory and language learning. *Journal of Hacettepe University Faculty of Education*, *3*, 135–140.

Dongyu, Z., Fanyu, & Wanyi, D. (2013). Sociocultural theory applied to second language learning: Collaborative learning with reference to the Chinese context. *International Education Studies*, *6*(9), 165–174.

Eaton, S. E. (2010). *Formal, non-formal and informal learning: The case of literacy, essential skills, and language learning in Canada*. Eaton International Consulting Inc.

Elman, J. (1991). Distributed representations, simple recurrent networks, and grammatical structure. *Machine Learning, 7*(2-3), 195–225. doi:10.1007/BF00114844

Furniss, E. (2014). *Perspectives on policy and practice: indigenous language and education*. EAC.

Godwin-Jone, R. (2016). Augmented reality and language learning: From annotated vocabulary to place-based mobiles games. *Language Learning & Technology, 20*(3), 9–19.

Hulin, R., & Na, X. (2014). A study of Chomsky's universal grammar in second language acquisition. *International Journal on Studies in English Language and Literature, 2*(12), 1–7.

Jacob, W. J., Cheng, S. Y., & Porter, M. K. (2015). Global review of indigenous educations: issues of identity, culture, and language. In W. Jacob, S. Cheng, & M. Porter (Eds.), *Indigenous Education: Language, Culture, and Identity*. Springer.

Joanisse, M. F., & McClelland, J. L. (2015). Connectionist perspectives on language learning, representation and processing. *Wiley Interdisciplinary Reviews: Cognitive Science, 2015*. doi:10.1002/wcs.1340 PMID:26263227

King, L., & Schielmann, S. (2004). *The challenge of Indigenous Education: Practice and Perspectives*. UNESCO.

Krashen, S. D. (1983). Bilingual education and second language acquisition theory. In C. F. Leyba (Ed.), *Schooling and Language Minority Students: A Theoretical Framework* (2nd ed.). Legal Books Distributing.

Krashen, S. D. (2018). *The conduit hypothesis: how reading leads to academic language competence*. Language Magazine.

Lan, Y. J. (2015). Contextual EFL learning in a 3d virtual environment. *Language Learning & Technology, 19*(2), 16–31.

Menezes, V. (2013). Second language acquisition: reconciling theories. *Open Journal of Applied Sciences, 2013*(3), 404-412. Doi:10.4236/ojapps.2013.37050

Northern Territory Government of Australia. (2017). *Guidelines for the Implementation of Indigenous Languages and Cultures Programs in Schools*. Department of Education.

Ozfidan, B., & Aydin, H. (2017). Curriculum related issues in bilingual education. *Higher Education Studies*, *7*(4), 25–34. doi:10.5539/hes.v7n4p25

Paiva, V. L. M. O. (2014). Main second language acquisition theories: From structuralism to complexity. *Revista Contexturas*, *23*, 112–124.

Pathan, H., Memon, R. A., Memon, S., Khoso, A. R., & Bux, I. (2018). A critical review of Vygotsky's socio-cultural theory in second language acquisition. *International Journal of English Linguistics*, *8*(4), 232–236. doi:10.5539/ijel.v8n4p232

Rabin, S. (2010). *Introduction to Game Development* (2nd ed.). Boston, MA: Course Technology.

Ramadan, R., & Widyani, Y. (2013). Game development life cycle guidelines. *2013 International Conference on Advanced Computer Science and Information Systems*, 95-100.

Schumann, J. H. (1986). Research on the acculturation model for second language acquisition. *Journal of Multilingual and Multicultural Development*, *7*(5), 379–392. doi:10.1080/01434632.1986.9994254

Song, S. (2018). *Second language acquisition as a mode-switching process – an empirical analysis of Korean Learners of English*. Palgrave Macmillan UK. Doi:10.1057/978-1-137-52436-2

Statista. (2016, December). *Number of video gamers worldwide in 2016, by region (in millions)*. Retrieved from https://www.statista.com/statistics/293304/number-video-gamers/

Sugiharto, S. (2010). The robustness of the comprehension hypothesis: A review of current research and implications for the teaching of writing. *Journal of Social Sciences and Humanities*, *18*(2), 417–425.

Tobias, S., & Fletcher, D. (2011). Learning from computer games: a research review. In S. D. Wannemacker, S. Vandercruysse, & G. Clarebout (Eds.), *Serious Games: The Challenge*. Springer.

Tsalapatas, H., Heidmann, O., Alimisi, D., & Houstis, E. (2013). A serious game-based approach for situated learning of vehicular languages addressing work needs and cultural aspects. In *proceedings of the 7th International Technology, Education and Development Conference* (pp. 5059-5065). Valencia, Spain: IATED.

UNESCO. (2015). *Multilingualism in cyberspace: indigenous languages for empowerment*. San José, Costa Rica: UNESCO Regional Conference for Central America.

United Nations. (2018). *Indigenous languages. The united nations permanent forum on indigenous issues*. UN Department of Public Information.

Valente, A., Johnson, W. L., & Vilhjálmsson, H. H. (2006). The tactical language and culture training system: a demonstration. *Proceedings of The Twenty-First National Conference on Artificial Intelligence and Eighteenth Innovative Applications of Artificial Intelligence Conference*, 1955-1956.

Vetter, E. (2014). Combining formal and non-formal foreign language learning: First insights into a German-Spanish experiment at university level. *Studies in Applied Linguistics*, *2014*, 39–50.

Wattanasoontorn, V., García-Hernández, R. J., & Sbert, M. (2012). Serious games for e-health care. In Y. Cai & S. L. Goei (Eds.), *Simulations, Serious Games and Their Applications*. Springer.

Wilkinson, P. (2016). A brief history of serious games. In *Entertainment Computing and Serious Games, LNCS 9970* (pp. 17–41). Springer. doi:10.1007/978-3-319-46152-6_2

ADDITIONAL READING

Can, T., & Simsek, I. (2015). The use of 3D virtual learning environments in training foreign language pre-service teachers. *Turkish Online Journal of Distance Education*, *16*(4), 114–124.

Chalak, A., & Ahmadi, B. (2017). Integration of serious games in teaching English as a foreign language to Iranian children. *International Journal of Foreign Language Teaching & Research*, *5*(17), 77–87.

Chomksy, N. (1986). *Knowledge of Language: Its Nature, Origin and Use*. Praeger.

Crain, S., & Lillo-Martin, D. (1999). *An Introduction to Linguistic Theory and Language Acquisition: An Introduction to Human Impacts on the Environment*. Blackwell Publishing.

Devlin, B. C., Disbray, S., & Devlin, N. R. F. (Eds.). (2018). *History of Bilingual Education in the Northern Territory: People, Programs, and Policies*. Springer.

Galla, C. K., & Goodwill, A. (2017). Talking story with vital voices: Making knowledge with indigenous language. *Journal of Indigenous Wellbeing*, *2*(3), 67–75.

Gasser, M. (1990). Connectionism and universals of second language acquisition. *Studies in Second Language Acquisition*, *12*(02), 179–199. doi:10.1017/S0272263100009074

Gómez Chova, L., Candel Torres, I., & López Martínez, A. (2012). *Edulearn12 Proceedings*. Barcelona, Spain: IATED.

Jacqueline-Andersen, P. (2018). *The Indigenous World*. Copenhagen, Denmark: International Work Group for Indigenous Affairs.

Marsh, T. (2015). Slow serious games, interactions and play: Designing for positive and serious experience and reflection. *Entertainment Computing*, *14*, 45–53. doi:10.1016/j.entcom.2015.10.001

Mocinic, A. (2011). Bilingual education. *Metodicki Obzori*, *6*, 175–182.

Muller, C. (2017). *Serious Games for Global Education: Digital Game-Based Learning in the English as a Foreign Language (EFL) Classroom*. Berlin: Peter Lang Gmbh. doi:10.3726/b11802

Nava, A., & Pedrazzini, L. (2018). *Second Language Acquisition in Action: Principles from Practice*. London: Bloomsbury Academic.

Thompson, C. (2018). The role of practice within second language acquisition. In C. Jones (Ed.), *Practice in Second Language Learning*. Cambridge University Press. doi:10.1017/9781316443118.004

Vygotsky, L. S. (1978). *Mind in Society: The Development of Higher Psychological Processes*. Cambridge, MA: Harvard University Press.

KEY TERMS AND DEFINITIONS

Bilingual Education: Teaching system through which the use of two languages is encouraged while the curriculum is covered.

Formal Learning: Learning acquired in a guided environment, where the topics are established a priori and evaluation of acquired skill are present.

Indigenous Language: Language spoken within an ethnic community where the language is part of their identity and some traits of their customs are preserved through it.

Psycholinguistic: Psychology branch that studies how language is acquired by human being and how the information is processed for acquiring knowledge.

Serious Game: Video game developed with the objective to acquire knowledge over a specific topic as progress is made in the game.

Chapter 4

Temporal Asynchrony of Socio–Technical Devices in Distance Learning?
Origins of Cleavage Between Academics and Learning Communities

Xavier Inghilterra
https://orcid.org/0000-0001-6149-7207
Université de Lorraine, France

ABSTRACT

This chapter is based on a research that has been focusing on social sharing device effects and on students' practices of collaboration, communication, and mediation. The author has analyzed the recurring temporal split between academic environment and students' sphere in a context of distance learning. The goal is to understand the origin of the collaborative process of collective apprentice which is illustrated in the communities of apprenticeship outside the academic institution. A netnographic observation was conducted with Bachelor and Master's degrees in a private training center. The author assumes the information and communication socio-technical devices participate in the horizontalization of student practices. The author has highlighted the paradox of these learning communities, which are, unwittingly, in a process of social domination by having choosing a priori a decentralized structure. In light of the social criticism of the time, the observation reveals that digital technologies cause a temporal acceleration.

DOI: 10.4018/978-1-5225-7435-4.ch004

INTRODUCTION

In a first chapter issued in December 2013, we presented the results of research carried out among students registered in distance learning centers. We concluded that social networking formerly used in the private sphere is now in common use in academics. Some universities and training centers have taken coercive measures such as stopping access to Ethernet network. As for us, we think a collaborative process is a much better way to encourage active learning such as microblogging. Indeed, this interactional model is more appropriate as a computer-mediated communication device. Hence, we have been focusing on how students become familiar with a socio-technical tool implemented by professors. We have also identified the artefacts of microblogging on peer to peer mediation. To do so, we have undertaken participant observation by teaching the curriculum of Information and Relation Management, which represents our empirical field.

Our study lasted 4 months from November, 2012 to February, 2013 and the target audience was composed of 276 Bachelor students attending 5 courses of an hour (callconf). Twitter was used as a mediation channel combined with an institutional platform (LMS) and a students' blog. The aim was to initiate interactions between learners during callconfs and extend them afterwards in the private sphere. The gap between academic and personal environments promotes growing knowledge between peers. The first results were contrasting: pro microblogging students were a minority. Indeed, imposing on them a particular device can be crippling because freedom is essential to any learning community. On the contrary, those who became familiar with Twitter appreciated its flexibility such as the use of a community hashtag, for instance #ConfcallRS, giving them a sense of belonging. It came out that these collectives were naturally prone to intermediation: some students take the role of tutors, spontaneously initiating a mediation with their fellow classmates. Considering the emerging need to renew or diversify the various means of mediation, microblogging permits a dialogic style, communicational modalities and information sharing all of which essential to learning communities.

In this new chapter, we will deal with action research based on the conclusions of the previous experiment. That time, we have experimented a non-participant observation in which socio-technical devices were chosen by students themselves to create their own personal learning environment. The goal is to bring out the efficiency of collaborative learning observed in these epistemic communities.

THE EPISTEMIC FRAMEWORK OF THE RESEARCH

This study on collaborative distance learning was made among Bachelors of a private second-degree school. The socio-technical devices we studied were the institutional platform on the one hand (discussion forums) and students' social networks on the other hand (Google+ and Facebook). This research is focused on distance learning communities. Our empirical field is based on non-participant observations among students in Bachelor and Master using socio technical devices. They attend lessons in a private school with a strong anchoring in industrializing distance training, in other words its management and organization are directly inherited from industrial model (Depover, Deschryver, & Monasta, 1999). Through a socio technical approach our goal is to analyze students' practices of collaboration, mediation and communication which value peer to peer learning rather than academics.

This study highlights a recurrent phenomenon in distance learning: students prefer dealing with their peers to asking for their tutors' help online. Not only do they favor their constant availability but mostly their reactivity which becomes community ritual. It came out that the gap opposing the academic sphere and the students' sphere is partly due to distinct timeframes: a vertical one, called ENT, present in the school and a horizontal one, characterized by exchanges between students through the EPA. As a result, we can notice a temporal asynchrony triggering itself a misappropriation or poaching (Ricœur, 2006). Indeed, they transfer academic resources towards the EPA. Furthermore, our observation reveals that digital technologies cause a temporal acceleration of interactions. As described in literature reviews (Josèphe, 2008a; Rosa, 2010; Virilio, 2010a; Vitalis, 1994) mobile phones are responsible for it. Yet, these learning communities, which establish resolutely horizontal structures, do not seem aware of the long-term consequences of this bolting.

From the two thousands onwards, collaborative uses have been developing in the wake of web 2.0. technologies to the point of becoming the ultimate online practice in other words social sharing. Nowadays, learners have a wide range of information resources and can rely on their peers any time and anywhere on social networks. They privilege direct contact that is to say without any intermediary, as well as reactivity all together reinforcing in return their trust in the latest. Although non hierarchical by its very nature, social web has ended up establishing horizontality as a model of interaction between peers in many socio economic sectors. It is also evident that higher education or training students resort to these horizontal discussion uses, independently of the institution, before addressing to their referent tutors. The usual teaching model dating from Comenius in use for centuries and consisting in a transmission from knowledge holders to learners, is coming to an inexorable end at a time when lecture theatres are getting more and more deserted. As a result, alternative methods influenced by Siemen's connectivist model (Siemens, 2006) but also very close to Vygotsky's neoconstructivism (Vygotskij, Sève, Sève, & Clot, 1985), have emerged such as Open Universities, MOOCs or P2PU. They have been a great success. Considering distance learning used to be seen as a "handicap" in the past, it is no longer true. On the contrary, in an era of connected individualism, its essential values are now put forward such as permitting students attending the same education lessons on line massive interactions between themselves, as well as growing enrichment of knowledge and efficiency learning.

DATA COLLECTION METHODOLOGY

This scientific study is part of a social and epistemic paradigm. Let us consider the exogenous aspects of social origin and the endogenous ones of epistemic nature. Indicators of our groups' sociability and collective contribution can be measured thanks to proteiform materials and methodological multidisciplinarity. In effect, the latest both combines a vast interactionist field aimed at analyzing digital rituals and an informationist field studying social networks analysis (SNA), *a verbatim* interviews and sociometrics. In the actual research, a real understanding of the collective learning process is made relevant by collecting as many indicators as possible. That is the reason why we are going to focus on the following ones:

1. Interaction rites which are analyzed by inventorying socio-affective and socio-cognitive signs during interactions. To do so, we have resorted to the coding of the functions of parts of messages (Henri & Rigault, 1996) who define four functional levels in exchanges depending on their social, organizational, cognitive or metacognitive vocation (see Table 1 to 3 in appendix).
2. Formal or informal knowledge: our observation has for a goal to make out what students acquire between peers in a strictly institutional environment, as well as in a collaborative way. Therefore, we will have to underline the dichotomy between didactic resources they find in the institutional ENT and the ones they produce themselves and share in their EPA. These informal exchanges between themselves constitute informal knowledge which represents a major point in this research.

To get a better comprehension of these indicators, we have followed this multidisciplinary combination based on interaction traces analysis, content analysis, online questionnaires, semi-guiding interviews and focus groups.

INDUSTRIALIZING DISTANCE TRAINING

The institutional framework of this research is characterised by the industrialization of training. The entrepreneurial approach based on technologization, rationalization and ideologization (Vidal, Grandbastien, & Moeglin, 2010) gives an advantage to competition, lowering the cost of training. It's all about making compromises between tutors' intervention and the economy of scale made in the management and logistics of distance learning. For the past few years, many schools have also taken the option of mass training with a socio constructivism input as a precept. In the end it comes out that there is a standardization of the teaching process. On the other hand, training devices based on Learning Management System have now reached a functional maturity. Considering their use has become obvious, it is regrettable it too often replaces tutors' mediation.

Sociology of practices (Jouët, 2000) suggests to clarify first and foremost the background in which social sciences see the impact of technique on our society. Two epistemologies are frequently opposed: technical determinism in which social evolution is encouraged by technical innovation and social determinism in which technical development increases social inequalities. However as social sciences researchers, we are supposed to be vigilant concerning training industrialization. That's why we privilege usability study in the way it enables to analyse rationally a socio technical device of information and communication (Akrich, Callon, & Latour, 2006) and prevents any determinism.

THE CONCEPT OF SOCIO TECHNICAL DEVICE OF INFORMATION AND COMMUNICATION

According to Agamben, not only are individuals influenced by their technological environment but they are also its actors (Agamben, 2006). In this epistemic perspective, we are referring to scientific works from laboratory I3m's researchers[1]: "figuring out world's shifts by underlining technologies' interactions with their environment". They have interpreted processes like collaboration or co-building and have tried to prove that ICTs have a long time impact by modifying uses on media, cultural and organisational levels.

These researches, issued from critical thought, aim at rethinking mediation at work in any socio-technical device. For Françoise Bernard, this concept of socio-technical device which was first elaborated for critical thinking purposes, later became by generalising, a concept to function (Bernard & Durampart, 2013). However, Foulcaud considers this device also presents a dominant strategic role. This is precisely the acceptation we are referring to in this study. As for Quéré, institutional trust is a phenomenon which needs to be looked at carefully through the prism of the mechanisms of deference on the one hand and of public space on the other hand (Quéré, 2005). It relies on a specific device, in other words on "trust-based device".

Among the I3m laboratory, the concept of socio technical device of information and communication is a unifying paradigm. These researches originating from Critical Theory question the status and role of mediation in each socio technical device. Analysing processes such as constructivism or connectivism, they prove that digital technologies modify, in the long-term, using habits of mediation, culture and organisation. By resorting to CMC, we have recourse to computer sciences and the input of mediated communication. The new ways of connectivity permit to tame distance (Jacquinot, 1993) and the notion of CMC also called socio-technical mediation plays a major role in our research.

CRITICAL THEORY

We have also noticed this quest for visibility can sometimes reveal a will to stage oneself. Considering the fact that students can post their own topics of discussion and can occupy media space on the EPA or ENT, it appears that some of them are getting more and more self-centred. Is this tendency relevant of a quest for recognition? That is what we are putting forward in reference to the Recognition Theory (Honneth, 2013) of Frankfurt School. Thus, our aim is to highlight individuals' standard expectations within socio-technical devices and most particularly self-recognition among peers. Our study both emphasizes inherent temporalities of the EPA and the ENT and the acceleration phenomenon which characterizes students' sphere. That is the reason why our theoretical anchoring is influenced by Frankfurt School's Critical Theory as far as self-recognition is concerned, as well as by Rosa's Social Acceleration (Rosa, 2010) due to technical innovation, social change and pace of life.

TEMPORALITY IN AN ERA OF CONNECTED INDIVIDUALISM: ANTHROPOLOGY OF A "MOBINAUTE"

Time is another key issue to take into account to analyse virtual communities' practices. Because of the development of ICTs, ubiquitous computing and mobile devices, users' communicational abilities have undergone major changes. With ATAWAD access giving total mobiquity with the omnipresence of mobile networks (WIFI, 4G), internauts also have the possibility to host their personal data in distant servers. The cloud became so obvious that the end of local storage work was much expected in favour of the « all connected ». With the emergence of connected individualism (Flichy, 2004) it is now time for distant collaboration and participative work. It has become common use to share on dedicated social networks permitting to store and share all kinds of data (texts, photos, videos, bookmarks, bibliographies, blogs, music...). These major achievements highlight users' « ubiquity myth » (Musso, Ponthou, Seulliet, Viginier, & Charlès, 2007). However, it's a utopia to believe you can be efficient anywhere and anytime on various tasks.

In an era of multitasking and real time, internauts' cognitive overload can have many psychosocial consequences in terms of public health. The main thing is the progressive blurring of the frontier between professional environment and personal sphere also called « privacy ». However mobile phones and smartphones in particular, are the archetypes of mobiquity that causes both a space and time desynchronization. Indeed, there is no clear limit between presence and absence in the way that omnipresent mobile phones are essential to maintain continuous interpersonal links (Licoppe, 2009). According to Christian Licoppe, connected presence encouraged by mobile phones is a communication which is not incompatible with absence but which cannot stand silence. In effect there is a growing phobia of being cut out from social networks (ibid., p. 29). That is the reason why SMSs have known such a growth in a context of phatic communication between peers where instantness prevails. Immediacy, ephemerality and boundary remodelling between private and public spheres are what Tisseron calls this new « *extimité* » (Tisseron, 2007).

For Pascal Josèphe, this tendency to temporal acceleration is characteristic of digital technologies and of contemporary social practices (Josèphe, 2008b). In his essay entitled « La société immédiate », the author denounces the following actual trend: the replacement of time mediation by the instantness cult. Our economic and technic models reduce the time between the expression of their needs and their satisfaction. The result of this speeding up is a temporal discordance between individual and social time causing an explosion of collective life rhythm. « I want, I take », « I feel like it, I consume ». Josèphe wonders if immediacy is not bringing us back to uncivilized times. Indeed, digital technology is not only a sign of beneficial progress. A radical change in our relation to the world and others is taking place. Post-modern society tends to forget the past and no longer believes in a better future which results in favouring even more the present through immediacy. With this idea of time, emphasized by the omnipresence of socio-digital networks, the whole of social life is affected such as medias, politics, justice, economy, arts … Let us refer to Pascal Josèphe's thesis on the need for instantness noticed among the studied individuals. The interaction marks we have observed actually reveal that communicational rhythm is intensifying significantly because of mobile terminals, mostly used by digital natives. This is also Paul Virilio's opinion when he talks about « la révolution dromologique », thinking that the acceleration of the world is worrying as far as its effects on Man, the economy and the Environment are concerned (Virilio, 2010b).

METHODOLOGY OF THE RESEARCH

The Advantages of Netnography on the Epistemology of ICSs

It is common use in praxeological sociology to have recourse to ethno-methodology in order to study social groups. Beyond formal analysis, we take into account members' posture inside a collective. According to Garfinkel, it is all about having the required skills to join the « village » (Garfinkel, Barthélemy, & Quéré, 2007). But in the case of virtual communities, « classical » ethno-methods have their limits. However, netnography allows a close immersion of the researcher in the heart of the observation without taking part in it.

Observing while participating or participating while observing is nearly as obvious as eating a burning hot ice cream (Favret-Saada, 2009).

A Multidisciplinary Methodology

In this study, we deal with the effects of socio-technical devices on the practices of collaboration, communication and mediation between students. Our goal is to put forward the collaborative process at the origin of collective learning which is much significant among learners. On the one hand, it is important to distinguish what they learn thanks to the institution and, on the other hand, the knowledge they acquire together between peers (Benghozi, Bitouzet, Soulier, & Zacklad, 2001). That is why we make a distinction between teaching resources exported from the ENT and those produced by students themselves and shared via their EPA. These exchanges constitute informal knowledge that plays a major role in this research. We think these socio-technical devices of information and communication participate in the horizontalization of collective uses. To apprehend collaborative process, we resort to a definitely multidisciplinary methodology combining both interactionist and informationist fields: qualitative methods such as the categorization of the learning activity and the analysis of interaction rituals and quantitative ones for instance *a verbatim* analysis or social networks analysis.

From a methodological perspective, we used a systematic hypothetico-deductive method as our empirical approach. Our experimental field is composed of 314 individuals from Bachelor and Master degrees registered in distance learning. Our corpus is made of 1405 messages taken from various devices: discussion groups in the ENT and community spaces created by students on Facebook and Google+. Our measurement ranges from November 2014 to May 2015 that is to say 6 months' non-participant observation.

THE RESULTS OF THE OBSERVATION

Antagonistic Temporalities

Since ubiquitous computing conquered the domestic and professional spheres, users have taken the habit of being constantly connected. During online training, pervasive communication is being established among learning communities and becomes essential by reducing geographical distance and linking people together. Proximity is materialised by a phatic communication giving a rhythm to students' everyday routine and annihilating their sense of isolation. A virtuous emulation is emerging from the group and the first collaborations are being established in an informal way. In the closest communities a real mutual aid plan appears between students who motivate each others. Interaction time is a protean notion which takes different shapes according to the generation. First, we observe a « vertical » temporality whose answer time ranges from a few hours to a few days: this is institutional time used by tutors and educational coordinators in other words the X generation (Prensky, 2007). The second temporality is « horizontal » and corresponds to interaction latency between students: it is particularly quick, nearly instantaneous because of mobile terminals. But if reactivity is too long, exchanges can be compromised. As a matter of fact, students and tutors are developing in two orthogonal temporalities causing temporal a synchronism. It might explain why learners misuse institutional ENT.

This desynchronization accentuates even more the already obvious gap between tutors and students. Without giving more credit to Prensky's theory on digital natives (Prensky, 2010), we think time relation differs according to the generation. In the extracts below, we can notice two temporalities: institutional time which is longer versus students' time which is fast.

Extract 1. *A verbatim* analysis

[...] Ok + I know last year, + in February 2014, I immediately set my phone on Google+ [:] then I had requests from the group so + I wanted to be able to answer as fast as possible in fact [:] I set the phone like that straight away + it was a bit different with the learning deck ++ that is to say emails' platform + we check them every day at 5 pm while posts are received the second that follows! /// it allows me to answer people at once [...]

Extract 2. *A verbatim* analysis

[...] you know tutors + are always there for us, nothing to complain about, they answer as soon as they can, but sometimes it's a bit longer /// then I will not say that +++ finally tutors + they say they connect once a day, 'cause 24h is a bit long. We wish he had the answer earlier +++ you know + tutors aren't necessarily available all the time, every minute +++ if there's an answer from a student, why not ?

In addition, a second point has to be made as for the answering time slots. On the side of the institution, they match with the "working" hours, generally from 9 in the morning to 6 in the evening. Talking about learners, however, there is no precise or unconventional time slot. Since smartphones were part of their everyday life, their communicational uses have become pervasive. What's more, we have noticed that they do not have any greeting salutations at the beginning and the end of their interactional sequences (Amato & Boutin, 2013). Is time perception variable to that point, depending on socio-technical devices and their use ? It has to be made clear that these « all digital » and « unlimited internet » natives have never known alternate connection slots till the mid 2000's. In effect, the arrival of broadband and mainstream internet marked the end of minute-based billing forcing users to disconnect each time from the analogical modem. In practice, the very first internauts who were conditioned by online and offline slots do not have the same relationship to time. Later internauts have a phatic way of communicating which is never clearly expressed through any standard form of greeting such as « hello! », « see u later », giving a sense of no real beginning or ending (Jakobson & Vine, 1985). Indeed, there is no need for close exchanges which can start again at any time.

The communication channel is always implicit and they just have to start a chat to revive it with the same intensity and rhythm. In context of vertical temporality, students cannot know when they get an answer from their tutors to a question they have asked on the ENT. On the contrary, the slightest « bottle into the sea » on the EPA will find an echo by at least a member of the constantly connected community. This leads us to think the studied population tends to favour quick answers to the detriment of reliability.

Extract 3. *A verbatim* analysis

[...]+++ if I react quickly it's because I get it ! if I don't know, it's true I still want to verify and control it /// but it's like we told before about reactivity, because if we are blocked on a subject, if I don't get an answer half an hour later, I put it away and then I'll forget it or I'll learn something false +++

Extract 4. *A verbatim* analysis

[...] no, I appreciate spontaneity but I'll still verify the answer (laughs) /// at least I'm going to see if it's right [...] calculate the answer again ... /// but if it's a definition + yes I trust [...] that's it.

Extract 5. *A verbatim* analysis

[...] So + after me ++ I manage with computer tools to get information and verify it but technically speaking, I think reactivity is most important.

Reactivity as a Token of Trust

Nowadays, web devices, social networks and smartphones provide an elaborate feedback to the protagonists of the interaction giving them a delivery notification, the hour of reception, if the message is read or not, if the addressee is answering or if he has modified it before sending it... These are so many precious indicators for the speaker to qualify his partner as reliable or not. The confidence he will grant, will depend on his reactivity. The more a device is mediatised the more the user can appreciate the other's reactivity and the more trust he will feel through interaction. That is the reason why time and interactional reactivity in particular constitute a recurrent digital ritual in the learning communities we studied (Amato & Boutin, 2013) According to other postmodern thinkers, there is another artifactual repercussion: media times.

For Vitalis, multimedia activities such as online games and internet globally head to become socializing factors progressively replacing human mediation maintained by family and school for instance (Proulx & Vitalis, 1999). Students cherish immediateness and channels functioning on the short term that provide them with gratification straight away. Their economic model actually relies on huge communicational potentials supposed to give impatient individuals a sense of instant happiness. Furthermore, the artefact entailed by internet technological mediation and smartphones, increases this feeling of immediacy.

Acceleration at Work

In his social critique of time, Rosa puts forward what he calls « acceleration pathologies » and social link transformation (Rosa, 2010). During our research we have noticed some phenomenons of desynchronization, of functional dichotomy between private and professional spheres, and of injunction to stay online all the time. For these students, the meaning of continuous time along with strong reactivity is the first reason for the gap between the institution and the learning audience. If the unrestrained rhythm of exchanges invites us to a questioning of the relevance of the answers in such a short interval, we can wonder what the generalization of optical fibre and its real time effects will cause on an interactional level. Besides, new socio-technical devices have emerged like Snapchat and Messenger, privileging immediateness with the broadcasting of videos limited to 10 seconds maximum and which cannot be watched again later on. These applications are very popular among youngsters. But this over-mediatised environment has without any doubt a negative influence on users' pace of life.

According to the most pessimistic forecast, the situation reaches its height creating a desynchronization which could compromise social progress (ibid.). The targeted students have resorted to real « reactivity races » motivated by an increasing visibility and quest for leadership. This is the paradox of these horizontal communities who, by doing so, become ironically the victims of social domination. To dominate someone, it is easy to make him speed up (Viveret & Le Doze, 2014). On the opposite, horizontal collaboration could be a fruitful heuristic to decrease the pace in an all living together society.

Social Recognition

The search for visibility, sometimes exaggerated to the point of looking like staging is also an artefact of socio-technical devices of information and communication. By letting them post their own chat topics and occupy digital space from ENT or EPA, some learners are in quest for recognition. The first illustration is an intermediation phenomenon. Some of them distinguish themselves from the others by playing the role of mediators among the community. In this study, we use to call them Tutors « T2 » meaning second tutors or tutor assistants. Most of the time this intermediation is spontaneous but it can become self-centred. In this case, the race for reactivity may be assimilated to a fight for recognition. Today's social networks constitute amazing catalysts of contemporary expressivism. They have the specificity to give free rein to a type of visibility favouring a presentation of oneself free from co-presence constraints. In other words, what an individual would not dare saying in the other's presence, is less difficult to say with distance. This is also valid from a temporal point of view. Pervasivity or injonction to remain constantly on line are symptomatic of the virtual communities (Metzger, Badillo, Chabot, Chevalier, & Collectif, 2004).

A Model of Hybrid Governance

We have been wondering what could justify such a situation from these students originally attracted by "symmetric" sharing and collaboration. For self-centred individuals, it is generally all about being visible through a digital presentation of oneself (Domenget, Larroche, Peyrelong, & Merzeau, 2015) motivated by a quest for recognition (Honneth, 2013). For the most altruistic of them, these are discrete practices with a community ideology as a leitmotiv. Anyhow, this intermediation is evocative of a new era. Today's model both allies the potentials of a decentralised network and of a hierarchical structure. On one side is informal knowledge acquired outside the institution and on the other is academic training. This "way of doing" (Bautier et al., 2015), constitutes a fertile ground for mediation between peers. That is the reason why Turq's horizontal hierarchy (Turcq, 2013) is an unprecedented socio-economic form: connected individualism with a pyramidal structure. Consequently, it is easy to understand why this hybrid environment creates a tension between these two opposed temporalities.

CONCLUSION

In this study, we have been underlying the acceleration theory since it has led us to understand time logics symptomatic of our students' uses. It means there is, in their practices, a tendency to favour short time for spontaneity and reactions in the moment rather than longer time when the quality or richness of interaction prevail. Doesn't reactivity tend to supplant long time? By privileging mobile terminals which are reducing more and more communicational latency, students are differentiating themselves one more time from academic practices, increasing the already existing gap.

Observed temporality and acceleration lead us to consider life from the perspective of social domination and hierarchical relationships. Horizontal communities in such distance learning schools have the particularity to be ephemeral structures, only appearing for the time of the training. It doesn't prevent them from having "strong" socio-affective links in the sense that they maintain a pervasive communication. "Short" time and immediateness represent one of the most important criteria for distorting institutional ENT to community EPA. The latest's rythm is governed by digital technologies which engender this acceleration effect, always producing more interactive velocity.

A Critical View of Temporal Acceleration

The technological artefact of networks via mobile terminals is noticeable through individuals' constant connection. The "race for reactivity" they are experiencing is motivated by a wish to be visible, also seen through peer to peer intermediation. This acceleration is worrying in the way that it is meant to increase in the coming years with the evolution of technological devices. Considering these exchanges in which interactional richness prevails, we can wonder what will happen to "real time" ones with the generalization of optic fiber and high-speed internet. Whether it's about time speeding or disintermediation, it has to be noted that users attracted by a participative model find themselves unwittingly in a hierarchical relation ruled by algorithms. It's the principle of scoring and evaluation between peers which is notably illustrated on platforms termed as "collaborative economy" platforms.

In such a context, life rhythm is speeding up among the younger ones, increasing furthermore the gap with the older generations and with tutors in this case. We can deplore this pernicious process of social domination among this population due to time acceleration, as well the psycho-social risks in the long term. Therefore, it is legitimate to reflect on the consequences of this paradox: How can such a reticular structure between peers which has had emancipatory effects thanks to knowledge production and its transmission, evolve if it adopts an even more vertical and centralized architecture? Even though we are getting more acquainted with the origin of the gap between academic and personal spheres, we still have to find the means to harmonize the rhythm between the users of a same digital device, which is a real challenge considering new educational device.

REFERENCES

Agamben, G. (2006). *Qu'est ce qu'un dispositif? (Payot & Rivages)*. Paris: Editions Payot & Rivages.

Akrich, M., Callon, M., & Latour, B. (2006). *Sociologie de la traduction: textes fondateurs*. Paris, France: Presses de l'École des Mines.

Amato, S., & Boutin, É. (2013). Rites d'interaction et forums de discussion en ligne : Une approche nethnospective de comportements de déférence et de civilité. *Les Cahiers du numérique, 9*(3), 135-159. doi:10.3166/LCN.9.1.25-38

Bautier, É., Crinon, J., Eloy, F., Joigneaux, C., Kakpo, S., Rayou, P., & Rochex, J.-Y. (2015). Supports pédagogiques et inégalités scolaires: études sociologiques (S. A. Bonnéry, Éd.). Paris, France: la Dispute.

Benghozi, P.-J., Bitouzet, C., Soulier, E., & Zacklad, M. (2001). *Le mode communautaire: vers une nouvelle forme d'organisation*. Retrieved from http://hal.archives-ouvertes.fr/hal-00262785

Bernard, F., & Durampart, M. (2013). *Savoirs en action: culture et réseaux méditerranéens* (Vol. 1). Paris, France: CNRS.

Depover, C., Deschryver, N., & Monasta, A. (1999). *Guide de soutien aux projets de formation en alternance*. Mons, Belgique: Université de Mons-Hainaut, Unité de technologie de l'éducation.

Domenget, J.-C., Larroche, V., Peyrelong, M.-F., & Merzeau, L. (2015). *Reconnaissance et temporalités: une approche info-communicationnelle*. Paris, France: l'Harmattan.

Flichy, P. (2004). L'individualisme connecté entre la technique numérique et la société. *Reseaux, 124*(2), 17–51. doi:10.3917/res.124.0017

Garfinkel, H., Barthélemy, M. T., & Quéré, L. T. (2007). *Recherches en ethnométhodologie* (B. Dupret & J.-M. de Queiroz, Trans.). Paris, France: Presses universitaires de France.

Henri, F., & Rigault, C. R. (1996). Collaborative Distance Learning and Computer Conferencing. In T. T. Liao (Éd.), *Advanced Educational Technology: Research Issues and Future Potential* (pp. 45-76). Springer Berlin Heidelberg. Retrieved from http://link.springer.com/chapter/10.1007/978-3-642-60968-8_3

Honneth, A. (2013). *La lutte pour la reconnaissance* (P. Rusch, Trans.). Paris, France: Gallimard, impr.

Jacquinot, G. (1993). Apprivoiser la distance et supprimer l'absence? ou les défis de la formation à distance. *Revue française de pédagogie*, 55–67. Retrieved from http://www.jstor.org/stable/41200347

Jakobson, R., & Vine, B. (1985). Verbal art, verbal sign, verbal time (K. Pomorska & S. Rudy, Éd.). Oxford, UK: Blackwell.

Josèphe, P. (2008). *La société immédiate: essai* (Vol. 1). Paris, France: Calmann-Lévy.

Jouët, J. (2000). Retour critique sur la sociologie des usages. *Reseaux*, *18*(100), 487–521. doi:10.3406/reso.2000.2235

Licoppe, C. (Ed.). (2009). L'évolution des cultures numériques: de la mutation du lien social à l'organisation du travail. Limoges, France: Fyp éd.

Metzger, J.-P., Badillo, Y., Chabot, E., Chevalier, Y., & Collectif. (2004). *Médiation et représentation des savoirs*. Editions L'Harmattan.

Musso, P., Ponthou, L., Seulliet, E., Viginier, P., & Charlès, B. (2007). *Fabriquer le futur 2: l'imaginaire au service de l'innovation*. Paris, France: Village mondial : Pearson education France.

Prensky, M. (2007). *Digital game-based learning*. Paragon House.

Prensky, M. (2010). *Teaching Digital Natives: Partnering for Real Learning*. Corwin Press.

Proulx, S., & Vitalis, A. (1999). *Vers une citoyenneté simulée: médias, réseaux et mondialisation*. Rennes, France: Apogée.

Quéré, L. (2005). Les « dispositifs de confiance » dans l'espace public. *Reseaux*, *132*(4), 185. doi:10.3917/res.132.0185

Ricœur, P. (2006). *Parcours de la reconnaissance: trois études*. Paris, France: Stock.

Rosa, H. (2010). *Accélération: une critique sociale du temps* (D. Renault, Trans.). Paris, France: La Découverte, impr. 2010.

Siemens, G. (2006). *Knowing Knowledge*. Lulu.com.

Tisseron, S. (2007). *L'intimité surexposée*. Paris.

Turcq, D. (2013). *Le management augmenté: faire face à la complexité*. Paris: Boostzone éd.

Vidal, M., Grandbastien, M., & Moeglin, P. (Eds.). (2010). Formation à distance : principe de provocation et innovations: Vol. 8. Cachan, France: Lavoisier.

Virilio, P. (2010). *Le grand accélérateur*. Paris, France: Galilée.

Vitalis, A. (1994). *Médias et nouvelles technologies: pour une socio-politique des usages*. Rennes, France: Apogée.

Viveret, P., & Le Doze, C. (2014). *Vivre à la bonne heure*. Paris, France: les Presses d'Ile-de-France.

Vygotskij, L. S., Sève, F., Sève, F., & Clot, Y. (1985). Pensée et langage. Ed. sociales.

KEY TERMS AND DEFINITIONS

ATAWAD: The acronym of anytime, anywhere, any device. Since pervasive and ubiquitous computing, students use mobile devices whatever they are and whatever they do on the principle of informal learning.

CMC: The acronym of computer mediated communication. Contrary to face to face communication, distance learning involves mediatized devices to allow interactions between students and tutors on the principle of ubiquitous computing.

Confcall: Short for "conference call," which means that students are gathered in a virtual classroom in the context of distance learning. The technology we used in this research is based on voice over IP to join a group of learners for an online course.

ENT: The acronym of *environnement numérique de travail* and represents the academic platform such as Moodle. Tutors drop off training resources for students or post topics about courses or exercises on discussion groups. In the ENT, time is much slower than in the EPA.

EPA: The acronym of *environnement personnel d'apprentissage* and represents students' networks such as Facebook or Google+ environments to work together and keep in touch with each other. Because of their mobile practices, EPA is characterized by swifted temporalities and peer-to-peer interactions.

ICS: The acronym of information and communication sciences.

ICT: The acronym of information and communication technologies.

LMS: The acronym of learning management system. These kinds of platforms have emerged with industrializing distance training using SCORM standards. Management and organization in LMS are directly inherited from industrial model.

MOOC: The acronym of massive open online course. With the arrival of broadband internet, online courses put up with an unlimited number of enrolled students all over the world. Based on the theory of connectivism, MOOCs allow wide interactions between professors, teaching assistants, and students' communities in addition to traditional course materials. MOOCs are wide research domain in distance learning and emerged as popular means of education in 2012.

Netnography: A portmanteau word made of *network* and *ethnography*. Netnography is especially useful to observe online communities using both modern social networks tools and traditional ethnologic methods.

Open Universities (OU): A public academic institution in distance learning created in 1969 in the United Kingdom. Most of the students study off-campus all over the world but there is also a number of full-time post-graduate research based on 48-hectare university campus, as well as 1000 members of academics and research staff and over 2500 administrative, operational, and support staff.

Peer-to-Peer University (P2PU): Brings some of the characteristics of MOOCs, but is focused on people sharing their knowledge on a learning topic or shared by other users with a wiki-type mentality. Unlike typical massive open online courses, anyone can create a course as well as take one. P2PU is organized into schools that include especially social innovation, school of webcraft (backed by Mozilla), school of open (coordinated by Creative Commons), and a school of education (focused on pedagogy).

SNA: The acronym of social networks analysis. Row data collected online can be used for internauts' activity visualization. This sociometric approach provides more information about cohesion, centrality, proximity, and intermediation of the social networks observed.

Temporality: A central notion in this research because the asynchrony of practices is the origin of the cleavage between the institution and students. During the frenziest interactions of learning communities, we counted up to seven consecutive answers in a minute. Such a use requires mobile terminals.

Tutor Assistant: Called "Tutor T2" for second tutor in this study because of the intermediation phenomenon observed. Basically, some students play the role of tutors among the peers' community. More and more LMS are offering three different status that of student, tutor, and tutor assistant. This in-between status may be a fruitful heuristic for the massification of training.

APPENDIX

Table 1. Categorization of the functional levels of the activity of LMS (discussion groups)

Functions	Social	Organizational	Cognitive	Metacognitive
Common	50	23,	26,3	0
Sals technique	37,5	37,5	25	0
Engish	45,6	33,3	21	0
Finnce	40,5	51,9	7,6	0
Exas	84,3	3,9	11,7	0
Reprting	8,4	83,3	8,3	0
Ecoomy	4,3	69,5	17,4	4,3
Law	84,3	3,9	11,7	0
Mangement	25	45,	12,5	16,7
Communication	29,1	45,8	12,5	12,5
Leadership	18,2	72,7	9	0
Σ=	40,	39,8	15,4	3,3

Table 2. Categorization of the functional levels of the activity on Google+

Functions	Social	Organizational	Cognitive	Metacognitive
GARH Group	85,9	11,6	2,5	0
IMMO Group	88,9	8,9	1,4	0,3
Σ=	87,4	10,2	1,9	0,1

Table 3. Categorization of the functional levels of the activity on Facebook

Functions	Social	Organizational	Cognitive	Metacognitive
MORH Group	41,6	52,2	5,3	0,9
BFA P1Group	78,5	7,1	7,1	7,1
P1Entraide Group	42,5	57,4	0	0
Σ=	54,2	38,9	4,1	2,6

[1]I3m is a research laboratory working on Information and Communication Sciences and based in University of Toulon (EA-3820).

Chapter 5

Do I Know My Learners...?
The Conditions and Factors to Consider in Embedding Ubiquitous Technologies Into the Plan and Design of the Learning Process

Anna Liza Daunert
University of Mainz, Germany

Linda Price
University of Bedfordshire, UK

ABSTRACT

As digital technologies become an integrated part of our everyday lives, we need to consider how to harness their educational potential in higher education. However, despite considerable research into the use of technology in higher education, there still remains a gap between what teachers might perceive as valuable digital curriculum design and what students perceive as valuable digital learning experiences. One key component is how ubiquitous technologies can be harnessed to support students' learning experiences. In this chapter, the authors examine the implications of students' preferences and usage of u-technologies for designing teaching and learning curricula that positively exploit technology. This chapter builds on the research conducted by Daunert and Harteis that investigated pre-service teachers' preferences and experiences of u-technologies. The results of this cross-sectional survey are considered in relation to designing curricula in digital environments.

DOI: 10.4018/978-1-5225-7435-4.ch005

INTRODUCTION

Tomorrow is already here, in fact it probably arrived yesterday. Such is the pace of change in our modern digital global world; we always seem to be a step behind. We are in the middle of a digital revolution, where the pace of change is almost hard to chart. Nearly every week there is a new phone or device on the market and new applications appear on a daily basis. The internet now provides our daily news source as well as our communications, maps, calculations, encyclopedia, storage, health and well-being and a host of other things. And yet in higher education we still seem to brandish pedestrian, passive forms of education, fit for a bygone era. Western students arrive at our universities with a plethora of devices hoping to be excited by latest research and knowledge only to find that they are corralled into conventional teaching rooms where the most exciting use of technology they experience is PowerPoint. In fact, so great is the gap in understanding the educational potential of technology that students are often banned from using their phones in class. The argument being that it is a distraction: but in truth, it is not difficult to be distracted from a boring passive lecture.

As educators, we often ignore the potential and the ubiquity of technology at our peril. What kind of a world are we preparing students for if they are not well-versed in how to exploit technology in solving problems? We need to be preparing our students for a world in which they will have to answer questions not yet posed and where they will not yet have the knowledge to answer those questions. So future graduates will need to be able to harness the power of tomorrows technological advances in order to be relevant and effective in a digital global world. So how is our education currently preparing students for this future?

Without doubt, the explosion of digital devices that students can bring to their learning situation poses challenges for teachers. There are so many different devices that change with such speed and so many applications to know about and to use. So how would or could a teacher be knowledgeable about all of these? Perhaps that question belies a fundamental problem: do we still believe that a modern 21st century university education is best served by the 'sage on the stage' model? Is it our views of what constitutes a university education that is outdated and not fit for purpose? So perhaps it is the underpinning beliefs about higher education and the approaches to teaching that needs to change. So instead of teachers having to know everything about everything, they become the guide and the facilitators. That is not to say that teacher's knowledge of the subject matter is irrelevant – far from it. But there is a difference between envisioning the role as a content expert and someone who enables students to develop into active learners who have the skills to progress their expertise. Such a shift could liberate teachers from the pressure of feeling they need to know everything and liberate students from passive and outdated education that ill-prepares them for a digital world.

There has been much research into the use of technology in higher education. However, its use has often been perceived as being disconnected from pedagogical processes. Critics would argue that technologies have often been used *'regardless of whether or not they are pedagogically effective, and even in ignorance of the long tradition of pedagogical evidence and thought'* (Beetham & Sharpe, 2007, *p. 3)*. Recent Horizon Reports (Johnson, Adams Becker, Estrada, & Freeman, 2014) indicate that effective use of ubiquitous technologies is being impeded by low skills levels among staff who are not effectively supported in how to embed technology use effectively in their teaching. However, more recent research also points to more fundamental issues in relation to teachers underlying beliefs about teaching and how that impacts upon the effective use of technology. For example, Englund, Anders, and Price (2017) have shown that more student-centered beliefs about teaching lead to student-centered and active-learning approaches to using technology. Conversely, transmissive, content-centered approaches to teaching lead to passive content-centered approaches to using technology.

Content-centered approaches still pervade in many higher education institutions where the focus is on how to use the tool as opposed to how it can be used to support the whole educational enterprise. Technology as a tool or as a concept usually fails when it is not embedded into the curriculum (Kirkwood and Price, 2016). Currently, institutional foci in relation to using technology typically focus on technical aspects such as access and efficiency rather than the 'craft' and 'science' of teaching and learning. Such approaches are to the detriment of effective use of technologies for learning (Salmon, 2005). Much work is still to be done in order to adopt a holistic adaptation of the technology.

One of the challenges in re-orienting a vision for 21st century higher education is to understand how to harness the ubiquitous technologies that students use for pedagogical advantage. So how does one embed ubiquitous technologies into the curriculum to enhance students' learning experiences? Addressing such challenges requires educators to use technology wisely and sustainably, but more importantly, we need to begin with an understanding of how students are using technologies currently to support their learning. In the next section, we consider students preferences and usage of digital technologies in order to gain insights into how educators might harness ubiquitous technologies to support learning by using what students may consider as everyday things.

STUDENTS' PREFERENCES AND USAGE OF TECHNOLOGY

The study conducted by Daunert and Harteis (2014) provides a good basis from which to assess how students perceive the value of technology and how students use technology in their learning. It explored the preferences and usage of u-technologies with pre-service teachers in a German university. It explored the purpose of the usage and whether it was academic in orientation or leisure-oriented.

This cohort was considered as particularly relevant on the basis that, as pre-service teachers, their experiences with u-technologies might offer some insight into how they, as future educators, would view and use technology. The importance of this is that the teaching models we experience often influence the teaching models we later practice as teachers (Cheek & Castle, 1981; Chicoine, 2004; Frank, 1990; Goodlad, 1982; Herrington, Sparrow, & Herrington, 1999; Hornbach, 2004; Knowles, 1988; Pringle, 2006). Englund, Olofsson, and Price (2017) further showed that teacher's beliefs and approaches to teaching also affect how they use technology, so examining pre-service teachers perceptions and use of technology can provide valuable information as to how technology is and perhaps should be used to support learning.

The study also examined learners' personal views and experiences in utilizing u-technologies in order to obtain first-hand accounts of how much time the students devote to which u-technologies and for what purpose. Careful consideration of these points of view and first-hand experiences provide insights into the importance and significance with which they attach to the technologies in their own learning. This information is valuable in contributing to knowledge about how to improve practice developing curricula that exploit technologies to enhance student learning. It can help guide curriculum designers and educators who plan and design learning with u-technologies, especially among pre-service teachers.

PRE-SERVICE TEACHERS' PERSPECTIVES AND PRACTICES IN UTILIZING UBIQUITOUS TECHNOLOGIES

A summary of the survey results provides an overview of the perspective of pre-service teachers in a German university. Their preferred u-technologies and usage are examined and significance of these u-technologies for their learning.

A total of 331 respondents participated in the 2014 survey. The total number of female respondents was 65% and evidently higher than the male respondents: this reflects the population of education students in Germany. At the time of the survey, 76% of the sample were in their 3rd semester and 76% were within the age range of

20 to 22. The respondents were asked to choose from the given list or name their top 5 most preferred technological devices and web-based tools and applications. The results showed that the respondents' (N=331) preferences for technological devices were laptops (58.3%) and smartphones (25.4%). The first preference for web-based tools and applications was social networking (54.1%). The results showed that for their first preference there was variation within web-based tools as to what forms these took. For example, wikis (24.5%), media-sharing (15.4%), LMS (8.8%), blogs (5.1%), cloud-based (3.0%). However, the second preference for web-based tools and applications showed a wider dispersion among the respondents: i.e., 28.7% for media-sharing, 21.1% for wikis, 18.1% for social networking, 15.7% for LMS, 8.5% for blogs, and 6.3% for cloud-based tools.

Based on the results, the most widespread devices (laptop and smartphone) and the most widespread web-based tools (social-networking and wikis) are most preferred by the respondents. However, a considerable number of respondents chose other devices as well (e.g., PC, netbook, tablet, and iPod) as their preferred devices. As teachers, we may have perceptions about what digital tools and devices students should be familiar with, however, in reality, that may not be the case. As Kirkwood and Price (2005) have shown, even if students have familiarity with particular technologies, it does not mean that they know how to use them effectively for their learning. The data shows that only a few students chose content-sharing tools (0.9% and 0.6%) and LMS (8.8% and 15.7%) as their first and second preferences, yet these tools support activities that teachers consider important in the learning process. The point is, that we should not assume that students are acting in the way in which we, as teachers, perceive they should be acting.

As for the use of u-technologies, students were asked to record the total number of hours they actually spend per day using the specific u-technologies and whether it was for academic purposes or for leisure. The results showed that the majority of the respondents used wikis and social-networking tools for both leisure and academic purposes. In particular, 69.1% of respondents claimed to use wikis for up to 2 hours per day for academic purposes but only 13.9% up to 4 hours and 0.9% for up to 6 hours per day. This is plausible considering that wikis are a familiar feature within the LMS that is regularly used by the students in the university. However, a total of 51.2% claim to use social-networking tools for academic purposes for up to 2 hours per day, 22.3% up to 4 hours, 3.3% up to 6 hours, and 1.5% for up to more than 6 hours per day. Also, the respondents claim to use blogs for academic purposes (17.6% up to 2 hours and 4.5% up to 4 hours per day). Overall, this is a small percentage of the sample of pre-service teachers who report usage for educational purposes. This is contrary to other higher education settings in which blogs are reputed to play an important role in students' learning activities, especially in the education discipline.

Wee Sing Sim & Foon Hew (2010) reviewed blog usage in higher education and identified 6 categories of usage. These encompass learning journal or knowledge log, record of personal or everyday life, assessment tool, task management tool, tool for interaction and communication, and tool to express emotions or feelings (p. 154). However, in the 2014 survey, only a few respondents claimed to have used the web-based tools that would be expected for academic-oriented activities. Equally, the usage time was less than expected for academic activities. For example, 36.7% of respondents claimed to use the LMS for up to 2 hours, with only 8.8% respondents claiming to use it for up to 4 hours, and 1.8% claimed to use it for up to 6 hours per day. With regard to content-sharing, only 15.8% of respondents claimed to use these tools for up to 2 hours, 2.7% up to 4 hours, and 1.2% for up to 6 hours per day. Although the students can use their university LMS for exchanging ideas or discussion with their classmates, they mostly mention the use of Facebook, Skype, WhatsApp, and email for these purposes. They also make reference to using these tools as well as Dropbox for sharing notes or for collaborative activities.

The findings show that students have creatively adapted the functionalities of the web-based tools, like blogs and Facebook, into their everyday learning activities or into the academic context in general. This is hardly surprising: students want to be able to integrate and take advantage of the tools that they use and are familiar with in their everyday lives to support their learning. Tinto's model (1997, 1998) of academic and social integration purports that students who are adapted socially as well as academically into the academy are more likely to succeed. Hence, the use of u-technologies by students for academic and social purposes would indicate how students are enacting Tinto's model of academic and social integration in a digitally-mediated world to make learning and leisure work together seamlessly.

In addition, the respondents of the 2014 survey also provided their perspectives on the usefulness and significance of u-technologies by expressing their judgment on 10 statements according to a scale of 1 to 5; i.e., 1= the statement is definitely not true, 2 = it is rather not true or likely not true, 3 = it is partly true and partly not true, 4 = it is rather true or likely true, and 5 = the statement is definitely true (see Table 1).

The mean scores and the SDs of statement numbers 1, 2, 3, and 9 show that the respondents highly value the role of the technical devices in helping them accomplish their learning activities easily and quickly. The respondents also gave a high rating to statement numbers 3 and 4 showing agreement to the scaffolding role of technologies in their research work, keeping up-to-date by having easy access to information. However, the mean score and the SD of statement number 6 is apparently showing the high dispersion of the sample and some disagreement to the statement that they write their notes or documents only with their laptop or netbook or tablet. This would indicate that the use of digital medium or otherwise is likely to be dependent upon the context in which they are required to take notes.

As for the statements concerning the use of web-based tools, the respondents highly valued the role of email, chat, and forums (statement 7) as communication channels with their instructors and classmates. The moderate to slightly high rating of statement number 8 shows their agreement to the assumed role of blogs, wikis or other web-based collaborative tools in supporting the learning process. However,

Table 1. Students' evaluation of the usefulness and significance of u-technologies

Statements	N	SD	Mean
Statement 1: I can do most of my learning activities in the university easier and quicker with the help of technical devices than without.	329	0.87	4.17
Statement 2: If I use a technological device as a working tool, I often work faster and more effective.	329	0.87	3.50
Statement 3: My laptop/PC with internet connection is a great help to a big part of my research work because I do not necessarily have to go to the library.	329	0.83	4.23
Statement 4: I find accessibility and quick information update on the internet very helpful because it makes studying easier.	329	0.77	4.26
Statement 5: I use links and other web-based tools/applications very often because they support the learning process.	328	0.96	3.12
Statement 6: I write my notes/documents only with my laptop/netbook/tablet.	327	1.06	2.04
Statement 7: Communication with instructors or colleagues with the help of e-mail/chat/forum is a great advantage because it is a very convenient/practical and flexible way to reach someone.	329	0.82	4.30
Statement 8: I assume that blogs, wikis, or other web-based collaborative applications/tools support the learning process.	329	0.85	3.45
Statement 9: I cannot imagine myself studying/learning without a tech device with an internet connection.	329	0.99	4.19
Statement 10: I mainly use web-based applications or tools for my courses at the university.	327	0.92	3.02

the mean scores of statements 5 and 10 show a low to moderate rating given by the respondents, i.e., concerning the use of web-based tools and applications for their courses or for supporting the learning process in general. This likely reflects a desire to use tools that they are more readily familiar with and use for other purposes and in other contexts too. The results also indicate that, although there is a university-wide LMS with existing features that support synchronous learning, most courses are still designed and implemented similar to that of a content management system (CMS). This in effect means that there is limited opportunity for active learning and that the curricula, in such cases, largely stores content. This likely reflects the staff development needs of instructors and professors in how to effectively design the learning process with digital technologies. The findings imply that there is still a need to familiarize students and to train teachers or educators in effective use of technologies in order to scaffold learning.

Given the widespread use of LMS and the regular use of a university-owned LMS, the respondents did not regard it as useful in the learning process. This might reflect the limited use that has been made of the LMS in the design of the curricula which reflect a more CMS approach to designing the curricula. This can affect how the students value these tools in the context of learning. Students' awareness of the benefits and perceived usefulness of the tools for learning can determine their attitude towards them and, consequently, their decision to use them (Hartshorne & Ajjan, 2009). Limited or less practice and negative experiences in using an LMS could explain why students are adapting other tools that are originally created for leisure purposes, like Facebook, for their academic activities instead of simply using the collaborative tools embedded in their university LMS.

Thus, it is important to consider that there is a mismatch between the teachers' perceptions (as well as teachers' teaching practices with technologies) and the students' perceptions of their learning experiences in learning with technologies. This specifically reflects problems encountered and their assessment of the meaningfulness of learning in web-based environments (Löfström and Nevgi, 2007). This mismatch could negatively affect students' perceptions and their future usage of these technologies. Motivation and interest can be shaped or affected by prior experiences, in this context, the ability of preservice teachers to use the technology effectively in their future teaching practice. Hence, it is important to actively engage learners and make sure that they understand what they should do and why and how it could impact their learning (Kirkwood & Price, 2005).

Additionally, the competencies of the educators play a vital role. It is crucial that teachers are equipped with the knowledge and ability as to why, how, and when to best embed technologies into the teaching-learning process (Kirkwood & Price, 2016). Price and Kirkwood (2008) argue that considering staff development for HE teachers has focused on technological skills at the expense of understanding how to use technology effectively pedagogically. Training teachers in embedding technologies into their teaching practice can significantly change not only their beliefs about teaching but also "the comfort with using technologies". Teachers' longitudinal engagement in professional development can also consequently yield positive effects on the achievement scores of their students (Blanchard, LePrevost, Tolin, & Gutierrez, 2016). However, a more nuanced way of the considerable role of technology in supporting teaching and learning is not to consider what to do with the technology, but what the technology can do for the learner. So instead of prescribing for students what format or medium to use – part of the assessment could include a component where the student states why they have used a particular format or medium and why that approach is the best means to enable them to represent their work. This is a much more progressive means of conducting assessments and enable them to develop important discernment skills in format and use of technology matched with the required task. Such skills will be important in their future careers.

However, the teacher or educator is just one of the many factors in the whole educational system or context. For example, the failure of LMS in a university and the very low interest or motivation of students to use the available technologies in the university cannot be attributed to the teacher alone. Other factors are also highly influential. For example, the quality of the existing platform, accessibility, the administration and continuous monitoring of the infrastructure, and the easy access to IT support whenever problems are encountered, also affect perceptions of value (Alfadly, 2013). The majority of the respondents (90.9% of n=330) of the 2014 survey reported having encountered such problems with their eLearning platforms, which were classified into 2 categories, technical issues and (system and course) administrator-dependent issues. However, technical issues are the most frequently occurring problems they encountered, e.g., accessibility of features and links, problems to access course materials, difficulty to download or view course materials, login, and problems during the registration process.

The importance of the Daunert and Harteis's (2014) study is in demonstrating the importance and value of u-technologies among learners and how this may differ from teachers' expectations. Their actual use of the u-technologies for academic purposes does tend to complement what they are using for other purposes and reflect how they are using what might be considered their 'everyday things' to support their learning. The results showed the resourcefulness of the learners. However, in academia, we still tend to promote particular technologies that we feel are supportive of the learning experience. Perhaps, in our efforts to embed the use of ubiquitous technologies in higher education, we should recoil from a focus on which technology we think students should use and better enable them to use technologies of their choice, provided they can use them effectively or justify their use when appropriate. This is when the teacher or educator comes in as a facilitator or guide and as an evaluator in the learning process in order to guide the learners towards the best way of achieving their learning goals and to provide the necessary feedback by monitoring the learners' performance.

Hence, in order to embed the use of technology we should focus on the content and pedagogy, and provide support when necessary, e.g., metacognitive support (Kramanski & Michalsky, 2010); thus, the focus is on why we are doing things and not merely on how. Early exposure and training of pre-service teachers is a necessary step towards future good practice in designing and implementing courses that effectively use technologies. Englund, Olofsson, and Price (2017) have shown that inexperienced teachers who are introduced to staff development early in their teaching career progress faster and further towards student-centered approaches to teaching and learning than those who are experienced teachers. Kirkwood and Price (2005) also argue that it is necessary for teachers "to develop a better understanding of the issues surrounding the use of ICT, so that innovations are not driven by technology" (p. 270). While a combination of many factors and actors may influence how the curricula are designed and experienced, if we are to effectively embed technology into the learning process we need to focus on the purpose and what our students will gain from the experience rather than designing how they should experience it (Kirkwood & Price, 2016).

DESIGNING THE LEARNING PROCESS

In this section, we draw on the Universal Design for Learning (UDL) approach integrated with the adapted components of the ADDIE model of Instructional Design as a framework. We later highlight specific components of ADDIE (i.e., analysis and evaluation) that are complementary to the UDL approach. We argue for the value of this framework on the basis that the UDL approach is not technologically focused – but instead focuses on enabling students through multiple and flexible means to represent their learning, act and express their learning and engage in their learning. Additionally, the ADDIE model of instructional design complements the

UDL approach because it also highlights the individual learner and the learning needs even at the outset of the learning process. It also focuses on systematic monitoring of learning achievement or performance outcomes through the alignment of the learning needs, the goals or intended learning outcomes, assessment methods and tools, and learning activities. Thus, both approaches complement each other in focusing on the learner and on the learning process, which we consider as a necessary condition for fostering effective learning. As the findings and their implications showed, which we presented in the previous sections of this chapter, the diversity of learners is prevalent not only in their preferences of technologies but also in their use of u-technologies for their learning. It also showed the resourcefulness or creativity of the learners in adapting available web-based tools for their learning activities. For these reasons, we call for a (re)focus on the learner and the learning process and consider individual learning needs and learning approaches in planning and designing the curriculum; thus, providing the learners a curriculum that is inclusive and authentically support and foster effective learning.

The Universal Design for Learning (UDL) Approach

The UDL framework was first defined by David H. Rose of the Harvard Graduate School of Education and the Center for Applied Special Technology (CAST) in the 1990s. The CAST website offers a detailed description and information on the principles and the background of the UDL framework. CAST (2018) argues the importance of considering the diversity of learners. Hence, the UDL approach has been developed to accommodate these individual approaches to learning. It is also based on the assumption that people learn according to the three broad networks in the human brain, which are responsible for: 1) recognition (the "what" of learning); 2) skills and strategies (the "how" of learning); and 3) caring and prioritizing (the "why" of learning). Consequently, the curriculum should be designed to help learners achieve all three and that the curriculum should be flexible. Flexible means that it is designed for individual learning while it takes into account other important aspects of the curriculum, like goals, methods, materials, and assessment.

In designing a curriculum that can work for everyone, UDL is implemented based on three overarching principles of learning that offer multiple options for all learners; these are:

1. Provide multiple means of Representation (the "what" of learning). Learners differ in the ways that they perceive and comprehend information that is presented to them. For example, those with sensory disabilities (e.g., blindness or deafness); learning disabilities (e.g., dyslexia); language or cultural differences,

and so forth may all require different ways of approaching content. Others may simply grasp information quicker or more efficiently through visual or auditory means rather than printed text. Also learning, and transfer of learning, occurs when multiple representations are used because it allows students to make connections within, as well as between, concepts. In short, there is not one means of representation that will be optimal for all learners; *providing options for representation is essential.*

2.   Provide multiple means of Action and Expression (the "how" of learning) Learners differ in the ways that they can navigate a learning environment and express what they know. For example, individuals with significant movement impairments (e.g., cerebral palsy), those who struggle with strategic and organizational abilities (executive function disorders), those who have language barriers, and so forth approach learning tasks very differently. Some may be able to express themselves well in written text but not speech, and vice versa. It should also be recognized that action and expression require a great deal of strategy, practice, and organization, and this is another area in which learners can differ. In reality, there is not one means of action and expression that will be optimal for all learners; *providing options for action and expression is essential.*

3.   Provide multiple means of Engagement (the "why" of learning). Affect represents a crucial element to learning, and learners differ markedly in the ways in which they can be engaged or motivated to learn. There are a variety of influences that impact individual engagement including neurology, culture, personal relevance, subjectivity, and background knowledge, along with a variety of other factors presented in these guidelines. Some learners are highly engaged by spontaneity and novelty while others are disengaged, even frightened, by those aspects, preferring strict routine. Some learners might like to work alone, while others prefer to work with their peers. In reality, there is not one means of engagement that will be optimal for all learners in all contexts; *providing multiple options for engagement is essential. (Extract taken from CAST, 2011, p. 5)*

These 3 principles of UDL can guide teachers or educators in determining and eliminating the barriers that interfere in the learning process and thus help students reach their goals. These allow students to be able to attend to the way in which the learning is represented, the way in which they can demonstrate their achievement and the way in which they engage with their learning (see Appendix for the UDL guidelines or visit http://udlguidelines.cast.org for details on the UDL framework and guidelines).

In summary, UDL is an educational framework that is prevalent in the Canvas VLE community for guiding the development of flexible learning environments. It is based on educational research and it recognizes that learning, and how learners engage with learning, can be unique to them. Hence, it emphasizes the need to accommodate multiple approaches to learning in order to meet the needs of diverse learners. This is because there is not a single optimal design for everyone. Universal design approaches mirror good practice in areas which are typically designed to accommodate a wide variety of users, including those with disabilities. Embedding features that help those with disabilities ultimately benefits everyone. Hence, using a UDL approach from the beginning helps make education more inclusive and effective for everyone.

Therefore, UDL ensures that:

- All students have meaningful access to the curriculum where assessment strategies accurately appraise their achievements and not the means by which they demonstrate those achievements.
- Educators have the opportunity to provide an inclusive education curriculum for diverse learners.
- Educators can help address legislative requirements by providing an inclusive curriculum from course conception, rather than through post learning design re-adjustments.
- All students have the opportunity to work more independently and understand what support they need.
- Educational technology is used in a more effective manner for all students.

The UDL approach, thus, provides concrete guidelines for implementing a flexible and inclusive curriculum, which strongly focus on providing multiple options that optimize the learning experiences of each learner and help them reach their goals. However, teachers and educators also need a guideline on how to get there (i.e., to accomplish the appropriate tasks) in order to effectively implement the guidelines. For this reason, we use the components of instructional design because they complement the basic principles of the UDL approach. Thus, we adapted the ADDIE model of instructional design to not only integrate the analysis and evaluation components with the UDL principles but also to serve as an organizing framework for teachers and educators.

ADDIE and the Instructional (Systems) Design Process

Instructional design (ID) means "more than just creating instruction", it focuses on "establishing and maintaining efficient and effective human performance, it is guided by a model of human performance" and a lot more (see Rothwell & Kazanas, pp.3-6). The main goal of instructional design is to increase efficiency and effectiveness where there is a need for performance improvement, such as the learning context in higher education. There are a few models of the instructional design process (for example, Dick & Carey and the ISD model), but here we focus on the ADDIE model of instructional design, especially on the important components common to all ID models (i.e., analysis, evaluation, and assessment) because they complement the UDL framework. The basic principles of UDL can be linked with the components of ADDIE, which can provide a more systematic approach of planning and designing the learning process that aims to implement the concrete guidelines of the UDL approach.

The ADDIE model has five components with sub-steps or subcomponents that are otherwise considered as the main components in other ID models. The main components of ADDIE have diverse interpretations in different learning contexts, like training, curriculum development, professional development, etc. We adapt the components with the emphasis on the importance of analysis and evaluation components. The analysis component puts emphasis on the outset of the learning process while the evaluation component focuses on the process and the result or the end of the learning process. Evaluation is a very important component because, according to Gagne, Wager, Golas, and Keller (2005), "Evaluation activities can reveal where revisions are required in each of the other four components" (p. 22).

The following is a summary of ADDIE Model Components and Subcomponents, with additional descriptions or some parts deleted and/or slightly rephrased (Gagne, et al., 2005, p. 21).

1. Analysis (adapt as needs assessment/analysis; context or resource analysis)
   a. Determine the learning needs or performance problems and determine which type of instruction is the solution.
   b. Conduct an analysis to determine the target cognitive, affective, and motor skill goals for the course.
   c. Determine what skills the entering students are expected to have, and which will impact learning in the course.
   d. Analyze the time available and how much might be accomplished in that period of time.

2. Design
   a. Translate course goals into performance outcomes and major course or unit objectives.
   b. Determine the instructional topics or units to be covered, and how much time will be spent on each.
   c. Sequence the units with regard to the course objectives.
   d. Identify the major objectives to be achieved during each unit.
   e. Define lessons and learning activities for each unit.
   f. Develop specifications for assessment of student performance for each unit.
3. Development
   a. Make decisions regarding the types of learning activities and materials.
   b. Prepare draft materials and/or activities.
   c. Revise, refine, and produce materials and activities
   d. Produce adjunct materials
4. Implementation
   a. Implement and provide help or support as needed
5. Evaluation (as a recurring process: formative and summative)
   a. Implement plans for student evaluation
   b. Implement plans for program evaluation
   c. Implement plans for course maintenance and revision

Although theories and assumptions on learning abound, the main assumptions of constructivism continue to appeal to the proponents of modern and contemporary approaches to teaching and learning. There are proponents of constructivism who contend that the learning process occurs at the cognitive or psychological level of an individual while there are those who support the assumption that learning also occurs at the social level. Learning is thus a complex process and a complex concept.

The main assumption of constructivism is that "people actively build or construct their knowledge of the world and of each other" (Cobb, 2000, p. 277; see also Huang, 2002; Lock & Strong, 2010; Wertsch, 2010). Learning can also be defined as the acquisition or modification of knowledge and skills, which can be explained in various contexts depending on how it occurs in a specific environment. It is a continuous process of construction of new knowledge and reconstruction of an already existing one. It can happen either at the individual level or at the group level. Thus, it is a continuous process of construction, reconstruction, and collaboration (Daunert & Harteis, 2014). However, learning should be goal-oriented in that the learning context should enable improvement of performance or achievement as well as assessment, i.e., whether learning is effective or not. Effective learning means that learning is successful or effective given that there is a match between two important variables: 1) the needed or desired learning performance and 2) the learning outcome or the result of the learning performance (Rothwell & Kazanas, 2008). This match can be determined through regular monitoring and assessment of the learners' performance. This should be considered when planning and designing the learning process. As Glaser (1990) argues, assessment practices should be intertwined with teaching and learning in that testing instruments should be developed to guide learners in improving their performance.

Hence, in designing learning that aims to foster effective learning, it is important to take the individual learner into account. Gagné (1977; 1985; see also Seel, 2003) recommends that educators should answer some important questions that will serve as the basis for the design of the learning process. They should consider these important questions:

1. Which skills or competences should be learned?
2. Which kinds of stimulation external to the learner can best support the internal processes that are necessary to learning?

Similarly, Seel (2003, p. 239 trans.) explains that the best starting point is to consider the interaction between the student and the requirements or conditions of the learning tasks in that personal conditions (e.g., cognitive and motivational dispositions, learning styles, and prior knowledge) are linked with the environmental conditions and task-based conditions (e.g., information resources and learning time). All the aforementioned factors and conditions for effective learning provides the rationale for focusing on the individual learner and the vital role of assessment and evaluation in the learning process. Therefore, adapting the components of instructional design highlights the importance of conducting an analysis and/or needs assessment as an important step in effectively designing the learning process.

Conducting a needs assessment is usually the first step in the ISD model. The purpose of needs assessment is to uncover, more precisely than performance analysis does, what the performance problem is, who it affects, how it affects them, and what results are to be achieved by training [or instruction]. Needs assessment is very important because all subsequent steps in the ISD model depend on its results (cited from Rothwell, 200; Rothwell & Sredl, 2000, in Rothwell & Kazanas, 2008, pp. 60-61).

Adapted Framework: UDL and ADDIE

The UDL guidelines are described in detail on the CAST website. In this chapter, we developed a general framework that adapted the main components of the UDL.

The UDL Guidelines are a tool used in the implementation of Universal Design for Learning, a framework to improve and optimize teaching and learning for all people based on scientific insights into how humans learn. The UDL Guidelines can be used by educators, curriculum developers, researchers, parents, and anyone else who wants to implement the UDL framework in a learning environment. These guidelines offer a set of concrete suggestions that can be applied to any discipline or domain to ensure that all learners can access and participate in meaningful, challenging learning opportunities. (CAST, 2018)

Taking the UDL guidelines into account, the goal is to get to the bottom of each column (representing the principles of UDL and their subcomponents), specifically to the executive functions as self-directed and self-actualizing learner. Thus, the upper columns have the function of guiding learners to get to the executive functions. Similarly, the ADDIE model has flexible components and subcomponents that serve as a road map to teachers or educators in planning and designing training, instruction, professional development, or any learning process. To describe the adapted framework, we framed the main components of UDL and ADDIE to demonstrate how they complement each other in planning and designing the learning process for diverse learners (see Figure 1).

Highlighting the Role of Evaluation, Assessment, and Feedback

Considering the adapted framework (i.e., linking UDL with ADDIE), we emphasize the vital role of evaluation, assessment, and feedback. Based on the adapted framework, the outset of the learning process is as important as any of the phases of the learning process. Thus, needs analysis or the analysis component plays a vital role in the whole context, specifically towards determining and defining the goals and the intended learning outcomes. This component paves the way for a systematic evaluation and assessment of learning and, thus, provides a basis for systematically aligning the intended learning outcomes, assessment methods and tools, and teaching-learning media and activities.

Figure 1. Adapted framework with UDL and ADDIE combined

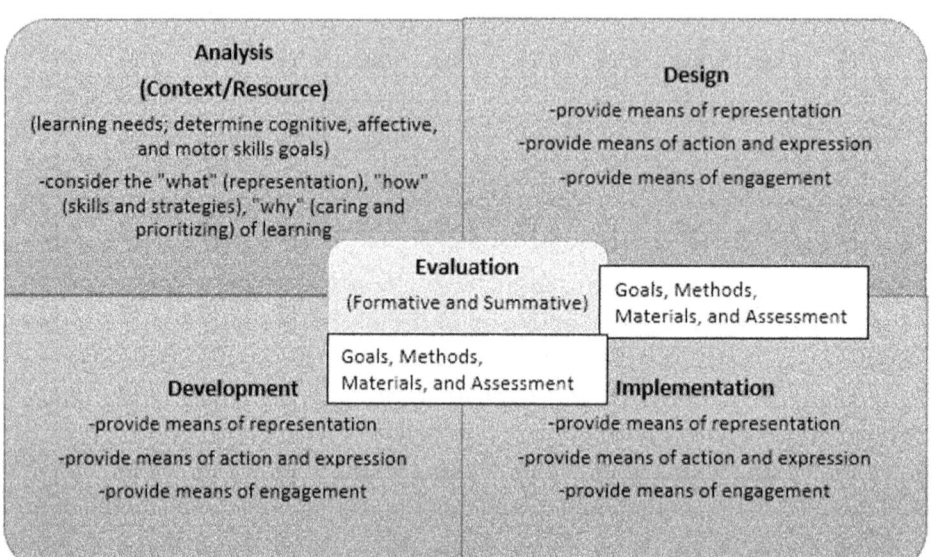

Evaluation activities (i.e., both formative and summative evaluation methods) can help determine where revisions are required in each of the components (Gagne, et al., 2005) or at any stage of the learning process. Evaluation during the process and of the whole process also pave the way for (constructive) feedback on the programs or training, which could consequently yield improved learning performance or the achievement of learning goals.

Assessment is a very powerful tool in driving student learning. Research has shown that academic feedback is more strongly and consistently related to achievement than any other teaching behavior (Kirkwood & Price, 2008). This relationship is consistent regardless of grade, socioeconomic status, race, or academic context. When feedback and corrective procedures are used, most students can attain the same level of achievement as the top 20% of students (Bellon, Bellon, & Blank, 1991).

The use of authentic and consistent assessment practices is a way towards improving student achievement or learning performance. To underpin this, we could also draw upon the guidance provided by the academic framework and the concepts of 'Constructive Alignment' (Biggs, 1999). At its simplest level, constructive alignment requires the module intended student learning outcomes, to link with how the students are assessed and what activities they have to engage with in order to achieve success (see Figure 2).

Figure 2. The relationship between intended learning outcomes, assessment, and teaching and learning activities. Adapted from: Using Biggs' Model of Constructive Alignment in Curriculum Design from Open Educational Resources of UCD Teaching and Learning, University College Dublin

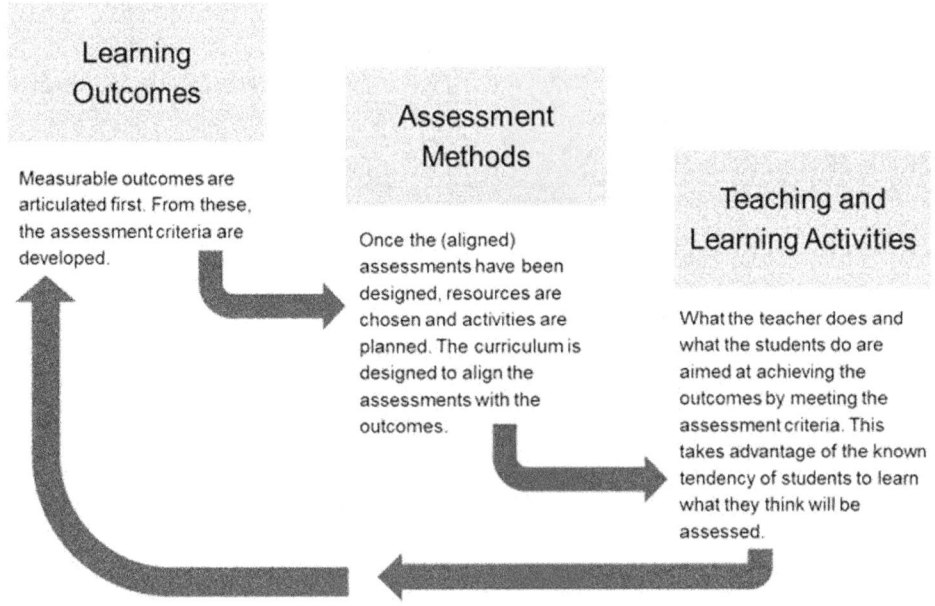

CONCLUSION

As teachers, instructional designers, and educators in general, we need to consider in our planning and designing of the learning process how we can effectively enable students to engage with and reflect their learning. In order to use technologies well in supporting this aim, we need to capitalize on the ubiquitous technologies that they already use in order to allow them to seamlessly and effectively support their learning. Given how rapidly technology is changing, we cannot hope to be knowledgeable about all technologies and tools and their relative merits. Nor do we have time to teach students how to use these rapidly changing technologies given our busy teaching schedules. However, we can and should provide the necessary support and guidance. Besides, as the Daunert and Harteis (2014) study has shown, students are not using the technologies we provide them in either the frequency or depth that we might have anticipated: they prefer to use technologies they are familiar with to support their learning. So why bother focusing on 'which tools'? Instead, we should focus on 'which learning' and on how we can best support the learning process in which students will be able to achieve the desired learning outcome or desired learning performance. The use of the UDL model integrated with the components of instructional design provides a principled framework enabling the design of curricula that embraces technology and enables students to develop skills more fitting for the 21st century.

REFERENCES

Ajjan, H., & Hartshorne, R. (2008). Investigating faculty decisions to adopt Web 2.0 technologies: Theory and empirical tests. *The Internet and Higher Education*, *11*(2), 71–80. doi:10.1016/j.iheduc.2008.05.002

Alfadly, A. A. (2013). The efficiency of the "Learning Management System (LMS)" in AOU, Kuwait, as a communication tool in an E-learning system. *International Journal of Educational Management*, *27*(2), 157–169. doi:10.1108/09513541311297577

Beetham, H., & Sharpe, R. (2007). *Rethinking pedagogy for a digital age: designing and delivering e-learning*. London: Routledge. doi:10.4324/9780203961681

Bellon, J., Bellon, E., & Blank, M. A. (1991). *Teaching from a Research Knowledge Base: A Development and Renewal Process*. New York, NY: Macmillan Publishing Company.

Biggs, J. B. (1999). *Teaching for Quality Learning at University*. Buckingham, UK: SRHE & Open University Press.

Blanchard, M. R., LePrevost, C. E., Tolin, A. D., & Gutierrez, K. S. (2016). Investigating Technology-Enhanced Teacher Professional Development in Rural, High-Poverty Middle Schools. *Educational Researcher*, *45*(3), 207–220. doi:10.3102/0013189X16644602

CAST. (2011). Universal Design for Learning Guidelines version 2.0. Wakefield, MA: CAST.

CAST. (2018). *Universal Design for Learning Guidelines version 2.2*. Retrieved from http://udlguidelines.cast.org

Cheek, H. N., & Castle, K. (1981). The Effects of Back-to-Basics on Mathematics Education. *Contemporary Educational Psychology*, *6*(3), 263–277. doi:10.1016/0361-476X(81)90008-4

Chicoine, D. (2004). Ignoring the Obvious: A Constructivist Critique of a Traditional Teacher Education Program. Educational Studies. *Journal of the American Educational Studies Association*, *36*(3), 245–263.

Cobb, P. (2000). Constructivism. In A. E. Kazdin (Ed.), *Encyclopedia of Psychology* (Vol. 2, pp. 277–279). New York: American Psychological Association and Oxford University Press, Inc.

Daunert, A.L. & Harteis. (2014). Pre-service teachers' perspectives and practices in utilizing ubiquitous technologies for academic-oriented learning and knowledge management. In J. Pelet (Ed.), *E-Learning 2.0 Technologies and Web Applications in Higher Education* (pp. 254-272). Hershey, PA: Information Science Reference. doi:10.4018/978-1-4666-4876-0.ch013

Englund, C., Olofsson, A. D., & Price, L. (2017). Teaching with technology in higher education: Understanding conceptual change and development in practice. *Higher Education Research & Development, 36*(1), 73–87. doi:10.1080/0729436 0.2016.1171300

Frank, M. L. (1990). What Myths about Mathematics Are Held and Conveyed by Teachers? *The Arithmetic Teacher, 37*(5), 10–12.

Gagné, R. M. (1977). *The Conditions of Learning.* New York: Holt, Rinehart & Winston.

Gagné, R. M. (1985). *The Conditions of Learning (4ᵗʰ ed.).* New York: Holt, Rinehart & Winston.

Gagné, R. M., Wager, W. W., Golas, K., & Keller, J. M. (2005). *Principles of Instructional Design* (5th ed.). Belmont, CA: Wadsworth/Thomson Learning Inc.

Glaser, R. (1990). Toward new models for assessment. *International Journal of Educational Research, 14*, 475–483.

Goodlad, J. I. (1982). Response: Let's Get on with the Reconstruction. *Phi Delta Kappan, 64*(1), 19–20.

Hartshorne, R., & Ajjan, H. (2009). Examining student decisions to adopt web 2.0 technologies: Theory and empirical tests. *Journal of Computing in Higher Education, 21*(3), 183–198. doi:10.100712528-009-9023-6

Herrington, T., Sparrow, L., & Herrington, J. (1999). Investigating mathematics education using multimedia. *Journal of Technology and Teacher Education, 7*(3), 175–186.

Hornbach, C. (2004). Response to Masafumi Ogawa, "Music Teacher Education in Japan: Structure, Problems, and Perspectives. *Philosophy of Music Education Review, 12*(2), 201–204. doi:10.1353/pme.2005.0005

Huang, H. M. (2002). Toward constructivism for adult learners in online learning environments. *British Journal of Educational Technology*, *33*(1), 27–37. doi:10.1111/1467-8535.00236

Johnson, L., Adams Becker, S., Estrada, V., & Freeman, A. (2014). *Horizon Report: 2014 Higher Education Edition*. Austin, Texas: The New Media Consortium. Retrieved from http://www.nmc.org/pdf/2014-nmc-horizon-report-he-EN.pdf

Kirkwood, A., & Price, L. (2008). Assessment and student learning: A fundamental relationship and the role of information and communication technologies. *Open Learning: The Journal of Open and Distance Learning*, *23*(1), 5–16. doi:10.1080/02680510701815160

Kirkwood, A. & Price, L. (2016). *Technology-Enabled Learning: Handbook*. Commonwealth of Learning.

Kirkwood, A., & Price, L. (2016). *Technology Enabled Learning: Handbook*. Commonwealth of Learning.

Kirkwood, A. T., & Price, L. (2005). Learners and Learning in the 21st Century: What do we know about students' attitudes and experiences of ICT that will help us design courses? *Studies in Higher Education*, *30*(3), 257–274. doi:10.1080/03075070500095689

Knowles, J. G. (1988). A Beginning Teacher's Experience: Reflections on Becoming a Teacher. *Language Arts*, *65*(7), 702–712.

Kramanski, B., & Michalsky, T. (2010). Preparing preservice teachers for self-regulated learning in the context of technological pedagogical content knowledge. *Learning and Instruction*, *20*(5), 434–447. doi:10.1016/j.learninstruc.2009.05.003

Lock, A., & Strong, T. (2010). *Social Constructionism. Sources and stirrings in theory and practice*. Cambridge, UK: Cambridge University Press. doi:10.1017/CBO9780511815454

Löfström, E., & Nevgi, A. (2007). From strategic planning to meaningful learning: Diverse perspectives on the development of web-based teaching and learning in higher education. *British Journal of Educational Technology*, *38*(2), 312–324. doi:10.1111/j.1467-8535.2006.00625.x

Price, L., & Kirkwood, A. (2008). Technology in the United Kingdom's higher education context. In S. Scott & K. Dixon (Eds.), *The 21st century, globalised university: Trends and development in teaching and learning* (pp. 83–113). Perth, Australia: Black Swan.

Pringle, R. M. (2006). Preservice Teachers' Exploration of Children's Alternative Conceptions: Cornerstone for Planning to Teach Science. *Journal of Science Teacher Education, 17*(3), 291–307. doi:10.100710972-006-9017-4

Rothwell, W. J., & Kazanas, H. C. (2008). *Mastering the instructional design process. A systematic approach* (4th ed.). San Francisco: Wiley.

Salmon, G. (2005). Flying not flapping: A strategic framework for e-learning and pedagogical innovation in higher education institutions. *ALT-J, 13*(3), 201–218. doi:10.3402/rlt.v13i3.11218

Seel, N. (2003). Psychologie des Lernens (2. Auflage). München: Ernst Reinhardt (UTB).

Tinto, V. (1997). Classrooms as communities. Exploring the educational character of student persistence. *The Journal of Higher Education, 68*(6), 600–623.

Tinto, V. (1998). Colleges as communities. Taking research on student persistence seriously. *Review of Higher Education, 21*(2), 167–177.

Wee Sing Sim, J., & Foon Hew, K. (2010). The use of weblogs in higher education settings: *A review of empirical research. Educational Research Review, 5*(2), 151–163. doi:10.1016/j.edurev.2010.01.001

Wertsch, J. V. (2010). Vygotsky and recent developments. In P. Peterson, E. Baker, & B. McGaw (Eds.), *International Encyclopedia of Education* (Vol. 3, pp. 231–236). Academic Press. doi:10.1016/B978-0-08-044894-7.00490-5

KEY TERMS AND DEFINITIONS

Academic-Oriented Learning: Refers to the learning process and learning activities that are intended to achieve academic or scholarly objectives. The learning process involves activities that will fulfill the learner's goals or objectives in his/her formal studies in an educational institution, for instance, in a higher education institution.

Effective Learning: Learning is successful or effective given that there is a match between the needed or desired learning performance and the learning outcome or the result of the learning performance.

eLearning: Learning can be defined as the acquisition or modification of knowledge and skills, which can be explained in various perspectives depending on how it occurs in a specific context or environment. Hence, eLearning is a learning process, which specifically occurs in virtual learning environments. The learning process is primarily supported and mediated by information and communication technologies (ICT) or any form of electronic media, which include (web-based) learning platforms or learning management systems (LMS).

Knowledge Management: Pertains to all methods and tools that promote and support the access to knowledge as well as sharing, distribution, and application of knowledge, which could further improve the quality of performance in an organization. The core activities in knowledge management include generating, storing, sharing, distributing, and applying knowledge.

Learning: Generally defined as the acquisition or modification of knowledge and skills, which can be explained in various perspectives depending on how it occurs in a specific environment or context. It is a continuous process of construction of new knowledge and reconstruction of an already existing one. It can happen either at the individual level or at the group level. Thus, it is a continuous process of (re)construction and collaboration.

Ubiquitous Technologies or U-Technologies: Refer to widely used technological devices and web-based tools or applications. Their use is very prevalent nowadays (i.e., a vast number of people around the world utilize them every day).

APPENDIX

Table 2. A depiction of the UDL framework by CAST

	Provide multiple means of Engagement Affective Networks The "WHY" of Learning	**Provide multiple means of Representation** Recognition Networks The "WHAT" of Learning	**Provide multiple means of Action and Expression** Strategic Networks The "HOW" of learning
A C C E S S	**Provide options for Recruiting Interest** • Optimize individual choice and autonomy • Optimize relevance, value, and authenticity • Minimize threats and distractions	**Provide options for Perception** • Offer ways of customizing the display of information • Offer alternatives for auditory information • Offer alternatives for visual information	**Provide options for Physical Action** • Vary the methods for response and navigation • Optimize access to tools and assistive technologies
B U I L D	**Provide options for Sustaining Effort & Persistence** • Heighten salience of goals and objectives • Vary demands and resources to optimize challenge • Foster collaboration and community • Increase mastery-oriented feedback	**Provide options for Language & Symbols** • Clarify vocabulary and symbols • Clarify syntax and structure • Support decoding of text, mathematical notation, and symbols • Promote understanding across languages • Illustrate through multiple media	**Provide options for Expression & Communication** • Use multiple media for communication • Use multiple tools for construction and composition • Build fluencies with graduated levels of support for practice and performance
I N T E R N A L I Z E	**Provide options for Self-Regulation** • Promote expectations and beliefs that optimize motivation • Facilitate personal coping skills and strategies • Develop self-assessment and reflection	**Provide options for Comprehension** • Activate or supply background knowledge • Highlight patterns, critical features, big ideas, and relationships • Guide information processing and visualization • Maximize transfer and generalization	**Provide options for Executive Functions** • Guide appropriate goal-setting • Support planning and strategy development • Facilitate managing information and resources • Enhance capacity for monitoring progress
G O A L	*Expert learners who are purposeful and motivated*	*Expert learners who are resourceful and knowledgeable*	*Expert learners who are strategic and goal-directed*

CAST (2018). Universal design for learning guidelines version 2.2. Wakefield, MA: Author.

Chapter 6

Higher Education and Web 2.0:
Barriers and Best Practices From the Standpoint of Practitioners

Pedro Isaias
The University of Queensland, Australia

Paula Miranda
Polytechnic Institute of Setubal, Portugal

Sara Pífano
Information Society Research Lab, Portugal

ABSTRACT

The abundance of evidence of Web 2.0's value in educational settings has provided both educators and researchers with prized information about the application of a panoply of technologies. The experience that this evidence portrays can be used to meaningfully direct teachers in their own ventures of Web 2.0 implementation. In online learning environments, any collaboration between the students must occur with the support of technology, so it is fundamental that technology functions as an enabler, maximizing the opportunities that online settings offer, and that students can tap into those technologies to enhance their learning experience. This chapter focuses on the implementation of Web 2.0 within higher education from the viewpoint of e-learning experts. It reports on the findings of on online questionnaire that examined both the barriers and the best practices of implementation and that was applied internationally among researchers and teachers in the higher education sector.

DOI: 10.4018/978-1-5225-7435-4.ch006

INTRODUCTION

Web 2.0, as originally coined by O'Reilly (2007), refers to a stance towards the use of the Web, rather than a technology in itself that is associated with several precepts namely collective intelligence, user participation, content edition, software that improves the more it is used, and rich user experience. As it evolved, Web 2.0 began to reach different sectors of society with the development of tools, sites and applications that people could use namely for recreational, business, health and educational purposes. Within educational contexts its use is been widely documented and explored (Echeng, Usoro, & Ewuzie, 2016; Isaias, Miranda, & Pifano, 2017; Karvounidis, Chimos, Bersimis, & Douligeris, 2018; Marosan, Josanov, & Savic, 2015; Pieri & Diamantini, 2014; Rogers-Estable, 2014; Soomro, Zai, & Jafri, 2015; Virtanen & Rasi, 2017).

In an attempt to depict existing Web 2.0 technologies, Bower (2015) study attests to the existence of more than 200 different technologies with applicability in learning and teaching. Education's partnership with Web 2.0 causes learning to become more interactive and collaborative, giving students the possibility of generating and exchanging their own content (Isaias, Miranda, & Pifano, 2009). Regardless of a wide variety of educational benefits Web 2.0 technologies' potential persists unattained (Jimoyiannis, 2015). This reality results in a pressing need to examine the barriers to its implementation as well as the best practices that can guide educators in their innovative experiments with these technologies. In order to address the existing barriers and maximise the benefits that Web 2.0 purports, a scrupulous implementation plan needs to be put in place. There are several aspects that teachers must take into account when applying Web 2.0 to their courses. It is important to begin with a careful selection of the technology that is more suitable (Holenko Dlab, Candrlic, & Sabranovic, 2016) for the attainment of the specific learning goals. Where needed, teacher training should be encouraged (Baltodano, 2016). Also, the tools that are selected need to be intuitive, so that the students can easily use them (Pieri & Diamantini, 2014). It is equally essential stimulate student participation, as the more students participate, the more that will motivate others to contribute (Chen, Yen, & Hwang, 2012).

This chapter begins with a theoretical background about the use of Web 2.0 in higher education, the obstacles associated to its implementation and recommended guidelines for its deployment. It then describes the methods that were used in this research and presents the results that were obtained via the online questionnaires. It concludes with a discussion of this study's outcomes and their significance for the context of Web 2.0 implementation in higher education courses.

WEB 2.0 TOOLS WITHIN THE HIGHER EDUCATION SECTOR

Web 2.0 is appreciated for its positive impact on student social interaction and community building (Safran, Helic, & Gütl, 2007), on the empowerment of the students in the creation of their own learning scenarios (Bates, 2011) and on the possibility to collaboratively construct knowledge (Virtanen & Rasi, 2017). Moreover, Web 2.0 enables students to embrace a more self-regulated ethic of learning (McLoughlin & Lee, 2010), it increases their interest and satisfaction (Karvounidis et al., 2018) and scaffolds communication and discussion activities (Watty, McKay, & Ngo, 2016).

At the same time some incredulity exists still. The scepticism that remains around the use of Web 2.0 for pedagogical purposes can be attributed to claims that it can cause students to be distracted from their learning goals (Bubas, Coric, & Orehovacki, 2011) and that their participation might be dependent of assessment (Echeng & Usoro, 2016). Also, teachers seem to have insufficient expertise on how to operate these technologies effectively (Rogers-Estable, 2014) and they have to take on the added responsibility of having to actively and frequently contribute with content (Baxter, Connolly, Stansfield, Tsvetkova, & Stoimenova, 2011).

Web 2.0 has been thriving in various sectors of society, which results in an overwhelming amount of tools, platforms and websites that were designed to serve multiple purposes. In Bower (2016) study, the author conducted an extensive review of Web 2.0 technology, where he identified more than 200 technologies with application for learning and teaching, from a universe of 2,000 links. He then proposed a typology based on 37 types of technology, organised into 14 clusters:

- Text based tools (creation, editing and exchange of text documents and text based discussions – ex. Google Docs (http://docs.google.com) and Twitter (http://twitter.com);
- Image based tools (creation, editing and sharing of images and mindmapping – ex. Flickr (http://flickr.com) and FlockDraw (http://flockdraw.com);
- Audio tools (recording and sharing audio recordings – ex. SoundCloud (http://soundcloud.com) and Soundation (http://soundation.com);
- Video tools (creation, editing and sharing video files) - ex. YouTube (http://youtube.com) and Muvee (http://muvee.com);
- Multimodal production tools (organisation, sequencing and exchange of multimodal content) – ex. Padlet (http://padlet.com) and Prezi (http://prezi.com);

- Digital storytelling tools (creation and exchange of stories, comics and animation) – ex. Mixbook (http://mixbook.com) and Powtoon (http://powtoon.com);
- Website creation tools (development of websites or web pages) – ex. WordPress (http://wordpress.org);
- Knowledge organisation and sharing (file sharing, social bookmarking, Really Simple
- Syndication (RSS)) – ex. Dropbox (http://dropbox.com)
- Data analysis tools – (data collection, collaborative data analysis) – ex. SurveyMonkey (http://surveymonkey.com)
- Timeline tools (chronological organisation of content) – ex. Tiki-Toki (http://tiki-toki.com)
- 3D modelling tools (3D design) – ex. Tinkercad (http://www.tinkercad.com/)
- Assessment tools (creation of online assessment activities) – ex. Quizlet http://quizlet.com
- Social networking systems (online profile creation and content sharing) – ex. Facebook http://facebook.com
- Synchronous collaboration tools synchronous exchange of content) – ex. Zoom http://zoom.us

The comprehensive list presented by Bower (2016) constitutes not only a valuable resource to search for relevant tools, but also a detailed illustration of the amount of tools that are available. While, this is an opportunity for teachers to innovate in their courses and diversify the type of learning technology they select to support teaching and learning, it can present a challenge with concern to understanding which tools will result in more value. Hence selecting the most appropriate tools can become a complex part of Web 2.0 implementation (Grosseck, 2009).

BARRIERS AND BEST PRACTICES FOR WEB 2.0

In the implementation of Web 2.0 in higher education settings, to maximise the possibility of success, an inclusive understanding of the obstacles that may emerge during the process is essential. Also, the deployment of Web 2.0 has a higher possibility of succeeding if previous experiences and knowledge are taken into account, to offer insight into the best practices that need to inform it.

Obstacles for Implementation

According to Gregory and Lodge (2015) the academic workload of teachers in higher education can be a silent impediment to the adoption of technology within the learning environment, hence, it is important to implement workload models that are flexible and that can assist a sounder deployment of learning technologies. Similarly, the lack of time is equally mentioned as a common obstacle preventing teachers from the development of innovative teaching approaches with technology (Reed, 2014). Tus, the fact that deploying and using technology for learning can be significantly time consuming and the inadequate perception that exists about the workload it demands, are two important deterrents of using learning technologies from the viewpoint of the teachers (Kregor, Breslin, & Fountain, 2012). In the context of Web 2.0 in particular, the teachers' workload can equally increase. Since Web 2.0 tools are abundantly used for communication purposes and can be accessible at any time, their use may cause an increase of communication volume that the teachers have to manage, which adds to their existing workload (McLoughlin & Alam, 2014).

There is also the issue of the skills that technology implementation requires. The lack of adequate skills is often cited as an impediment of technology deployment in education (Reed, 2014; Rogers-Estable, 2014). The ability to understand and proficiently use Web 2.0 has become an essential e-skill that employees expect their workforce to have. Although higher education institutions have an important contribution to make for the development of these skills among their students, there is still a lack of institutional initiatives that focus on student training (Buchem & Hamelmann, 2011). This deficiency exists equally at the level of institutional teacher training with concern to Web 2.0 (Soomro et al., 2015), which needs educational institutions to assume their crucial part in teacher training (Fan, Radford, & Fabian, 2016) (Yuen, Yaoyuneyong, & Yuen, 2011). The innovative potential that Web 2.0 affords needs to be cultivated by an institutional settings of faculty encouragement and reward (Bates, 2011, p. 39).

There are other vital concerns related namely to copyright (Miranda, Isaias, & Pífano, 2016; Olaniran, Burley, & Chang, 2013), privacy (Bubas et al., 2011; Feldmann, 2014), intellectual property (Waycott, Sheard, Thompson, & Clerehan, 2013), technical complications (Tétard, Patokorpi, & Packalén, 2009) and security (An & Williams, 2010). Moreover, the wide array of existing technologies is an advantage, but in certain situations it can actually be an impediment due to the uncertainty that they cause as to what technologies are more adequate (Grosseck, 2009). Moreover, as difficult as it might be to be up-to-date with the continuous changes that technology undergoes (Zelick, 2013), the deployment of Web 2.0

requires teachers to be confident with their use and able to master their features for the benefit of learning (Jimoyiannis, 2015). Additionally, the introduction of Web 2.0 tools implies that the teachers need to cultivate more creative strategies to address the particularities of distributed environments that are outside of institutional support (Ovelar, 2010).

Implementation Recommendations

Given the overwhelming amount of Web 2.0 tools and applications, it is crucial to have defined criteria to assist the selection of the most appropriate. Firstly, teachers should base their selection on a pedagogical approach (Isaias et al., 2017). Guidance from pedagogical approaches can benefit the implementation of Web 2.0 and enhance higher education practice (Buchem & Hamelmann, 2011). The consideration for appropriate pedagogical approaches, such as constructivism, connectivism (Bates, 2011), collaborative learning needs to be incorporated into the implementation process, (Yuen et al., 2011) to guarantee that technology is effectively integrated (Karvounidis, Chimos, Bersimis, & Douligeris, 2014). As such the selection of the most adequate Web 2.0 tool needs to be conditioned by a pedagogical approach that the teacher embrace as a guide to their teaching (Bates, 2011). Another important criteria influencing technology selection is its capacity to motivate and engage the learners and to depict the course material (Bubas et al., 2011). Additionally, the Web 2.0 tools need to be chosen according to their value to a specific purpose (Homola & Kubincová, 2009), in this case learning. Hence, the tools need to have learning value in order to be deployed (Isaias et al., 2017). Finally, the subject itself is an equally important criterion (Bates, 2011; Karvounidis et al., 2014), as some tools fit better with particular disciplines (Kumar, 2009).

As one of the great motivators of user's contribution to web-based communities, content (Ewing, 2008), is essential in any Web 2.0 initiative. User-generated content is enabled by Web 2.0 that is responsible for converting learners from passive consumers of content to actual creators of content (Yuen et al., 2011). Students' addition of content can constitute motivate their peers to participate and cooperate (Jimoyiannis, 2015). Since the students can openly voice their opinions in Web 2.0 tools, some teachers advise the monitoring of their participation to guarantee that abusive language and inappropriate online behaviour is restricted (Waycott et al., 2013). The teachers' role is key in terms of content as they create and elucidate on the content that is generated by the learners (McLoughlin & Alam, 2014). The teachers should be an example of active contribution, namely with feedback (Baxter et al., 2011) and the provision of relevant content like course resources, relevant links and reading materials (Kumar, 2009).

User-generated content can assume a diverse number of formats, namely text, audio and video (Shang, Li, Wu, & Hou, 2011). As such, with the use of Web 2.0 students can add content that they have authored in a panoply of formats (Jimoyiannis, 2015). This is one of the aspects that students perceive as positive about these tools (Lai & Ng, 2011), hence, it needs to be considered when implementing Web 2.0 in order not to limit the possibilities of the students in terms of content creation and exchange. Specially in the context of e-learning, students demand integrated communication features that can ensure their interaction with their peers and social support (Feldmann, 2014). Thus, it is key to select a tool that includes the provision of communication features (Dlab, Candrlic, & Sabranovic, 2016). If these features are not built-in in the selected Web 2.0 technology, then additional tools need to be integrated to enable learners' interaction (Tétard et al., 2009).

Despite the fact that user-friendliness is one of Web 2.0's most prised characteristics for its capacity of user empowerment in terms of content creation (Benito-Ruiz, 2009), there are, nonetheless, some reports of learners' discontentment with the lack of intuitiveness that certain tools have, (Pieri & Diamantini, 2014), which can have a detrimental effect on their willingness to participate (Cole, 2009). Usability is an important aspect of Web 2.0 implementation in the sense that the tools need to be functional (Bubas et al., 2011). Ease of use is a vital driver of students' participation (Echeng et al., 2016) which needs to be ensure via multiple strategies, namely ensuring the availability of help resources (Bubas et al., 2011) (Chapman & Russell, 2009), the provision of training to the learners before they are required to use the tools (Jimoyiannis, Tsiotakis, & Roussinos, 2012) (Rahimi, van den Berg, & Veen, 2013) (Echeng & Usoro, 2016) and a use of an experimental period (Baxter et al., 2011).

Collective intelligence is one of the core precepts of Web 2.0 and it grows proportionally to the number of participating user (Constantinides & Fountain, 2008). This is one of reason why it is so important for the success of Web 2.0 application to reach critical mass. The participation of the users not only increased the value of Web 2.0, it is what makes it work. Moreover, a high number of users is a valuable driver for other users to join (Chen et al., 2012). The more user a platform has, the more users it is likely to have. There are several strategies that can be employed to motivate students to participate, more specifically, the development of a reward arrangement (Baxter et al., 2011), the attribution of grades to their participation, which can also impact the quality of their contributions (Echeng & Usoro, 2016), and the monitoring of the learners' participation (Tétard et al., 2009).

METHODOLOGY

Web 2.0's implementation can greatly benefit from the experience of educators. Hence, in order to identify the core barriers of Web 2.0 integration in higher education and to determine the best practices that should drive its use, this study designed an online questionnaire to be administered among researchers and teachers internationally. Online questionnaires are prised instruments of data collection in circumstances where the population is geographically dispersed. Also they are financially appealing and save time (Wright, 2005).

The respondents were selected via a sample of convenience and they were invited by email to participate. The questionnaire intended mainly to assess the respondents' proficiency in terms of Web 2.0, their experience with its technologies, the learning environments where they had applied them, the barriers hindering their implementation and the best practices underlying their incorporation in instructional scenarios. Hence, the questionnaire was divided into three groups of questions. The first group pertained to the collection of the respondents' demographic data, namely age, gender and professional occupation. The second group was composed of questions about the respondents' use of and experience with Web 2.0 tools in the courses they teach and their level of proficiency in Web 2.0 technology. The final group explored the barriers and the factors for the can lead to an effective implementation of Web 2.0.

The data that derived from the questionnaires was analysed in SPSS 20, through the use of descriptive statistics.

RESULTS

The online questionnaire originated a total of 176 complete responses, but for the purpose of this chapter only the respondents who have declared to have used Web 2.0 in e-learning contexts will be considered. Hence, a total of 70 responses will be analysed in this section. The data collection reiterated some of the beliefs of existing literature with regards to implementation barriers, as well as to the factors that can lead to a more successful application of Web 2.0.

Respondents Profile and Their Experience With Web 2.0

Most of the respondents were male (57.1%) while 42.9% were female participants. Only 2.9% of the sample was under 30 years old, 17.1% was between the ages of 30 and 40, 42.9% was 51-60 years old and 10% was between the ages of 61 and 70 years old. The online questionnaire was distributed internationally and received questions from experts from 22 countries, such as Germany, United Kingdom, Spain, Portugal, United States and Croatia. With regards to their professional occupation, the majority of the participants reported being in teaching positions 78.6%, such as professor, associate professor and lecturer. Those working in research corresponded to 15.7% of the sample.

Since all the participants claimed to have used Web 2.0 tools in their e-learning courses, they were asked about the tools that they used the most, using a five point Likert scale (1- rarely to 5-very often) to classify their use of the tools (*Figure 1*).

The mean values show that forums, video sharing and social networks are used more often by the participants. Despite that fact that these values are above 3 and reflect an above the average frequency, they reflect the absence of an expressive use of higher ratings pertaining to frequency. The percentage of participants who declared to use these three tools often or very often was 64.3%, 55.7% and 50% respectively. The remaining tools are used only sometimes or rarely. Despite the fact that all the participants have used Web 2.0 tools in their courses, they don't seem to implement them very frequently. In order not to restrict the responses of the participants to the tools that were listed in the questionnaire, they were provided with the opportunity to add other tools that they might have used/currently use in their courses. The 33

Figure 1. Mean values for Web 2.0 tools usage

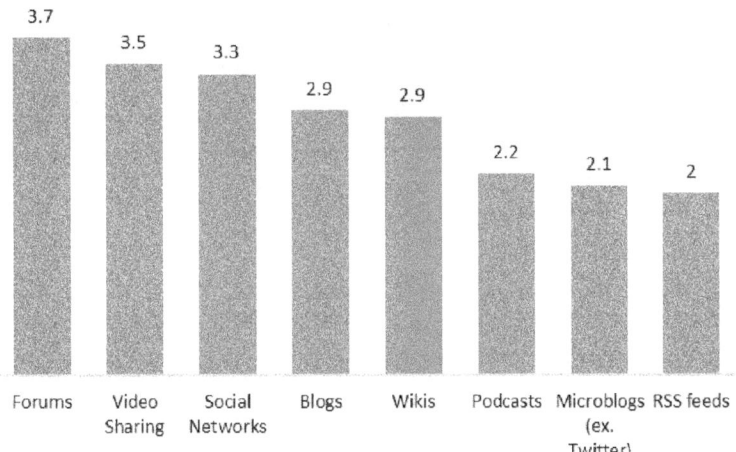

participants, who supplemented the initial list of tools, highlighted their use of social bookmarking, file sharing, mindmaps and collaborative platforms.

With the purpose of understanding the sample's level of expertise, the respondents were asked to classify their level of proficiency when it comes to using Web 2.0 tools (Figure 2).

With regards to the use of Web 2.0 tools, the sample demonstrated a varying degree of proficiency. While, solely 4.3% of the participants classified themselves as being not proficient, only a modest majority (64%) claimed to be proficient or very proficient. Also, 31.4% of the sample claimed to be somewhat or moderately proficient.

Barriers and Best Practices of Web 2.0's Deployment

Prior to approaching the practices that can lead to an effective application of Web 2.0 tools in the context of higher education, it was important to assess what type of obstacles can negatively impact its deployment. The respondents were given the option of selecting as many items as they would like and they could also propose other items besides the ones that were listed. Figure 3 portrays their responses.

Figure 2. Level of proficiency in using Web 2.0 tools

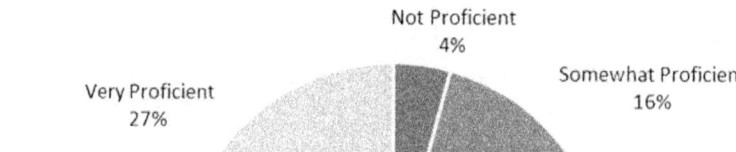

Figure 3. Barriers affecting the implementation of Web 2.0

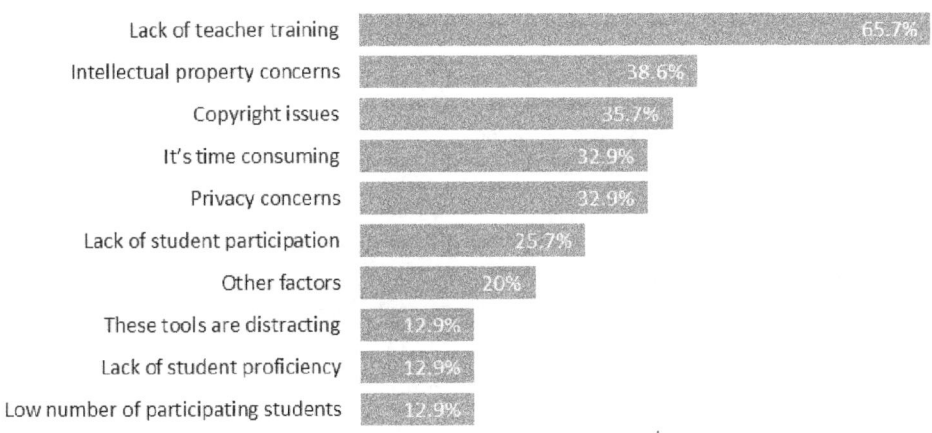

In terms of the barriers, the participants highlighted the lack of teacher training (65.7), intellectual property concerns (38.6%), copyright issues (35.7%), privacy concerns (32.9%) and the fact that it is time consuming (32.9%). The lack of teacher training was clearly the predominant factor according to the experts, with circa 27 percentage points over the second factor in the chart. On the other hand, the fact that these tools are distracting, the lack of student proficiency in using the tools and a low number of participating students were deemed as not very impactful as barriers to implementation having each gather solely 12.9% of the responses. Moreover, the 20% of the respondents, who added other factors, mentioned the lack of support from the higher education institutions, the fact that some students don't access to the necessary technology, the cost, faculty's hesitancy and lack of commitment to adopt and the fact that sometimes the use of Web 2.0 tools cannot be made mandatory.

With concern to the factors that can lead to an effective application of Web 2.0 tools in the context of higher education, the experts also had the option of selecting as many items as they would like and they could equally suggest additional items to complement the ones that were listed (Figure 4).

In terms of the aspects that they consider to be important for a fruitful implementation, they pointed out the need to select a Web 2.0 tool with learning value (55.7%), the students' participation (52.9%), selecting a Web 2.0 tool that is easy to use (51.4%), the integration of features that enable student interaction (50%), the availability of relevant content (48.6%) and enabling content creation in multiple formats such as photo, video, text, (45.7%). Managing the quality of the students' contributions and a high number of participating students were also selected by 25.7% and 18.6% of the participants, but they were the factors to which was attributed less significance.

Figure 4. Factors that assist the effective deployment of Web 2.0

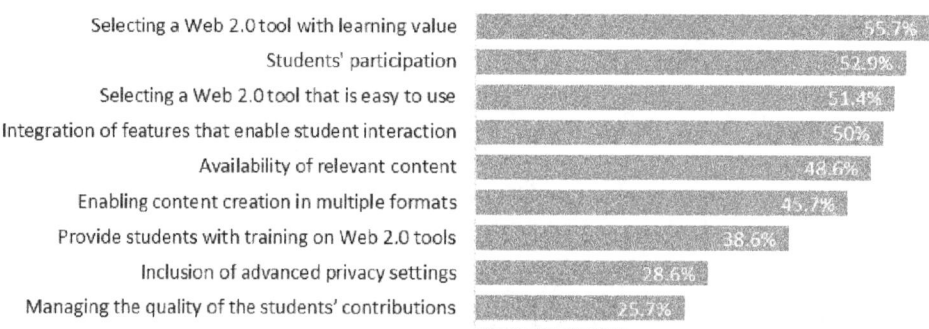

The last section of the questionnaire presented the participants with several practices associated with the implementation of Web 2.0, which were grouped into five main elements: Web 2.0 technology selection, student participation, high number of active students, ease of use, and features for content generation and communication. The experts were asked to rate them in accordance to their level of agreement, using a six point Likert scale (1- totally disagree to 6 - I don't know). These factors were selected to be further scrutinised due to the importance that the current literature on the subject attributes to them, as was described in section 2.

The selection of the most adequate technology is an intricate process that requires teacher to account for several aspects including pedagogy, training, the subject itself and the learning value of the tool (Figure 5).

Figure 5. Aspects to consider when selecting a Web 2.0 tool

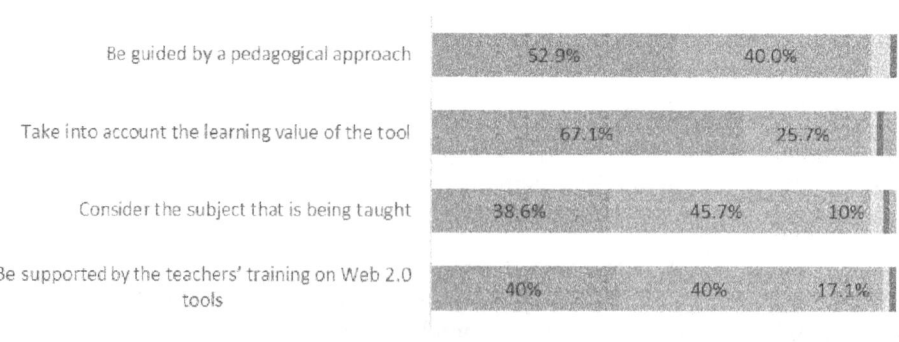

All the practices related to technology selection itemised in the questionnaire had very high agreement levels ranging from 80% to 93% of total agreement. In particular, the experts highlighted the need to use a pedagogical approach to guide the deployment of Web 2.0 and to consider the learning value of the tool (each with 93%).

Web 2.0 value is intrinsically connected with user participation, as it is one of its most fundamental precepts. As such, in the context of higher education, it becomes necessary to encourage the participation of students. According to the respondents' levels of total agreement, to motivate students to participate, intellectual property concerns need to be addressed (73%); copyright issues need to be discussed (73%); their participation should be graded (63%); and advanced privacy settings should be used (59%). There was one other item associated with student participation, which stated that their participation should be mandatory, but it had only 46% of total agreement ratings. This practice also had 21% of total disagreement and 33% of non-committal ratings, which for this scale correspond to "neither agree nor disagree" and "I don't know".

With regards to the statements associated to a high number of active students, they all received high total agreement levels (Figure 6).

More specifically, the experts agreed that a high number of active students can be achieved by encouraging student interaction (89%) and collaboration (87%). Despite having total agreement levels of 81% and 71% respectively, the statements "encourages other students to participate" and "will bring more value to the tool", also registered a significant percentage of non-committal ratings (14% and 26% respectively). This seems to demonstrate that part of the respondents are unsure as to the impact that a high number of students in itself has on students' participation and what value it brings to the tool.

Figure 6. Statements associated with a high number of students

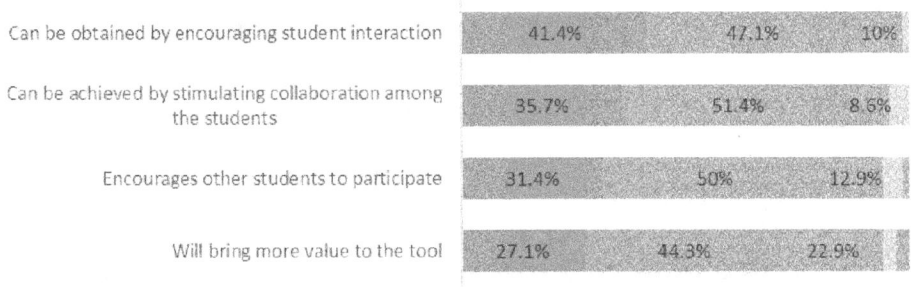

With concern to ease of use, it represents one of the core advantages of using Web 2.0 tools in higher education, as their intuitiveness allows for teachers and students to operate them with minimal technical expertise. The percentage of total agreement for this aspect of implementation demonstrated that according to the participants, to guarantee ease of use, user friendly tools should be selected (94%), educational institutions should provide teachers with training on Web 2.0 (86%), help resources need to be available (84%), an experimentation period should be used (64%) and the teachers should provide students with training on Web 2.0 (63%). Although the majority of the participants agreed with all the statements, they revealed significant neutrality in terms of the need for an experimentation period and the provision of training by the teachers, with 24.3% of the participants selecting the neither agree nor disagree option for each statement. This might be due to the fact that an experimentation period will not always be possible because of time constraints associated with the academic calendar and also the fact that some teachers might require training themselves.

Lastly, with concern to features for content generation and communication, an expressive majority of the respondents agreed with the features and options that were listed in the questionnaire (Figure 7).

Above all, the participants highlighted the need for tools to enable communication among the students (96% of total agreement) and for features to add content in a variety of formats, such as videos, text, photos. With regards to the existence of an option to add comments to the contributions, 16% of the participants were neutral about its need.

Figure 7. Respondent's views on the need for features for content generation and communication

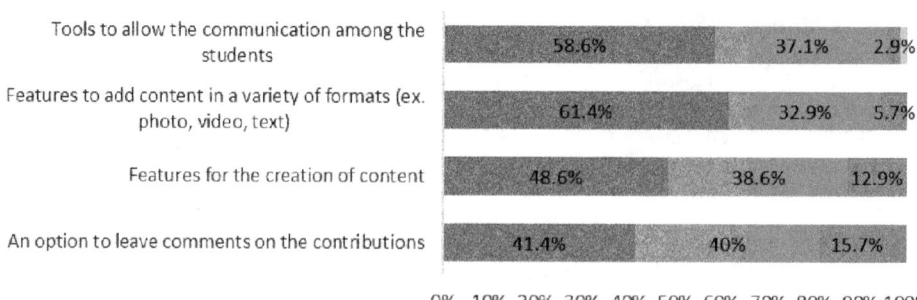

Considering all the statements presented to the respondents from all five elements, six in particular had total agreement percentages above 90% (Figure 8).

Three aspects were especially underlined by the participants: the existence of features for communication and content addition in multiple formats; the required user-friendliness of the tools; and technology selection which should be guided by a pedagogical approach and consider the learning value of the tool. In contrast, the three aspects that gathered more disagreement were the fact that the students' participation should be mandatory (21.4% of total disagreement), that the teachers should provide students with training on Web 2.0 (11.4%) and that advanced privacy settings should be used (10%).

DISCUSSION

The characteristics of online learning require technology to be used to both maximise the affordances of web-based learning environments and minimise the difficulties that derive from the absence of face-to-face education. Web 2.0 is a valuable technological partner with proven benefits to the learning experiences of the students. Nonetheless, its implementation remains surrounded by several barriers that hurdle its wide application to higher education. This chapter aimed to provide insight into the barriers as well as the best practices that can be followed by teachers to ensure an effective deployment of Web 2.0 in their course.

Figure 8. Best practices for Web 2.0 implementation in higher education

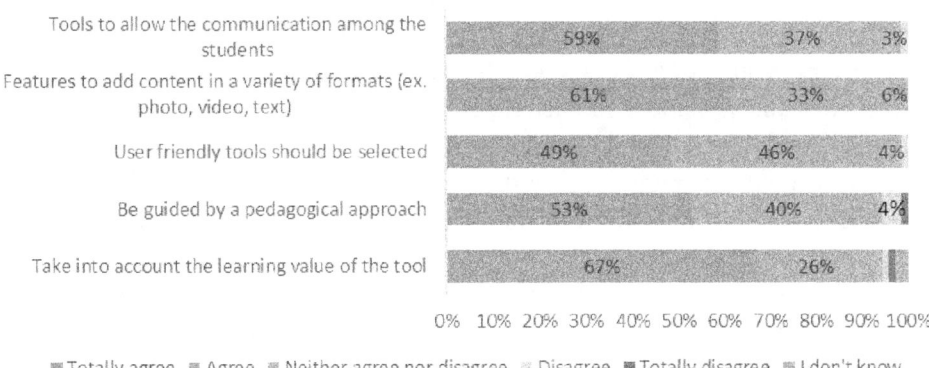

The online questionnaire that was distributed among international higher education was based on a thorough review of relevant literature and while it surveyed the barriers of implementation, it focused mainly on the best practices. The fact that all the respondents reported to have used Web 2.0 tools in their e-learning courses attested their suitability for this study. Also, the fact that an expressive majority reported to occupy teaching positions assists their expertise in this subject. The results demonstrated that forums, video sharing and social networks are the Web 2.0 tools that the respondents use more often. Nonetheless, the results on the frequency of use of specific Web 2.0 tools showed that, despite the fact that all of them have used Web 2.0, the participants do not deploy them very frequently. With concern to the sample's expertise in terms of Web 2.0 tools, based on the respondents' self-assessment, their proficiency levels varied mostly between the majority of those who saw themselves as being proficient or very proficient and a significant percentage of those who reported to be somewhat or moderately proficient.

With regards to the barriers that seem to be impeding the implementation, five factors were most often selected by the respondents: lack of teacher training, as was equally defended by current studies (Jimoyiannis, 2015; Reed, 2014; Rogers-Estable, 2014); intellectual property concerns as mentioned in Waycott et al. (2013); copyright issues, which also had a sound support from previous studies (Miranda et al., 2016; Olaniran et al., 2013); privacy concerns, a factor often mentioned in the literature (Feldmann, 2014); and the fact that it is time consuming, similarly to what was argued by Reed (2014) and Kregor et al. (2012). On the other hand, the factors that the majority of the respondents considered as contributors to an effective deployment of Web 2.0 were: the need to select a Web 2.0 tool with learning value, as advocated by Homola and Kubincová (2009) and Isaias et al. (2017); the students' participation, which was highlighted in previous studies (Jimoyiannis, 2015); selecting a Web 2.0 tool that is easy to use, as was widely defended in relevant literature (Benito-Ruiz, 2009; Bubas et al., 2011; Cole, 2009; Echeng et al., 2016); and the integration of features that enable student interaction, as was equally argued by Feldmann (2014) and Dlab et al. (2016).

Also, a significant percentage of the sample equally selected the availability of relevant content and enabling content creation in multiple formats (image, video, text) as important factors.

The further scrutiny of five main elements of Web 2.0 implementation, i.e. Web 2.0 technology selection, student participation, high number of active students, ease of use, and features for content generation and communication, allowed for a more detailed understanding of the best practices that support an effective implementation.

The analysis of all the practices pertaining to these elements showed that the respondents were in agreement with four in particular, the presence of features for communication and content addition in multiple formats, the necessary user-friendliness of the tools and the fact that technology selection should be guided by a pedagogical approach and consider the learning value of the tool. Conversely, three practices generated more disagreement: the fact that the students' participation should be mandatory, that the teachers should provide students with training on Web 2.0 and that advanced privacy settings should be used.

CONCLUSION

Within the context of Web 2.0's implementation, this chapter aimed to provide an overview of its barriers and to examine its best practices. The results collected from the questionnaires with international experts highlighted the lack of teacher training, intellectual property concerns, copyright issues, privacy concerns, and the fact that it is time consuming, as the most relevant impediments of Web 2.0's deployment in higher education. In opposition, the participants selected several practices as being conducive to Web 2.0's implementation, more specifically, the need to select a Web 2.0 tool with learning value, the students' participation, the selection of a Web 2.0 tool that is easy to use and the integration of features that enable student interaction. The information provided by the experts is valuable for both research and practice. In terms of research it adds to a significant number of studies that explore Web 2.0's value in higher education, providing further insight into the dynamic of its application. With concern to practice, it assists teachers to become aware of the challenges that they have to face and provides them with some guidance as to the practices that should inform their decisions in the implementation process.

Some of the limitations that impact this research include the reduced sample size and the use of a quantitative instrument for data collection. Future research should supplement the data provided by the online questionnaire with qualitative data to further analyse some of the options that the participants made. While the quantitative data provided insight into the barriers and best practices connected to Web 2.0's deployment, more in-depth methods, such as interviews or focus groups, could explore some of its more intricate ramifications and examine, in a more comprehensive manner, the real difficulties that educators experience.

REFERENCES

An, Y.-J., & Williams, K. (2010). Teaching with Web 2.0 technologies: Benefits, barriers and lessons learned. *International Journal of Instructional Technology and Distance Learning*, 7(3), 41–48.

Baltodano, M. M. (2016). ICT Training Requirements in Higher Education: Case Study of Training Programme for the Didactical Use of Web 2.0 Applications. *Educational Excellence*, 2(1), 15–27. doi:10.18562/IJEE.2015.0011

Bates, T. (2011). Understanding Web 2.0 and its implications for e-learning. In M. Lee & C. McLoughlin (Eds.), *Web 2.0-Based E-Learning: Applying Social Informatics for Tertiary Teaching* (pp. 21–42). Hershey, PA: IGI Global. doi:10.4018/978-1-60566-294-7.ch002

Baxter, G. J., Connolly, T. M., Stansfield, M. H., Tsvetkova, N., & Stoimenova, B. (2011). Introducing Web 2.0 in education: A structured approach adopting a Web 2.0 implementation framework. In *Proceedings of the 7th International Conference on Next Generation Web Services Practices (NWeSP)* (pp. 499-504). IEEE. 10.1109/NWeSP.2011.6088230

Benito-Ruiz, E. (2009). Infoxication 2.0. Handbook of research on Web, 2, 60-79.

Bower, M. (2015). A typology of Web 2.0 learning technologies. *EDUCAUSE, 8*.

Bower, M. (2016). Deriving a typology of Web 2.0 learning technologies. *British Journal of Educational Technology*, 47(4), 763–777. doi:10.1111/bjet.12344

Bubas, G., Coric, A., & Orehovacki, T. (2011). Strategies for implementation of Web 2.0 tools in academic education. *Proceedings of the 17th European University Information Systems International Congress*.

Buchem, I., & Hamelmann, H. (2011). Developing 21st century skills: Web 2.0 in Higher Education-A case study. *Elearning Papers, 24*, 1-5.

Chapman, A., & Russell, R. (2009). *Shared Infrastructure Services Landscape Study: A survey of the use of Web 2.0 tools and services in the UK HE sector.*

Chen, S.-C., Yen, D. C., & Hwang, M. I. (2012). Factors influencing the continuance intention to the usage of Web 2.0: An empirical study. *Computers in Human Behavior*, *28*(3), 933–941. doi:10.1016/j.chb.2011.12.014

Cole, M. (2009). Using Wiki technology to support student engagement: Lessons from the trenches. *Computers & Education*, *52*(1), 141–146. doi:10.1016/j.compedu.2008.07.003

Constantinides, E., & Fountain, S. J. (2008). Web 2.0: Conceptual foundations and marketing issues. *Journal of Direct. Data and Digital Marketing Practice*, *9*(3), 231–244. doi:10.1057/palgrave.dddmp.4350098

Dlab, M. H., Candrlic, S., & Sabranovic, S. (2016). Criteria for Selection of a Web 2.0 Tool for Process Modeling Education. In M. Auer, D. Guralnick, & J. Uhomoibhi (Eds.), *Interactive Collaborative Learning. ICL 2016. Advances in Intelligent Systems and Computing* (Vol. 544). Cham: Springer.

Echeng, R., & Usoro, A. (2016). Enhancing the use of Web 2.0 Technologies in Higher Education: Students' and Lectures' Views. *Journal of International Technology and Information Management*, *25*(1), 6.

Echeng, R., Usoro, A., & Ewuzie, I. (2016). *Factors to Consider when Enhancing the Use of Web 2.0 Technologies in Higher Education: Students' and Lectures' Views for Quality Use*. Academic Press.

Ewing, T. (2008). Participation cycles and emergent cultures in an online community. *International Journal of Market Research*, *50*(5), 575–590. doi:10.2501/S1470785308200043

Fan, S., Radford, J., & Fabian, D. (2016). A mixed-method research to investigate the adoption of mobile devices and Web2.0 technologies among medical students and educators. *BMC Medical Informatics and Decision Making*, *16*(1), 43. doi:10.118612911-016-0283-6 PMID:27094813

Feldmann, B. (2014). Two decades of e-learning in distance teaching–from Web 1.0 to Web 2.0 at the University of Hagen. In L. Uden, J. Sinclair, Y.-H. Tao & D. Liberona (Eds.), *Learning Technology for Education in Cloud. MOOC and Big Data: Proceedings of the Third International Workshop* (pp. 163-172). Cham: Springer International Publishing. 10.1007/978-3-319-10671-7_16

Gregory, M. S.-J., & Lodge, J. M. (2015). Academic workload: The silent barrier to the implementation of technology-enhanced learning strategies in higher education. *Distance Education, 36*(2), 210–230. doi:10.1080/01587919.2015.1055056

Grosseck, G. (2009). To use or not to use web 2.0 in higher education? *Procedia: Social and Behavioral Sciences, 1*(1), 478–482. doi:10.1016/j.sbspro.2009.01.087

Holenko Dlab, M., Candrlic, S., & Sabranovic, S. (2016). Criteria for Selection of a Web 2.0 Tool for Process Modeling Education. In M. E. Auer, D. Guralnick & J. Uhomoibhi (Eds.), *Interactive Collaborative Learning: Proceedings of the 19th ICL Conference* (vol. 1, pp. 88-96). Cham: Springer International Publishing.

Homola, M., & Kubincová, Z. (2009). Taking advantage of Web 2.0 in organized education (a survey). In M. Auer (Ed.), *Proceedings of the Interactive Computer aided Learning (ICL) International Conference* (pp. 741-752). Kassel, Germany: Kassel University Press.

Isaias, P., Miranda, P., & Pífano, S. (2009). Towards An Effective E-Learning 2.0. In *Proceedings of the 1st International Conference on Education and New Learning Technologies (EDULEARN 09)* (pp. 4997-5004). Barcelona, Spain: IATED.

Isaias, P., Miranda, P., & Pifano, S. (2017). Model for The Effective Implementation of Web 2.0 In Higher Education from The Viewpoint of the Teachers. *Proceedings of the 10Th International Conference of Education, Research and Innovation (ICERI 2017)*.

Jimoyiannis, A. (2015). TPACK 2.0: Towards a Framework Guiding Web 2.0 Integration in Educational Practice. In M. S. Khine (Ed.), *New Directions in Technological Pedagogical Content Knowledge Research Multiple Perspectives* (pp. 83–108). Charlotte, NC: Information Age Publishing.

Jimoyiannis, A., Tsiotakis, P., & Roussinos, D. (2012). Blogs in higher education: Analysing students' participation and presence in a community of blogging. In M. B. Nunes, & P. Isaías (Eds.), *Proceedings of the IADIS International Conference on e-Learning* (pp. 228-235). Lisbon, Portugal: IADIS Press.

Karvounidis, T., Chimos, K., Bersimis, S., & Douligeris, C. (2014). Evaluating Web 2.0 technologies in higher education using students' perceptions and performance. *Journal of Computer Assisted Learning, 30*(6), 577–596. doi:10.1111/jcal.12069

Karvounidis, T., Chimos, K., Bersimis, S., & Douligeris, C. (2018). Factors, issues and interdependencies in the incorporation of a Web 2.0 based learning environment in higher education. *Education and Information Technologies, 23*(2), 935–955. doi:10.100710639-017-9644-8

Kregor, G., Breslin, M., & Fountain, W. (2012). Experience and beliefs of technology users at an Australian university: Keys to maximising e-learning potential. *Australasian Journal of Educational Technology, 28*(8). doi:10.14742/ajet.777

Kumar, S. (2009). Undergraduate perceptions of the usefulness of Web 2.0 in higher education: Survey development. *Proceedings of the 8th European Conference on e-Learning*, 308-314.

Lai, Y. C., & Ng, E. M. (2011). Using wikis to develop student teachers' learning, teaching, and assessment capabilities. *The Internet and Higher Education, 14*(1), 15–26. doi:10.1016/j.iheduc.2010.06.001

Marosan, Z., Josanov, B., & Savic, N. (2015). Technology leaders of computer and Web 2.0 usage in higher education: Case study. *Skola biznisa,* (2), 32-48.

McLoughlin, C., & Alam, S. L. (2014). A case study of instructor scaffolding using Web 2.0 tools to teach social informatics. *Journal of Information Systems Education, 25*(2), 125.

McLoughlin, C., & Lee, M. J. (2010). Personalised and self regulated learning in the Web 2.0 era: International exemplars of innovative pedagogy using social software. *Australasian Journal of Educational Technology, 26*(1). doi:10.14742/ajet.1100

Miranda, P., Isaias, P., & Pífano, S. (2016). *Higher Education Students' Perceptions of Positive and Negative Effects of Social Networking in Portugal. In Social Networking and Education* (pp. 111–127). Springer.

O'Reilly, T. (2007). What is web 2.0, design patterns and business models for the next generation of software. *Communications & Stratégies, 65*, 17–37.

Olaniran, B. A., Burley, H., & Chang, M. (2010). Social Issues and Web 2.0: A Closer Look at Culture in E-Learning. In S. Murugesan (Ed.), *Handbook of Research on Web 2.0, 3.0, and X.0: Technologies, Business, and Social Applications* (pp. 613–629). Hershey, PA: IGI Global. doi:10.4018/978-1-60566-384-5.ch034

Ovelar, R. (2010). Exploring how faculties use and rate Web 2.0 for teaching and learning purposes. *Proceedings of the 5th Doctoral Consortium at the European Conference on Technology Enhanced Learning, CEUR Workshop Proceedings 709.*

Pieri, M., & Diamantini, D. (2014). An e-learning web 2.0 experience. *Procedia: Social and Behavioral Sciences, 116,* 1217–1221. doi:10.1016/j.sbspro.2014.01.371

Rahimi, E., van den Berg, J., & Veen, W. (2013). A roadmap for building web2. 0-based personal learning environments in educational settings. In I. Buchem, G. Attwell, & G. Tur (Eds.), *Proceedings of the 4th International conference on Personal Learning Environments (The PLE Conference 2013).* Berlin: Academic Press.

Reed, P. (2014). Staff experience and attitudes towards technology-enhanced learning initiatives in one Faculty of Health and Life Sciences. *Research in Learning Technology, 22.*

Rogers-Estable, M. (2014). Web 2.0 use in higher education. *European Journal of Open, Distance and e-Learning, 17*(2), 130-142.

Safran, C., Helic, D., & Gütl, C. (2007). E-Learning practices and Web 2.0. *Proceedings of the Conference ICL2007.* Kassel, Germany: Kassel University Press.

Shang, S. S. C., Li, E. Y., Wu, Y.-L., & Hou, O. C. L. (2011). Understanding Web 2.0 service models: A knowledge-creating perspective. *Information & Management, 48*(4–5), 178–184. doi:10.1016/j.im.2011.01.005

Soomro, K. A., Zai, S. Y., & Jafri, I. H. (2015). Competence and usage of Web 2.0 technologies by higher education faculty. *Educational Media International, 52*(4), 284–295. doi:10.1080/09523987.2015.1095522

Tétard, F., Patokorpi, E., & Packalén, K. (2009). Using wikis to support constructivist learning: a case study in university education settings. In *HICSS '09 Proceedings of the 42nd Hawaii International Conference on System Sciences* (pp. 1-10). IEEE Computer Society.

Virtanen, J., & Rasi, P. (2017). Integrating Web 2.0 Technologies into Face-to-Face PBL to Support Producing, Storing, and Sharing Content in a Higher Education Course. *Interdisciplinary Journal of Problem-Based Learning, 11*(1).

Watty, K., McKay, J., & Ngo, L. (2016). Innovators or inhibitors? Accounting faculty resistance to new educational technologies in higher education. *Journal of Accounting Education*, *36*, 1–15. doi:10.1016/j.jaccedu.2016.03.003

Waycott, J., Sheard, J., Thompson, C., & Clerehan, R. (2013). Making students' work visible on the social web: A blessing or a curse? *Computers & Education*, *68*, 86–95. doi:10.1016/j.compedu.2013.04.026

Wright, K. B. (2005). Researching Internet-based populations: Advantages and disadvantages of online survey research, online questionnaire authoring software packages, and web survey services. *Journal of Computer-Mediated Communication*, *10*(3).

Yuen, S. C.-Y., Yaoyuneyong, G., & Yuen, P. K. (2011). Perceptions, interest, and use: Teachers and web 2.0 tools in education. *International Journal of Technology in Teaching and Learning*, *7*(2), 109–123.

Zelick, S. A. (2013). The perception of Web 2.0 technologies on teaching and learning in higher education: A case study. *Creative Education*, *4*(07), 53–93. doi:10.4236/ce.2013.47A2010

ADDITIONAL READING

Bejjar, M. A., & Boujelbene, Y. (2016). *E-Learning and Web 2.0: A couple of the 21st century advancements in Higher Education Mobile Computing and Wireless Networks: Concepts, Methodologies, Tools, and Applications* (pp. 2150–2170). IGI Global.

Bennett, S., Bishop, A., Dalgarno, B., Waycott, J., & Kennedy, G. (2012). Implementing Web 2.0 technologies in higher education: A collective case study. *Computers & Education, 59*(2), 524–534. doi:10.1016/j.compedu.2011.12.022

Biasutti, M. (2017). A comparative analysis of forums and wikis as tools for online collaborative learning. *Computers & Education, 111*, 158–171. doi:10.1016/j.compedu.2017.04.006

Bower, M., Hedberg, J. G., & Kuswara, A. (2010). A framework for Web 2.0 learning design. *Educational Media International, 47*(3), 177–198. doi:10.1080/09523987.2010.518811

Echeng, R., & Usoro, A. (2014). Acceptance factors and current level of use of Web 2.0 technologies for learning in higher education: A case study of two countries. *International Journal of Advanced Computer Science and Applications, 5*(5), 9–14. doi:10.14569/IJACSA.2014.050502

Isaías, P., Pífano, S., & Miranda, P. (2014). Higher Education and Web 2.0: Theory and Practice. In J. Pelet (Ed.), *E-Learning 2.0 Technologies and Web Applications in Higher Education* (pp. 88–106). Hershey, PA: IGI Global. doi:10.4018/978-1-4666-4876-0.ch005

Loureiro, A., Messias, I., & Barbas, M. (2012). Embracing Web 2.0 & 3.0 Tools to Support Lifelong Learning - Let Learners Connect. *Procedia: Social and Behavioral Sciences, 46*, 532–537. doi:10.1016/j.sbspro.2012.05.155

McHaney, R. (2012). *The new digital shoreline: How Web 2.0 and millennials are revolutionizing higher education*. Stylus Publishing, LLC.

Perikos, I., Grivokostopoulou, F., Kovas, K., & Hatzilygeroudis, I. (2015). *Assisting Tutors to Utilize Web 2.0 Tools in Education*. International Association for Development of the Information Society.

Ureña-Torres, J.-P., Tenesaca-Luna, G.-A., Arciniegas, M. B. M., & Segarra-Faggioni, V. (2017). Collaborative and active learning through web 2.0 tools applied in higher education. Paper presented at the Information Systems and Technologies (CISTI), 2017 12th Iberian Conference on.

KEY TERMS AND DEFINITIONS

E-Learning: Learning mode that is delivered exclusively online and is supported by the use of electronic resources. It includes both professional training and formal education courses.

Learning Technologies: Any type of technology that can be used to support learning in several contexts. They can be deployed in face-to-face education, blended approaches or online learning.

Online Questionnaire: An instrument for data collection that is part of survey research and it is delivered online. It can be used to collect both quantitative and qualitative data from the respondents.

Pedagogical Approaches: Strategies pertaining to the theories and practices that guide teaching.

User-Friendly Technology: Technology that is easy to understand and use, requiring little or no training to be operated by the user.

User-Generated Content: Content that is authored by internet users and derives from their participation in online platforms that enable the creation and/or edition of content in a variety of formats (text, audio, video, image).

Web 2.0: The second version of the web, also denominated Social Web or Read Write Web. It describes the web as a platform and it is supported by several core principals, such as, user-generated content, collective intelligence, user participation, ease of use, and openness.

Chapter 7

Exploring the Adoptions by Students of Web 2.0 Tools for E-Learning in Higher Education:
Web 2.0 Tools for E-Learning in Higher Education

Liliana Mata
Vasile Alecsandri University of Bacau, Romania

Georgeta Panisoara
University of Bucharest, Romania

Silvia Fat
University of Bucharest, Romania

Ion-Ovidiu Panisoara
University of Bucharest, Romania

Iulia Lazar
University of Bucharest, Romania & InfoCons Association Bucharest, Romania

ABSTRACT

Optimal public policies, including education, have been applied for the sustainable economic growth of the European Union. In European countries, the use of Web 2.0 tools for increasing the education quality is constantly expanding, even if it is divided into two categories. One category consists of developed countries, Organization for Economic Cooperation and Development (OECD) members where there are the strongest of computing tools companies. Another category consists of OECD partner countries which hopes to fulfill the OECD requirements. The main study aim is the exploration of Web 2.0 tools adoptions for e-learning in one OECD

DOI: 10.4018/978-1-5225-7435-4.ch007

candidate. A case study details how behavioral perceptions have been applied. Thus, a survey containing questions about socio-demographic characteristics alongside respondents' perceptions related to Web 2.0 tools for e-learning in higher education was applied. The research outcomes confirm the students' limited knowledge of Web 2.0. Authorities must indicate what measures are necessary for large-scale adoption of all Web 2.0 tools useful for education.

INTRODUCTION

Web 2.0 tools have been implemented due to various educational benefits. These are structured into different categories as a result of the analysis of the topical reference literature. The first category of benefits is represented by *technological aspects*: it provides interactive services where the users control their own data and information (Maloney, 2007); facilitates the sharing of user content and determines the creation, use, sharing and distribution of documents (Dearstyne, 2007); developing the "ability to effectively use technological tools to identify, access, manage, integrate, evaluate, analyze and create digital resources" (Martin, 2006). Dohn (2009) consider that the students who use Web 2.0 technologies voluntarily in their daily lives are motivated to use them in academic contexts and have the necessary technical skills.

Another category of advantages of Web 2.0 applications is identified from the *pedagogical* perspective: promoting active learning, social learning, using technologies based on interaction and communication (Ferdig, 2007); giving the opportunity to publish the works at global level (Ajjan & Hartshorne, 2008); examining issues in different ways, establishing new connections, and developing a new entity that can be shared globally (Maloney, 2007); involving students in individual and collaborative learning activities (Alexander, 2006); building interactions in more active and cooperative ways (Rhoads et al., 2013); increasing levels of learning in different fields of study, increasing vocabulary knowledge (Eren, 2015); encouraging a learner-centered approach to teaching and obtaining feedback from students (Archambault et al., 2010).

There are also *social-cultural benefits* of web 2.0 applications such as: facilitating the collaboration through document sharing portals (Dearstyne, 2007); enriching communication (Chua & Goh, 2010; Pânişoară, Sandu, Pânişoară, & Duţă, 2015); stimulating the collaboration with international partners and developing cultural competencies as a result of the use of a variety of digital communication tools (Ertmer et al., 2011); determines social connection and active user participation (McLean et al., 2007); providing effective services in helping students gain social awareness (Firat & Koksal, 2017).

From the *economic* point of view, the biggest benefit of Web 2.0 applications is that they are cheap or free (Salamon, 2003); providing a more active role for users involved in developing services by creating new content or modifying existing ones, personalizing the interface of websites, and reusing content on their personal sites (Corrocher, 2011). In this socio-economic and cultural context, different Web 2.0 educational applications have been developed.

Jimoyiannis et al. (2013) identified six interdependent dimensions to integrate the technological, social and learning features of Web 2.0 for teacher training: participatory Web, open Web, collaboration, sociability, open classroom, Web as a learning platform. Web 2.0 technologies and applications can contribute to the professional development of teachers by supporting online communities.

This study aims to explain the concept of Web 2.0, the motivation of the need to train students in the efficient use of Web 2.0 tools, especially those who have chosen a didactic career. A case study was chosen to highlight the adoption degree of Web 2.0 tools in higher education. To this end, students from a Romanian university were asked to express their opinion on the degree of adoption of ICT tools and apps.

Based on the results obtained from the application of a questionnaire, recommendations and the conclusions of the study were made.

BACKGROUND DATA

According to Okello-Obura and Ssekitto (2015), fast progress and expansion of information and communication technologies (ICT) reflected on growth in the importance of Web 2.0 tools which influenced how persons communicate into a virtual envinronment. Complementary, over the past decade, innovative strategies in education are widely promoted. These include the integration of ICT considering socio-economic and cultural context. Another factor influencing the adoption of ICT is the level of digital literacy of teachers needs to be fit educational requirements.

The new generation of mobile devices with Internet access has facilitated the expansion of the concepts of e-learning and mobile learning, which include, in addition to strategies and technical specifications, pedagogical aspects. The main aim was to improve traditional methods of teaching and learning, with the accent on each subject area.

E-learning is the interaction between the teaching/learning process and ICT. This concept refers to various computer-assisted learning solutions that can be organized in different levels of difficulty for all levels of education (primary, secondary, higher education).

A great help is provided by computer-aided applications for teaching and learning various topics. From the perspective of Mozhaeva and collaborators (2014), "modern e-learning progressed from the application of separate technologies (video, multimedia, e-mail, etc.) to system decisions among which Learning Management System (LMS) and social networks (SN) dominate "(Mozhaeva et al., 2014).

Developing e-learning programs contributes to fostering creativity and ability of students to participate at different learning activities. The use of e-learning can be done traditionally through a unidirectional approach or in a modern way through synchronous or asynchronous, group or individual systems. Regardless of the approach, all e-learning systems are based on interaction and interactivity. The use of modern e-learning tools results in an increase in the quality of communication, information transfer and, implicitly, feedback (Lau et al., 2018; Wan & Niu, 2018).

The ways in which e-learning is transposed into practice are multiple, such as the creation of virtual laboratories or classes. Particularly are promoted collaborative nature of learning. E-learning education offers the opportunity to stimulate the creativity and critical thinking of learners. The first steps in this area have been assimilated to the concept of Computer-Based Learning (CBL) (Dias, Hadjileontiadou, Diniz, & Hadjileontiadis, 2017; Han, Halim, Shariffuddin, & Abdullah, 2013; Tlili, Essalmi, Jemni, Kinshuk, & Chen, 2016). Using projectors, videos, videos, etc. for experimentation had attracted the interest of the students.

The major change e-learning market has emerged with the rapid development of the Internet (1980) and especially the emergence of the World Wide Web (1992) (Riva, 2001). The Web often contains the data in the text, images, and sound form that is available on the Internet. The data are organized understandably and kept on computers recognized as Web servers. The Internet is a collection of networks connected to each other to exchange data (Srinidhi, Dilip Kumar, & Venugopal, 2018). Web and Internet terms are used synonymously, although they are different from a technical point of view. The Web is an Internet service that can be used to instantly communicate with people around the world through messages. The latest information about events is available on the Internet. The Internet can be used to search for information on any topic, including any course you want to graduate to obtain a basic or an extra qualification. The Web refers to the assembly of data in the form of text, images, and sound available through the Internet (Gutiérrez, 2018). A Web browser is a software program that easy manipulation of both text and graphics and allows us to observe and cooperate with many resources on the Web (Daniel & Daniel, 2012). Supplementary programs recognized as add-ons were used to view simulation, video, or audio files. An add-on consists of a software program that adds features to the browser and increases the Internet experience and provides supplementary functions by allowing the Web browser to access and run files that are included in Web pages (Howard, Yang, Ma, Maton, & Rennie, 2018).

However, e-learning does not replace classical education, but adds value to the learning process, contributing to the improvement of the educational act. We must keep in mind that distance learning differs from traditional learning by adaptability, property specific digital tools: CDs, DVDs, e-books, and virtual applications. The use of digital tools in training facilitates creativity, interactivity, but also improves the assessment (Karakaya & Demirkan, 2015; Muldner & Burleson, 2015). Moreover, those who have performed in the traditional education or are not used to a learning process independently no accept easily e-learning methods. Thus, these tools are not so popular as expected.

As a paradigm of computer-assisted training, e-learning includes all three functions of the Internet: documentary, communication, collaboration (Chia & Pritchard, 2014). In this way it is born a new concept of design education (Tsvyatkova & Storni, 2018) that allows learners to create educational content and to choose their own way of training. Applications "open source" facilitates content creation original scientific applications to educational needs clearly outlined.

Nevertheless, scientists have always encountered problems in the distribution of scientific results because of incompatible document formats used in various ICT systems. By creating HTTP's HTML and HTTP protocols (Gutiérrez, 2018), resources have been created to be consulted by the general public. In this way the web apart, which took three successive stages of development (Lazar, 2018).

As described in the doctoral thesis of Lazar (Lazar, 2018), the term "Web 2.0" is used for the first time in 2005 by Tim O'Reilly (Newman, Chang, Walters, & Wills, 2016), and represents digital communities that integrate various data (Nugultham, 2012). Web 2.0 tools (such as social networking sites, Facebook, Twitter, blogs, wikis, YouTube) have become the most widely used Web 2.0 technologies (Conole, 2010 apud (Newman et al., 2016)). With these digital tools to provide educational content sharing and development of Web 2.0 contributes significantly to improving the educational act (Sapountzi & Psannis, 2018). Web 2.0 main aim (Lazar, 2018) is to support cooperation, creativity, communication, secure information sharing, as well as to sustain Web-design and to increase its functionality, because it has a dynamic character, unlike the static structure of Web 1.0 (Sapountzi & Psannis, 2018).

Certainly, the advantage of e-learning which was based on Web 2.0 potentialities (Kapenieks, 2013) is to promote multiple learning resources through the application of ICT in learning and teaching, contributing to educational progress.

WHAT IS WEB 2.0 TOOLS?

The explosion of user-created content on the Web with Web 2.0 technology has quickly contributed to improving communication, collaboration, and innovation. After Dohn (2009), the use of Web 2.0 becomes a necessary competence for the contemporary world and provides a useful set of "lifelong" abilities. Web 2.0 applications are based on the pedagogical foundations of constructivism (Ferdig, 2007). The new technology differs from Web 1.0 because the content is no longer defined by those who have knowledge of programming or web design. Balubaid (2013) consider that anyone with minimal web skills can contribute to Web 2.0. In this context, Lai & Turban (2008) found that Web 2.0 has reformatted Web use so that any user can consume, create and control the content at a low cost or at no cost and easily.

Macaskill and Owen (2006) define Web 2.0 as a web-based platform that allows users to access, contribute, describe, harvest, label, comment, and mark web-mediated content in various formats such as text, video, audio, images, and graphs. After O'Reilly (2007), Web 2.0 is a suite of applications that are interactive, rich in context and easy to use. Brandon (2008) mentions that Web 2.0 is the term commonly used to refer to advanced Internet applications to create social connections and better collaboration among users. The key technological properties of Web 2.0 refer to data-based services rather than software, to providing a large number of small channels to consumers (Clarke, 2008). According to Brengarth and Mujkic (2016), Web 2.0 is a network platform that connects all devices, regardless of the operating system they are using.

The use of Web 2.0 technologies has a great impact on education, so there is an increasing interest in conducting different studies on the use and its effects. Teachers and designers have begun to explore the use of Web 2.0 in educational activities. Schaeffert and Ebner (2010) emphasize the need to rethink Web 2.0-based teaching strategies, in line with student needs to deliver technology-based learning. Newland & Byles (2013) highlights that the educational process can be transformed by using cooperative learning, social structuring of knowledge and a different pedagogical approach using Web 2.0 technologies. Danciu and Grosseck (2011) have remarked a restructuring of the roles of students and teachers in terms of the use of Web 2.0 technologies.

Web 2.0 applications include different and various forms: blogs, instant messaging, internet telephony, social bookmarking, social networking sites (Facebook, Twitter, Google plus), wikis (Wikipedia, WikiSpaces), and video sharing sites (YouTube, TED), audio/video conferencing. In Table 1 there are presented the main examples of web 2.0 technologies by systematizing descriptions made by different authors (Ajjan & Hartshorne, 2008) and their educational applications (Alexander, 2006; Balubaid, 2013).

Table 1. Examples of web 2.0 technologies and their educational applications

No.	Web 2.0 technologies	Description	Educational applications
1	Blogs	Blogs are entries in user journal entries in the form of text, images, and links to web content, such as websites or other blogs.	They encourage search, interpretations, and evaluation of blogs, cultural events, news, examining changes over time.
2	Wikis	Wikis refer to collaborative sites that stimulate user interaction by adding, removing or editing the site's content.	They promote individual learning and promote collaboration through group editing and mutual evaluation.
3	Social media websites	They offer users the opportunity to create personal profiles and establish different networks that connect them with family, friends and other colleagues.	Sites could be used to establish academic connections or to foster cooperation and collaboration in the classroom. • Facebook and Twitter are used for sharing text-based information and social networking. • Google+ allows users to share selectively with specific groups within their personal network.
4	Video sharing sites		YouTube is used for sharing videos.
5	RSS (Really Simple Syndication)	A powerful tool that can be used to manage online information	RSS is a form of web encoding that allows us to view a continuous flow of useful information that can be in text or video format and can be permanently updated or modified[1].
6	Apps	Some of the most useful, and easily integrated, tools in education, e.g. Google Apps (Google Drive, Docs, Sheets, Slides, Forms, and Drawings), Google Sites, Google Calendar, Google Maps), DropBox, etc.	The most recommended tools for education are developed by Google for interactivity and exchange of best practices. These applications give to the educational act a collaborative dimension and an innovative character.

[1]http://www.businessdictionary.com/definition/Really-Simple-Syndication-RSS.html

ADOPTIONS OF WEB 2.0 TOOLS INTO ONE OECD'S PARTNER COUNTRY UNIVERSITY

Web 2.0 applications have been adopted because they have multiple benefits. Thus, the use of Web 2.0 tools for e-learning is constantly increasing, even if it is used in OECD members or OECD partner countries which are in the progression of adoption of Web 2.0 tools.

The main study purpose is an investigation of Web 2.0 acceptances tools for e-learning. A survey containing requests about perceptions of using different Web 2.0 tools was delivered to voluntary participants. The research instrument or questionnaire testing to improve users use Web 2.0 tools and applications in traditional educational activities was built upon interviews and discussions that took place with experts and specialists in the field. Purpose of the research subject of this study is to learn whether or not educational users are familiar with the tools and Web 2.0 applications. The survey was administered online to 247 students from Faculty of Psychology and Educational Sciences, University of Bucharest, Romania of which 234 responded.

Data on the representative sample of 234 voluntary respondents, distinguishing 41.5% already practicing and 58.5% not practicing in pre-university system education. Among research participants 95.7% are females and 4.3% are males. 95% of respondents use the Internet daily. The period covered by the experimental data collection was June-September 2018.

62% of participants use a computer or laptop together with a smartphone to access Web 2.0 tools for e-learning. This is the combination of ICT tools most often seen among those interviewed for using distance learning. Very few respondents do not use smartphones in the e-learning process, replacing it with the tablet (Figure 1). 13.2% only use the computer/laptop, or just the smartphone. We notice a sharp decrease in tablet use for educational purposes probably due to the lack of functionality. Even if the smartphone currently occupies a secondary place in user preferences, the trend is to increase the interest in use for educational purposes.

We note the lack of knowledge about the Web 2.0 concept, both in general and in particular in the distance learning area. The percentage of respondents who are already familiar with the possibilities of using Web 2.0 is low, namely 19% (Figure 2), and only 13% (Figure 2) in e-education. The highest percentages are those who have a superficial knowledge about Web 2.0 use, generally (Figure 2), respectively 51% and 52% (Figure 2) related to education.

Figure 1. The frequency of use of ICT tools

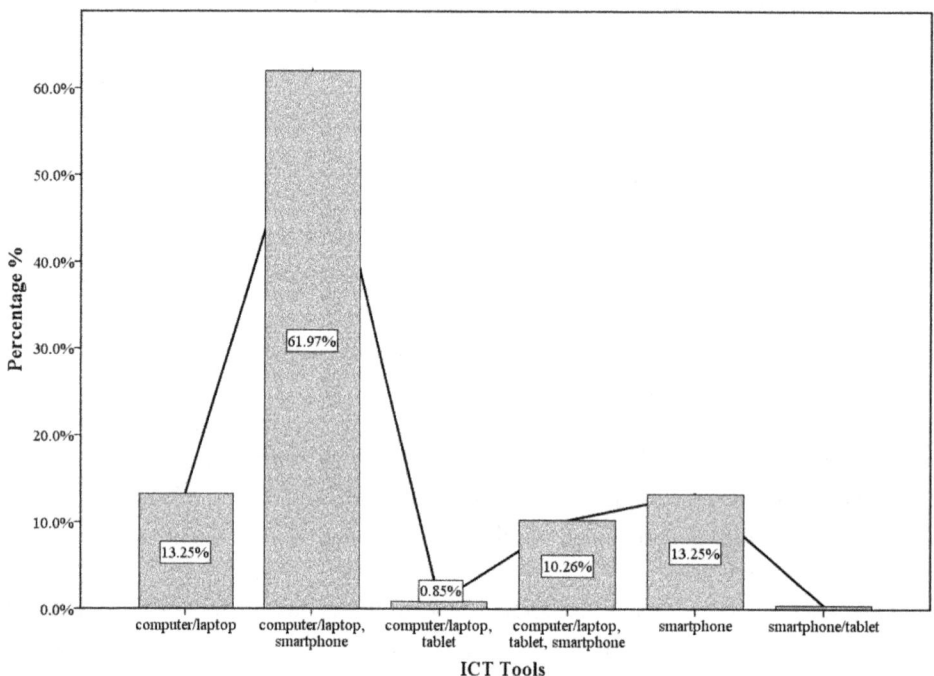

Figure 2. Participants percentage who are familiarized with Web 2.0 concept, generally (light gray color) and in education (dark gray color)

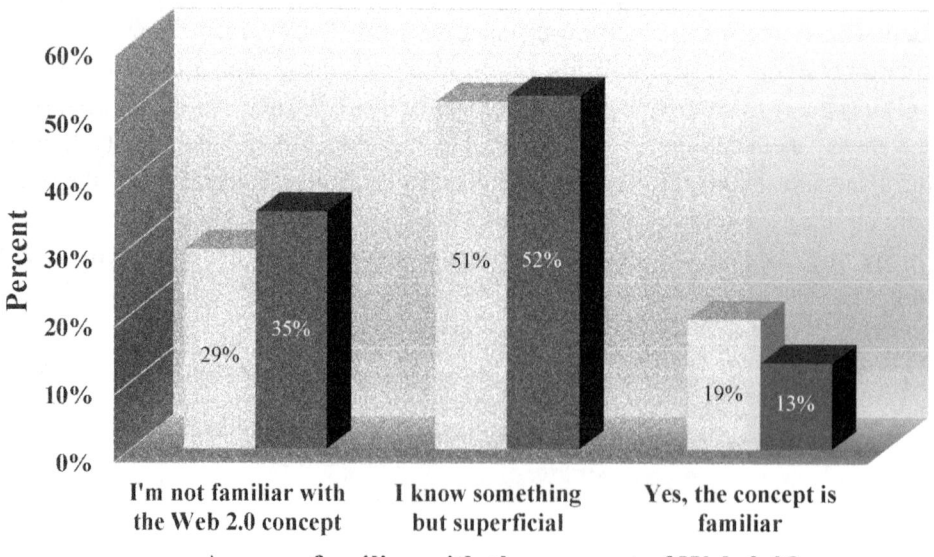

Very interesting is the distribution of users on different types of Web 2.0 tools (Figure 3 and Figure 4). These tools have been grouped into the following categories: social media websites, video sharing services, apps, and blogs. The association of two or more categories has also been investigated, as is the case with the non-use of these tools. RSS (Really Simple Syndication), a powerful tool that can be used to manage online information, was not found to be used by respondents.

Although respondents are familiar with social media websites, they are not used to their full educational potential. Definitely the most used are video sharing services associated with apps, even if the percentage of acquaintance is slightly lower than average (around 40%) (Figure 3 and Figure 4). This can be interpreted as a direct consequence of YouTube's simple instructions for using different educational apps. Students want to be trained in accessible, easy to understand and quick ways. They are not open to more complex applications that require additional intellectual effort over a longer period of time. This denotes superficiality and needs to be compensated by appropriate educational measures.

Figure 3. The percentage of use of different Web 2.0 tools associated with the perception of respondents' familiarity, in general

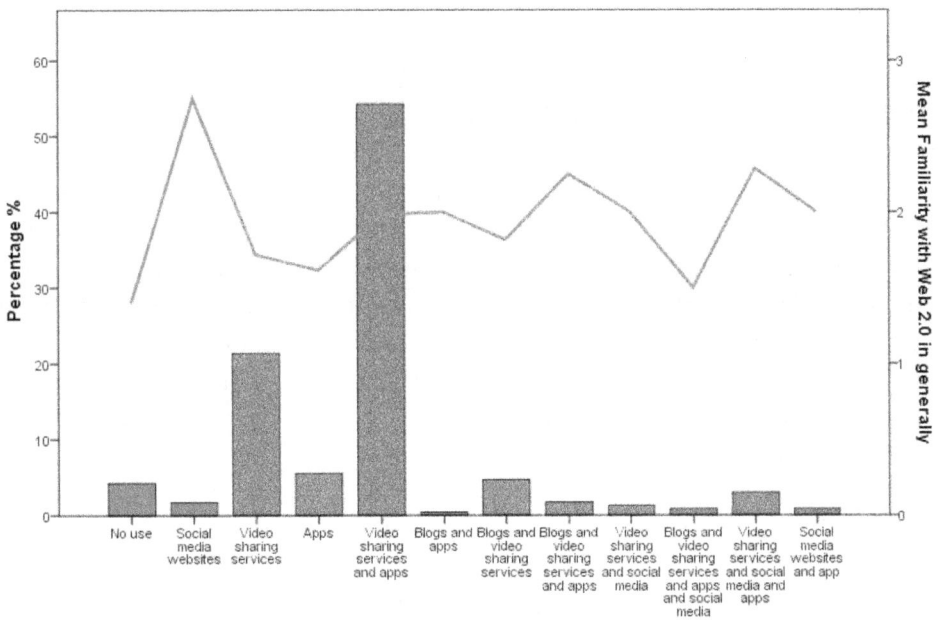

Figure 4. The percentage of use of different Web 2.0 tools associated with the perception of respondents' familiarity in education

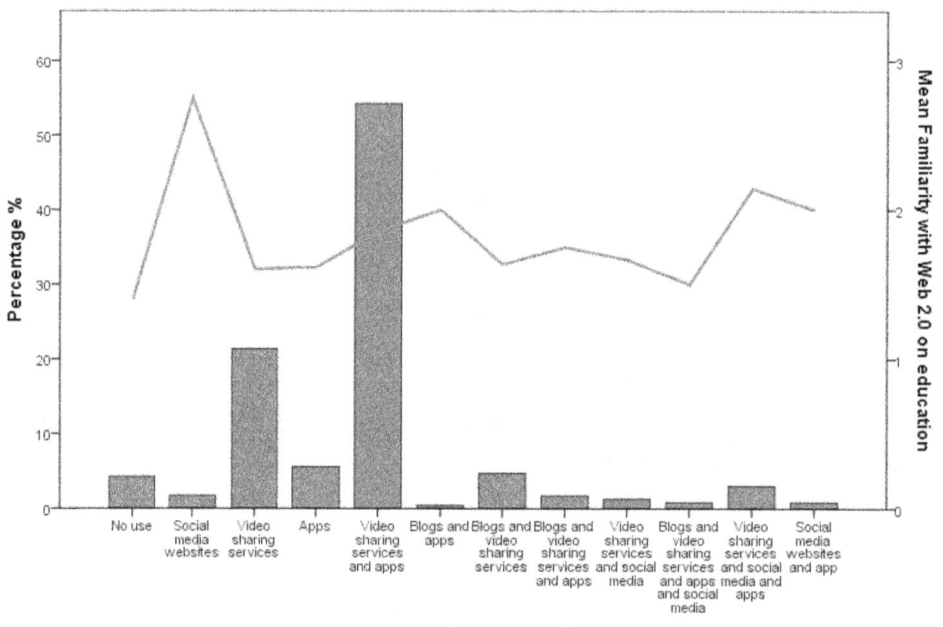

NECESSITY TO TRAIN STUDENTS WHO WILL BECOME TEACHERS ON THE USE OF WEB 2.0 TECHNOLOGIES AND APPLICATIONS

Preparing future teachers will include new experiences that will enable them to develop teaching activities based on the use of Web 2.0 technologies for use in their own classrooms. Cantu (2000) draws attention to the fact that pre-service teachers prove a limited knowledge of the effective integration of technology into the curriculum in the classroom. Unlike students who are motivated (Panisoara, Duta, & Panisoara, 2015) to use more and more new generation technologies such as social networks, blogs, wikis, and Web 2.0 applications, teachers rarely use them in teaching (Pence, 2007). In this context, there is important that future teachers to know how to use Web 2.0 tools to support and enhance their pupils' learning (Jimoyiannis et al., 2013). In order for Web 2.0 tools to become integrated into teacher training programs, they should be seen as adding significant quality to training processes (Peterson-Ahmad et al., 2018). Some teachers have initiated to use these new tools to classrooms, but as their practice in society expands, Albion (2008) observes there will be expectations for their wider application in schools.

With the introduction of new Web 2.0 technologies and applications in training future teachers, different pedagogical approaches have been created. Electronic portfolios (Albion, 2008; Evans & Powell, 2007), are a useful strategy for creating and supporting a sustainable learning community in teacher education, offering experiences that will encourage the use of Web 2.0 tools in class as a genuine practice. A specific method of integrating Web 2.0 technologies into teacher education is the participatory pedagogy process involving five steps (DePietro, 2013): asking students to use digital devices in the classroom; presentation course material and interaction with students using their devices; student interaction with the material, displaying certain behaviors while using technology; observing and recording behaviors that indicate how students tackle problems, solve problems, contribute ideas, and ultimately learn; creating a new device learning methodology.

Practically, there are already teacher training programs and studies based on the optimal application of Web 2.0 technologies and the identification their impact on professional development. Jimoyiannis et al. (2013) designed and implemented a specific program to train primary and secondary school teachers to use Web 2.0 tools in the classroom. The teacher's professional development program and study were achieved within a European project called Web2.0 European Resource Centre (http://www.web20erc.eu), aiming to develop a simplified technological and pedagogical framework for the use of tools Web 2.0 for educational purposes. The study's results have highlighted that the approach has contributed to building the knowledge and skills required by teachers to integrate Web 2.0 into their training. Another example relates to a teacher training course that included the integration of Web 2.0 tools into a lesson plan (Voithofer, 2007). Sadaf et al. (2012) explored the factors of preservice teachers' intentions to use Web 2.0 technologies in their future classrooms. A study conducted by Amundson (2017) on 590 pre-service teachers has led to the identification of the underlying factors of behavioral intentions to use Web 2.0 technologies. Peterson-Ahmad et al. (2018) analyze how pre-service teachers training programs can help them to utilize Web 2.0 platforms to support the students with disabilities.

It is essential that the formation of future teachers based on the use of Web 2.0 tools be introduced at the beginning of the programs, in order to allow an appropriate time for the development of authentic practice models before graduation. Pre-service teacher training programs for the use of Web 2.0 digital tools will help them to integrate them more effectively into teaching. Although there is growing concern about teacher training to effectively integrate these technologies into lessons, the way in which teacher education programs improve teachers' future use of Web 2.0 in teaching is still under discussion.

RECOMMENDATIONS TO SUPPORT INTEGRATION OF WEB 2.0 TOOLS IN EDUCATION

It is necessary to clearly explain the positive aspects, the opportunities as well as the negative ones, respectively the threats of the widespread use of each Web 2.0 tool used in education. The lack of in-depth knowledge of each instrument is definitely an impediment to its use. At least at first glance users are limited to using those tools that are easy to use and whose instructions are in video format.

In our opinion, the recommendations to support the integration of Web 2.0 tools in education are as follows:

- The increase of the use of e-learning platforms on which different applications are inserted;
- The use of different social networking facilities for e-learning classes;
- RSS promotion (Really Simple Syndication) to manage online information;
- The promotion of the use of blogs containing online formats, facilitating free expression of opinions and communication between users; a positive element is that debates can be archived and accessed at any time for use as examples, arguments, etc.;
- The promotion of the use of blogs containing different educational applications;
- The distribution of applications through educational forums.

Together with this, e-learning preferences of students and teachers were influenced by of adoption of ICT tools in higher education institution (Mozhaeva, Feshchenko, & Kulikov, 2014).

Respecting these recommendations will increase the adoption of Web 2.0 tools in education for less advanced countries, such as the OECD candidate states. The direct consequence will be reflected in increasing the degree of interactivity and faster realization of the exchange of information, leading to an increase in the quality of education.

CONCLUSION

The research results indicate that respondents have shown a superficial level of familiarity with Web 2.0 tools. The relevant experts of OECD countries need to find ways to extend the integration of Web 2.0 tools into education and learning for all European countries. The level of knowledge of their opportunities for increasing educational quality and the exchange of good practice between different peoples with different cultures is still low and therefore adequate policies are needed to narrow the gap between member countries and non-OECD member states.

REFERENCES

Ajjan, H., & Hartshorne, R. (2008). Investigating faculty decisions to adopt Web 2.0 technologies: Theory and empirical tests. *The Internet and Higher Education*, *11*(2), 71–80. doi:10.1016/j.iheduc.2008.05.002

Albion, P. R. (2008). Web 2.0 in Teacher Education: Two Imperatives for Action. *Computers in the Schools*, *24*(3-4), 181–198. doi:10.1080/07380560802368173

Alexander, B. (2006). A new way of innovation for teaching and learning. *EDUCAUSE Review*, *41*(2), 32–44.

Amundson, L. (2017). Web 2.0 Technologies: The Best-Fit Model for Preservice Teachers. *Journal of Technology and Teacher Education*, *25*(2), 131–154.

Archambault, L., Wetzel, K., Foulger, T. S., & Williams, M. K. (2010). Professional development 2.0. *Journal of Digital Learning in Teacher Education*, *27*(1), 4–11. doi:10.1080/21532974.2010.10784651

Balubaid, M. A. (2013). Using Web 2.0 Technology to Enhance Knowledge Sharing in an Academic Department. *Procedia: Social and Behavioral Sciences*, *102*, 406–420. doi:10.1016/j.sbspro.2013.10.756

Brandon, J. (2008). Web 2.0 definition for non-techies. *Computer World*. Retrieved from. http://blogs.computerworld.com/web_2_0_define_2_0

Brengarth, L. B., & Mujkic, E. (2016). WEB 2.0: How social media applications leverage nonprofit responses during a wildfire crisis. *Computers in Human Behavior*, *54*, 589–596. doi:10.1016/j.chb.2015.07.010

Cantu, D. A. (2000). Technology integration in preservice history teacher education. *Journal of the Association for History and Computing*, *3*(2), 1–19.

Chia, H. P., & Pritchard, A. (2014). Using a virtual learning community (VLC) to facilitate a cross-national science research collaboration between secondary school students. *Computers & Education*, *79*, 1–15. doi:10.1016/j.compedu.2014.07.005

Chua, A. Y. K., & Goh, D. H. (2010). A study of Web 2.0 applications in library websites. *Library & Information Science Research*, *32*(3), 203–211. doi:10.1016/j.lisr.2010.01.002

Clarke, R. (2008). Web 2.0 as syndication. *Journal of Theoretical and Applied Electronic Commerce Research*, *3*(2), 30–43. doi:10.4067/S0718-18762008000100004

Corrocher, N. (2011). The adoption of Web 2.0 services: An empirical investigation. *Technological Forecasting and Social Change*, *78*(4), 547–558. doi:10.1016/j.techfore.2010.10.006

Danciu, L., & Grosseck, G. (2011). Social aspects of web 2.0 technologies: Teaching or teachers' challenges? *Procedia: Social and Behavioral Sciences*, *15*, 3768–3773. doi:10.1016/j.sbspro.2011.04.371

Daniel, L. E., & Daniel, L. E. (2012). Internet History (Web and Browser Caching). In L. E. Daniel & L. E. Daniel (Eds.), *Digital Forensics for Legal Professionals* (pp. 213–218). Boston: Syngress. doi:10.1016/B978-1-59749-643-8.00031-6

Dearstyne, B. W. (2007). Blogs, mashups, and wikis: Oh my! *Information Management Journal*, *41*(4), 24–33.

DePietro, P. (2013). *Transforming Education with New Media: Participatory Pedagogy, Interactive Learning and Web 2.0*. New York: Peter Lang. doi:10.3726/978-1-4539-0831-0

Dias, S. B., Hadjileontiadou, S. J., Diniz, J. A., & Hadjileontiadis, L. J. (2017). Computer-based concept mapping combined with learning management system use: An explorative study under the self- and collaborative-mode. *Computers & Education*, *107*, 127–146. doi:10.1016/j.compedu.2017.01.009

Dohn, N. (2009). Web 2.0: Inherent tensions and evident challenges for education. *Computer-Supported Collaborative Learning*, *4*(3), 343–363. doi:10.100711412-009-9066-8

Eren, O. (2015). Vocabulary learning on learner-created content by using web 2.0 tools. *Contemporary Educational Technology*, *6*(4), 281–300.

Ertmer, P. A., Newby, T. J., Yu, J. H., Liu, W., Tomory, A., Lee, Y. M., ... Sendurur, P. (2011). Facilitating students' global perspectives: Collaborating with international partners using Web 2.0 technologies. *Internet and Higher Education*, *14*(4), 251–261. doi:10.1016/j.iheduc.2011.05.005

Evans, M. A., & Powell, A. (2007). Conceptual and practical issues related to the design for and sustainability of communities of practice: The case of e-portfolio use in preservice teacher training. *Technology, Pedagogy and Education*, *16*(2), 199–214. doi:10.1080/14759390701406810

Ferdig, R. (2007). Examining social software in teacher education. *Journal of Technology and Teacher Education, 15*(1), 5–10.

Firat, E. A., & Koksal, M. S. (2017). The relationship between use of Web 2.0 tools by prospective science teachers and their biotechnology literacy. *Computers in Human Behavior, 70*, 44–50. doi:10.1016/j.chb.2016.12.067

Gutiérrez, R. T. (2018). Understanding the role of digital commons in the web; The making of HTML5. *Telematics and Informatics, 35*(5), 1438–1449. doi:10.1016/j.tele.2018.03.013

Han, O. B., Halim, N. D. B. A., Shariffuddin, R. S. B., & Abdullah, Z. B. (2013). Computer Based Courseware in Learning Mathematics: Potentials and Constrains. *Procedia: Social and Behavioral Sciences, 103*, 238–244. doi:10.1016/j.sbspro.2013.10.331

Howard, S. K., Yang, J., Ma, J., Maton, K., & Rennie, E. (2018). App clusters: Exploring patterns of multiple app use in primary learning contexts. *Computers & Education, 127*, 154–164. doi:10.1016/j.compedu.2018.08.021

Jimoyiannis, A., Tsiotakis, P., Roussinos, D., & Siorenta, A. (2013). Preparing teachers to integrate Web 2.0 in school practice: Toward a framework for Pedagogy 2.0. *Australasian Journal of Educational Technology, 29*(2), 248–267. doi:10.14742/ajet.157

Kapenieks, J. (2013). User-friendly e-learning Environment for Educational Action Research. *Procedia Computer Science, 26*, 121–142. doi:10.1016/j.procs.2013.12.012

Karakaya, A. F., & Demirkan, H. (2015). Collaborative digital environments to enhance the creativity of designers. *Computers in Human Behavior, 42*, 176–186. doi:10.1016/j.chb.2014.03.029

Lai, L. S. L., & Turban, E. (2008). Group formation and operations in the Web 2.0 environment and social networks. *Group Decision and Negotiation, 17*(5), 387–402. doi:10.100710726-008-9113-2

Lau, K. H., Lam, T., Kam, B. H., Nkhoma, M., Richardson, J., & Thomas, S. (2018). The role of textbook learning resources in e-learning: A taxonomic study. *Computers & Education, 118*, 10–24. doi:10.1016/j.compedu.2017.11.005

Lazar, I. M. (2018). *Investigations on the relationship between the aspirational level and the acceptance of modern technology in education by learners* (Unpublished doctoral dissertation). University of Bucharest, Bucharest, Romania.

Macaskill, W., & Owen, D. (2006). Web 2.0 to go. *Proceedings of LIANZA Conference 2006.*

Maloney, E. (2007). What Web 2.0 can teach us about learning. *The Chronicle of Higher Education, 25*(18), B26.

Martin, A. (2006). Literacies for the digital age. In A. Martin & D. Madigan (Eds.), *Digital Literacies for Learning* (pp. 3–25). London: Facet Publications.

McLean, R., Richards, B. H., & Wardman, J. I. (2007). The effect of Web 2.0 on the future of medical practice and education: Darwikinian evolution of folksonomic revolution? *The Medical Journal of Australia, 187*(3), 174–177. PMID:17680746

Mozhaeva, G., Feshchenko, A., & Kulikov, I. (2014). E-learning in the Evaluation of Students and Teachers: LMS or Social Networks? *Procedia: Social and Behavioral Sciences, 152,* 127–130. doi:10.1016/j.sbspro.2014.09.168

Muldner, K., & Burleson, W. (2015). Utilizing sensor data to model students' creativity in a digital environment. *Computers in Human Behavior, 42,* 127–137. doi:10.1016/j.chb.2013.10.060

Newland, B., & Byles, L. (2014). Changing academic teaching with Web 2.0 technologies. *Innovations in Education and Teaching International, 51*(3), 315–325. doi:10.1080/14703297.2013.796727

Newman, R., Chang, V., Walters, R. J., & Wills, G. B. (2016). Web 2.0 - The past and the future. *International Journal of Information Management, 36*(4), 591–598. doi:10.1016/j.ijinfomgt.2016.03.010

Nugultham, K. (2012). Using Web 2.0 for Innovation and Information Technology in Education Course. *Procedia: Social and Behavioral Sciences, 46,* 4607–4610. doi:10.1016/j.sbspro.2012.06.305

O'Reilly, T. (2007). What is Web 2.0: Design patterns and business models for the next generation of software. *Communications & Stratégies, 65,* 17–37.

Okello-Obura, C., & Ssekitto, F. (2015). WEB 2.0 technologies application in teaching and learning by makerere university academic staff. *Library Philosophy and Practice (e-journal),* 24.

Panisoara, G., Duta, N., & Panisoara, I.-O. (2015). The Influence of Reasons Approving on Student Motivation for Learning. *Procedia: Social and Behavioral Sciences, 197,* 1215–1222. doi:10.1016/j.sbspro.2015.07.382

Pânişoară, G., Sandu, C., Pânişoară, I.-O., & Duţă, N. (2015). Comparative Study Regarding Communication Styles of The Students. *Procedia: Social and Behavioral Sciences, 186*, 202–208. doi:10.1016/j.sbspro.2015.04.066

Pence, H. E. (2007). Preparing for the real web generation. *Journal of Educational Technology Systems, 35*(3), 347–356. doi:10.2190/7116-G776-7P42-V110

Peterson-Ahmad, M. B., Stepp, J. B., & Somerville, K. (2018). Teaching Pre-Service Teachers How to Utilize Web 2.0 Platforms to Support the Educational Needs of Students with Disabilities in General Education Classrooms. *Education in Science, 8*(2), 1–9. doi:10.3390/educsci8020080

Rhoads, R. A., Berdan, J., & Toven-Lindsey, B. (2013). The open courseware movement in higher Education: Unmasking power and raising questions about the Movement's democratic potential. *Educational Theory, 63*(1), 87-109.

Riva, G. (2001). From real to Virtual Communities: Cognition, Knowledge, and Intention in the World Wide Web. In C. R. Wolfe (Ed.), *Learning and Teaching on the World Wide Web* (pp. 131–151). San Diego, CA: Academic Press. doi:10.1016/B978-012761891-3/50010-2

Sadaf, A., Newby, T. J., & Ertmer, P. A. (2012). Exploring Factors that Predict Preservice Teachers' Intentions to Use Web 2.0 Technologies Using Decomposed Theory of Planned Behavior. *Journal of Research on Technology in Education, 45*(2), 171–196. doi:10.1080/15391523.2012.10782602

Salamon, L. M. (2003). *The resilient sector: The state of nonprofit America.* Washington, DC: Brookings Institution Press.

Sapountzi, A., & Psannis, K. E. (2018). Social networking data analysis tools & challenges. *Future Generation Computer Systems, 86*, 893–913. doi:10.1016/j.future.2016.10.019

Schaeffert, S., & Ebner, M. (2010). New Forms of and Tools for Cooperative Learning with Social Software in Higher Education. In B. A. Morris & G. M. Ferguson (Eds.), *Computer-Assisted Teaching: New Developments* (pp. 151–156). Nova Publishing.

Srinidhi, N. N., Dilip Kumar, S. M., & Venugopal, K. R. (2018). Network optimizations in the Internet of Things: A review. *Engineering Science and Technology, an International Journal.* doi:10.1016/j.jestch.2018.09.003

Tlili, A., Essalmi, F., Jemni, M., Kinshuk, & Chen, N.-S. (2016). Role of personality in computer based learning. *Computers in Human Behavior*, *64*, 805–813. doi:10.1016/j. chb.2016.07.043

Tsvyatkova, D., & Storni, C. (2018). *Designing an educational interactive eBook for newly diagnosed children with type 1 diabetes: Mapping a new design space. International Journal of Child-Computer Interaction.* doi:10.1016/j.ijcci.2018.10.001

Voithofer, R. (2007). *Web 2.0: What is it and how can it apply to teaching and teacher preparation?* Paper presented at the American Educational Research Association Conference. Retrieved from http://education.osu.edu/rvoithofer/papers/web2paper. pdf

Wan, S., & Niu, Z. (2018). An e-learning recommendation approach based on the self-organization of learning resource. *Knowledge-Based Systems*, *160*, 71–87. doi:10.1016/j.knosys.2018.06.014

ADDITIONAL READING

Chen, Y.-C., Hwang, R.-H., & Wang, C.-Y. (2012). Development and evaluation of a Web 2.0 annotation system as a learning tool in an e-learning environment. *Computers & Education*, *58*(4), 1094–1105. doi:10.1016/j.compedu.2011.12.017

El Mhouti, A., Nasseh, A., Erradi, M., & Vasquèz, J. M. (2017). Enhancing collaborative learning in Web 2.0-based e-learning systems: A design framework for building collaborative e-learning contents. *Education and Information Technologies*, *22*(5), 2351–2364. doi:10.100710639-016-9545-2

Garcia, R., Falkner, K., & Vivian, R. (2018). Systematic literature review: Self-Regulated Learning strategies using e-learning tools for Computer Science. *Computers & Education*, *123*, 150–163. doi:10.1016/j.compedu.2018.05.006

Katsionis, G., & Virvou, M. (2008). Personalised e-learning through an educational virtual reality game using Web services. *Multimedia Tools and Applications*, *39*(1), 47–71. doi:10.100711042-007-0155-2

Newman, R., Chang, V., Walters, R. J., & Wills, G. B. (2016). Web 2.0—The past and the future. *International Journal of Information Management*, *36*(4), 591–598. doi:10.1016/j.ijinfomgt.2016.03.010

Schewe, K.-D., Thalheim, B., Binemann-Zdanowicz, A., Kaschek, R., Kuss, T., & Tschiedel, B. (2005). A Conceptual View of Web-Based E-Learning Systems. *Education and Information Technologies*, *10*(1), 83–110. doi:10.100710639-005-6749-2

Wang, M. (2011). Integrating organizational, social, and individual perspectives in Web 2.0-based workplace e-learning. *Information Systems Frontiers*, *13*(2), 191–205. doi:10.100710796-009-9191-y

KEY TERMS AND DEFINITIONS

Digital Technologies: A set of information and communications technology (ICT) which helps accurate and efficient modeling and simulation events.

E-Education: All educational solutions for distance training in which the methods of information and communication technology (ICT) are used, thus supporting individual learning.

Educational Policies: Solutions offered in an institutionalized framework for education quality management.

OECD Member Countries: The Organization for Economic Cooperation and Development (OECD) membership is attributed to developed countries that accept the principles of representative democracy and free market economy in Europe as well as outside Europe; currently are 36 OECD member countries.

OECD Partner Countries: Partner countries are not members of the OECD but are supported to improve governance and public management for development; partner countries may apply when they consider that fulfill the requirements to become full members of the OECD.

Professional Development: Personal development is achieved through activities aimed to improve skills and developing knowledge in a particular field.

Tools for E-Education: Tools for e-education are dynamic virtual space tools that encourage learners' collaboration, developing their creativity and digital abilities.

University of Bucharest: Is the second oldest modern university in Romania and represents a prominent academic organization centered on research and education.

Chapter 8
E–Learning Strategies for Emerging Economies in the Knowledge Era

Neeta Baporikar

ⓘ https://orcid.org/0000-0003-0676-9913

Namibia University of Science and Technology, Namibia & University of Pune, India

ABSTRACT

With the coming of the digital age over a period of the last three decades, the letter "e" is used to refer to the electronic world. Formerly known as computer-based training, e-learning has also come of age and is increasingly oriented to real-time learning, that is, activities facilitating simultaneous interaction between learners and instructors. Further, the knowledge explosion makes it more a necessity than a luxury even for emerging economies to consider the e-learning platforms and adopt e-learning strategies. The objectives of this chapter are to understand the essentials of effective e-learning strategies and identify the barriers and facilitators in embedding e-learning for emerging economies so as to align well in this knowledge era. The methodology adopted is in depth literature review and grounded theory approach. Contextual analysis and is restricted to effectiveness of e-learning from an emerging economy point of view.

DOI: 10.4018/978-1-5225-7435-4.ch008

INTRODUCTION

After hearing about the Digital Age in the 90's, e-Commerce, e-Business, e-Shopping and other terms beginning with the letter 'e' to refer to the electronic world and the Internet, when we talk today about e-Learning, we think of a site in the Internet or Intranet that is available to everybody, an illustrated encyclopedia in electronic format, or even a multimedia-based presentation. In fact, all these ideas are far beyond an e-Learning definition. Electronic learning is not only a kind of virtual or distance education to deliver content by electronic means through the use of the Internet, Intranet, or CD-ROM, but is aimed at effective learning in real time with activities facilitating simultaneous interaction between learners and instructors. Understanding the networked environments, with the onset of e-m-learning and knowledge management technologies, combined with other technologies, have an impact on organizations. Boettcher (1997) argued: "Now that the World Wide Web is providing a whole new context for teaching and learning, we have the need to return to the core principles of teaching and learning, and create a new model of teaching and learning." Therefore, if technology is applied in conjunction with pedagogical concepts, it can create an effective student-centered environment and enhance learning outcomes. A common thread among the plethora of definitions of knowledge management is that its objective is to identify and leverage the collective knowledge to compete and survive. One potential lever is e-learning, the creation and distribution of knowledge through the online delivery of information, communication, education, and training. It is well known that most e-learning materials format is a piece of content, followed by an evaluation question but here micro-learning may be of more use. After all in globalized world, with expectations swelling and increasing influence of social media and networking, organizations are also in the position to look for new ways to engage employees in learning and organization problem solving (Giurgiu, 2017).

Hence, the objectives of this chapter are to understand the essentials of effective ELearning Strategies and identify the barriers and facilitators in embedding ELearning for emerging economies so as to align well in this knowledge era. The methodology adopted is in depth literature review and grounded theory approach with contextual analysis and is restricted to effectiveness of ELearning from emerging economy point of view.

BACKGROUND

E-learning is certainly becoming the most accepted tool in organizations both as a training pedagogy and knowledge management. Corporations are discovering that ELearning has many of the same attributes as basic Knowledge Management processes, and thus can be a tool for Knowledge Management (Wild, Griggs, & Downing, 2002). Knowledge Management major aim is to establish a positive learning environment in which people can conduct all sorts of learning activities and share knowledge with other people in organization (Bukowitz & Williams, 1992; Hong & Kuo, 1999; Martensson, 2000). Liu and Wang (2009) argued that ELearning is the technology and tool supporting Knowledge Management and Knowledge Management is the premise and operational platform for it. Transfer and communication of tacit knowledge is considered crucial for effective learning yet it is the trickiest part. Tacit knowledge can be communicated through interaction, collaboration and conversations in communities/network of practices (Roknuzzaman, Kanai, & Umemoto, 2009). Ponce (2003) argued that data mining methods can be used in ELearning systems.

The basic concept of e-learning presupposes that electronic driven technologies can be used to facilitate and enhance learning process. Initially distance learning was used to supplement existing classroom instruction but over time, electronic online classes becoming primary form of interaction and information. The concept also meant that learners take control of their learning, setting their own goals and determining which learning method to be used (Stephen Brookfield, 1987). Further e-learning is part of the more encompassing concept of Distance Learning and cuts across numerous fields of thought and practice. In other words, it is a multi-disciplinary concept encompassing an array of academics, training and education, learning and knowledge, technology and investigation of individual markets segment.

From a business perspective, an aggressive and conservative forecast of business opportunities indicates that learning is expected to be a major product and services for many years to come, and e-learning will be deployed for this purpose. It also will have greater role in equalizing societies and economies as more emerging economies realize the potential and start adopting it on a wider basis. The United States Commission on Technology and Adult Learning defined e-learning as instructional content or learning experiences delivered or enabled by electronic technology (2001). On its part, the United Kingdom Department for Education and Skills in 2003 states that "if someone is learning in a way that uses information and communication technologies (ICT) they are using e-learning". Rosenbery (2001) defines e-learning as the use of

Internet technologies to deliver a broad array of solutions that enhance knowledge and performance. Doug Hum and Anne Ladoucour define it broadly as "using an electronic means to training that takes place over a network, the internet or an intranet (2001). Thus the elements of these conventional definitions include: information and communication technologies; network, 24/7 delivery on time and an electronic exchange of information for the purpose of learning. However as you can see, the above definitions are potentially limiting because for many organizations, e-learning simply means a CD-ROM, DVD and applications loaded unto single computer for computer-based training or instruction. Hence, it is time to derive a foundational definition of e-learning, where following set of logical statements can be advanced to have a more comprehensive definition:

1. E-Learning encompasses any form of learning transacted by way of digital technologies.
2. E-Learning delivery systems are subject to the dynamics of socio-technological evolution.
3. E-Learning may be synchronous or asynchronous, self-paced or instructor-led, a process or a single event, online or offline, or any combination of these modes.

Thus, taking these statements into consideration and for the purpose of this chapter and on-going research, the broad definitions proposed of e-learning are:

1. *"Electronic Learning can be defined as a learning experience involving the acquisition or transfer of knowledge delivered or transacted through electronic means"*.
2. "E-learning is an approach to build knowledge society through creation of knowledge management systems where the learning and learners are facilitated through electronic medium due to convergence of information, technology and communication".

Note: Again to restrict the definition of e-learning to Internet connection via networked computers is to ignore mobile devices and any emerging forms of ICT across all dimensions of the learning process. Restrictive definitions in terms of specific technologies are of limited long-term relevance to learning transactions in an electronic context. Hence any definition will be with reference to the time and will continue to change as technology is dynamic.

E-Learning: Concept of Learning

Burns *et al* (1997) defines flexible learning in terms of its flexible entry, course components, modes of learning and points of exit which offers the learner control and choice regarding the content, sequence, time, place and method of learning including flexible assessment processes. According to Rosenberg (2001), while e-learning may be seen as a form of flexible and distance learning, not all flexible and distance learning necessarily involves e-learning. Some authors distinguish e-learning from web-learning (Beer, 2000), or web-based training (Horton 2000). These authors emphasize the distinctiveness of the web as an educational medium that can be used to transfer information and knowledge rapidly without restriction of time and location, and potentially at a lower cost than alternative educational media or environments (Beer 2005). Horton defines web-based training as any purposeful, considered application of web technologies to the task of educating a fellow human being (2002). But by and large, web learning still remains a subset of electronic learning because the web technology is electronic in function.

Assumptions of E-Learning

The basic assumptions about e-learning which prevail are:

- Anytime, anyplace, any pace and speedily is one goal.
- Provides access to learners not presently served in traditional settings and enhances learning opportunities.
- Should be used as a strategic tool to support individual institutional missions but there are institutional structures and cultures that do not foster such an environment.
- Requires resource sharing and collaboration among providers and it can be enhanced by many kinds of partnership.
- Due to incorporated emerging information technologies, it provides both an opportunity and a challenge to adult educational institutions and corporate organizations to expand their missions.
- Most effective when staff, along with learners, acquires new knowledge and skills. Thus, on-going staff development is essential part of the process.

E-Learning Fallacies

Some of the fallacies of e-learning which exist in the globalized world are

- E-learning classes, especially online form of it, are fairly sterile and impersonal.
- Electronic online learning is only for people who have a lot of experience with computer skills to participate in online e-learning instruction.
- Classes are easier than conventional classes.
- Improper assessment.

E-LEARNING STRATEGIES

Efforts should be made to adapt the delivery system to best motivate and meet the needs of the learners, in terms of both content and preferred learning styles. Consider the following strategies:

- Assist in becoming both familiar and comfortable with the delivery technology.
- Make students/learners aware of and comfortable with new patterns of communication to be used in the course (Holmberg, 1985).
- Learn about students' backgrounds and experiences.
- Be sensitive to different communication styles and varied cultural backgrounds.
- Ensure that learners take an active role by independently taking responsibility for their learning.
- Be aware of learners meeting standards/deadlines, despite the lag time often involved in remote area or rural issues.

Morgan (1991) suggests that distant students who are not confident about their learning tend to concentrate on memorizing facts and details, as a result, they end up with a poor understanding due to surface learning approach rather than deep learning approach. But shift from surface to deep learning is not automatic. Brundage, Keane, and Mackneson (1993) suggest that adult students and their instructors must face and overcome a number of challenges. The challenges which need to be dealt include becoming and staying responsible, owning one's strengths, desires, skills, needs, providing opportunities for students to share their personal learning maintaining and increasing self-esteem, dealing with content, relating to others, ensure clear directions and realistic goals for group assignments (Burge, 1993). Clarifying what is learned, and redefining what legitimate knowledge is also matters. Brundage, Keane, and Mackneson (1993) suggest that adult learners may find it difficult to accept that their own experience and reflections are legitimate knowledge.

Teaching and learning as it is demanding and it becomes all the more for adults especially when they have to adapt to the technology based process. Hence it is pertinent to have a view of what is the uniqueness about e-learning vis-à-vis traditional learning as given in Table 1.

Benefits of E-Learning

As corporate leaders try to leverage the value of the value of their worker's ability to learn on the job and re-skill for new ones - the Internet provides new tool, not just a faster and less costly way of delivering the old training programmes. Also, an awareness of the tangible business benefits, as indicated by the statistics, is part of what drives the corporate e-learning market. Some of the benefits include:

1. **Speed:** Since IT has been used to speed up and streamline most aspects of business, it has also been applied to the often complex and costly process of training and e-learning is the ideal model for that purpose, now. Companies use e-learning to bring employees up to speed on new products, sales methods, financial practices or regulatory requirements.

2. **Savings:** Saving money is also an attraction for e-learning in the corporate training, if executed properly. For example, a client of Fuel, (an e-learning provider), a major telecommunications company saved 1.3million pounds on a course for one product by using e-learning. The course that involved substantial spending on equipment would have cost 1.4milion pound, but using e-learning and the creation of ' virtual' versions of the equipment cost just 100,000 pounds. But savings should not be considered as the main factor for adoption of e-learning in corporate place. It cannot be the only reason for

Table 1. E-learning vis-à-vis traditional learning

e-Learning	Traditional Learning
Student approaches	Teacher approaches
Active learning	Passive learning
Teachers guide to construct knowledge for learning	Teachers impart knowledge
Participation during online discussions	Participation by oral communication
Technology helps students explore their own ideas	Technology does not play major role
Technology help to find variety of teaching styles	Lack of variety due to lecture style

e-learning or it will fall. Seeing the potentials in e-learning, the IT giants are eager to gain a big slice of the IT market. IBM has a head start, having already achieved annual savings of well over $200million by adopting e-learning for its own activities.

3. **Flexibility:** E-learning, especially so called asynchronous or learning, offers companies a way of delivering training in a very flexible way. It helps companies rethink the way to assess, source, deliver, evaluate, manage the development of their staff at all levels, making the process, easier, faster and more effective.

4. **Skills Training:** E-learning process is being used for staff training in the skills needed for today's volatile and fast moving markets. There is a desperate need to transfer skill quickly, and e-learning is a veritable concept for this purpose.

5. **Access:** E-learning via the internet is advantageous in that it enables people to access up-to-date information as they perform important tasks. The concept of e-learning is changing from a course, consisting of 20 minutes to an hour of continuous material, to a 'learning object' which may be a few seconds to a few minutes of material. For example, a new employee might access a series of learning objects through very structured series of courses designed to explain the company and its products. Alternatively, an existing employee might use one of those same 30 seconds learning objects to help them solve a peculiar problem.

STRATEGIC ASPECTS OF E-LEARNING

Organizations are beginning to understand the fact that though e-learning could bring about savings and some other benefits highlighted above, the critical factor for adoption of e-learning is its ability to meet the corporate goals and objectives as well as making employees more productive. This means training and development should be managed along a company's overall strategy and performance, not as something apart from the main activities. Corporate organizations are advised to think long and hard about what they want to achieve from e-learning. The ground work takes time. For example, IBM a big player in the fragmented e-learning market encourages corporate organizations to carry out strategy study before taking any action, that is, e-learning should be viewed as an essential part of corporate strategy and not just as a fix for a problem.

Once organizations have decided what they want to achieve, businesses should think about content, the mix between online and classroom-based training, the type of IT systems and architecture they need and whether they want to outsource all or part of the process to outside experts. Most importantly they most consider how training ties in with their performance objectives. They need to see e-learning as part of the way to do business not in isolation. This approach is in line with the greater focus on return on investment as companies consider how to get the most out of the large sums they have spent on IT in the past decade. Corporations are now being encouraged to view their training activities from a broader perspective, so that these are integrated into their business. There is greater emphasis on tying learning to critical business goals. Learning is becoming a part of consolidated approach to performance enhancement. Some companies see this but many are not yet there. But sooner other companies will begin to pay attention to the benefits of e-learning.

ECONOMICS OF E-LEARNING

In the modern corporate organizations, there is hardly anybody that does not need to learn something about something, so the market for e-learning and learning management software is growing very fast.

The economics of e-learning are compelling because it reduces travel and material distribution costs and delivers content that is always up-to-date. The general believe is that e-learning over the Internet will be more successful than the e-learning of computer-based training (CBT) which preceded it. This is because the former requires only a web browser with standard multimedia extensions. CBT was more difficult to deploy, requiring compact disk player and proprietary software to be installed on each desktop computer. The learning management software market does not provide the training content, but the complete infrastructure required to use it. This includes user profiles, skills assessment, registration content delivery, training resource management, examination and so on.

A critical element is correlation tools that connect the learning activities with the organization's core business system in order to show the business impact in learning activities. The training manager cares about the traditional learning metrics of hour per employee or dollars per employee. However, chief executives only care about how training has impacted revenue, costs, and market share or customer satisfaction. The e-learning tools will demonstrate whether a salesman sells more products or the call center agent answers calls more quickly. Content can be delivered by a link to third party websites with which the organization has a contract. Some of these provide no feedback and others use industry standards interfaces that should back on the employees' progress and results to the learning management systems.

Although most content is run directly from the web, in low bandwidth environments it can be combined with a compact disk for audio and video that does not change frequently. Synchronous software also allows learning material to be downloaded to a portable computer and the progress and results uploaded to the server later. The high point in the e-learning market has historically been in customer facing application such as training customers, distributors, resellers, sales, and customer support and field service personnel. This radically changes revenue, as well as reducing the cost of customer support and field service. E-learning is now spreading to emerging economies where the aim is to improve the quality of human resources and increase accessibility to learning and acquisition of requisite knowledge and skills of human resources. The use of e-learning for formal qualifications varies by discipline and industry. However, when establishing an e-learning program, one of the first things considered is the cost of the system. Several cost components factor into the design of an electronic system like technology - hardware and software, transmission like satellite, microwave, maintenance and IT infrastructure, human resources for production to develop and adapt teaching materials, support cost like administrative costs, registration, advising/counseling, etc. (Threlkeld & Brzoska, 1994). Although the costs of offering distance education courses may be high, there are high costs associated with offering conventional courses.

Thus, the benefits of e-learning courses to the learner include:

1. Accessible training to and in rural areas.
2. Completion of course of study/training without suffering the loss of salary due to relocation.
3. Learners/Students are exposed to the expertise of the most qualified faculty.
4. As programmes become more efficient; program costs should decrease (Ludlow, 1994).

A classical model for those working in the training field is the one developed by Donald Kirkpatrick many years ago. That makes it possible even today to assess both traditional training delivered by an instructor in a classroom, as well as e-Learning that can be delivered using the Internet, Intranet or CD- ROM.

This model is composed of four progressive levels as given in Table 2.

According to Strother, there is an added level (level V) related to the Return on Investment or ROI, which should include a cost-benefit analysis. In this regard, using the evaluation data, the results are converted into monetary values and then compared with the cost of the training program in Level V.

Table 2. Progressive levels

Levels	Steps	Follow-up
Level 1	Reaction	How do learners feel?
Level 2	Learning	What did they learn?
Level 3	Behavior	Are they transferring the learning to their job?
Level 4	Results	How much does the training affect the company's bottom line?

E-Learning Benefits

Very often we hear statements about the importance of knowledge as a critical success factor for organizations in the global economy. Even though almost every firm is aware of the significance of knowledge, at times only some firms are clear about how to successfully manage and disseminate knowledge, and even more important, how to transform it into a source of better operating results. Organizations that have used knowledge to improve results are aware that in order to use it successfully, it should entail greater scope and not only use it to inform associates; it should transform abstract ideas and concepts into concrete and tangible experiences leading to results and improved productivity. Many times there is significant transformation that has made organizations rethink e-Learning not as an innovating technology but rather as a tool to improve operating performance. Many organizations, e-Learning is used as a way to substitute traditional training processes to improve critical skill and knowledge dissemination thus leading to logistics and economic rewards. With these results, it is reasonable to forecast that e-Learning implementation in the organizations will follow the patterns of successful organizations in developed markets: that is a greater number of firms will be taking advantage of e-Learning and as the there is a greater internal penetration it will allow more learners, departments, and business processes to take advantage of technology as well.

Current Scenario for E-Learning in Emerging Economies

The sharp increase in the eLearning in emerging economies (Figure 1) is due several trends including:

- Students glut aspiring to move into knowledge based jobs
- Changing demographics
- High rate of failures or poor graduation rates in university systems

- Reduced government funding to formal university programmes
- Massive national digitization efforts
- Rapid consolidation in the highly-fragmented education market
- Pronounced degree of commoditization in education
- Significant degree of formal education substitution

There are two major trends in emerging economies eLearning market: the proliferation (and fail rate) of university graduation rates and the growing number of students to pursue choice based learning rather than strict curricula based programmes. Prior to 2010, education and specially higher or professional education was university based but from early 2010 emerging economies started to invest in online education and started acquiring IT infrastructure.

Figure 1. Emerging economies primary factors driving e-learning market

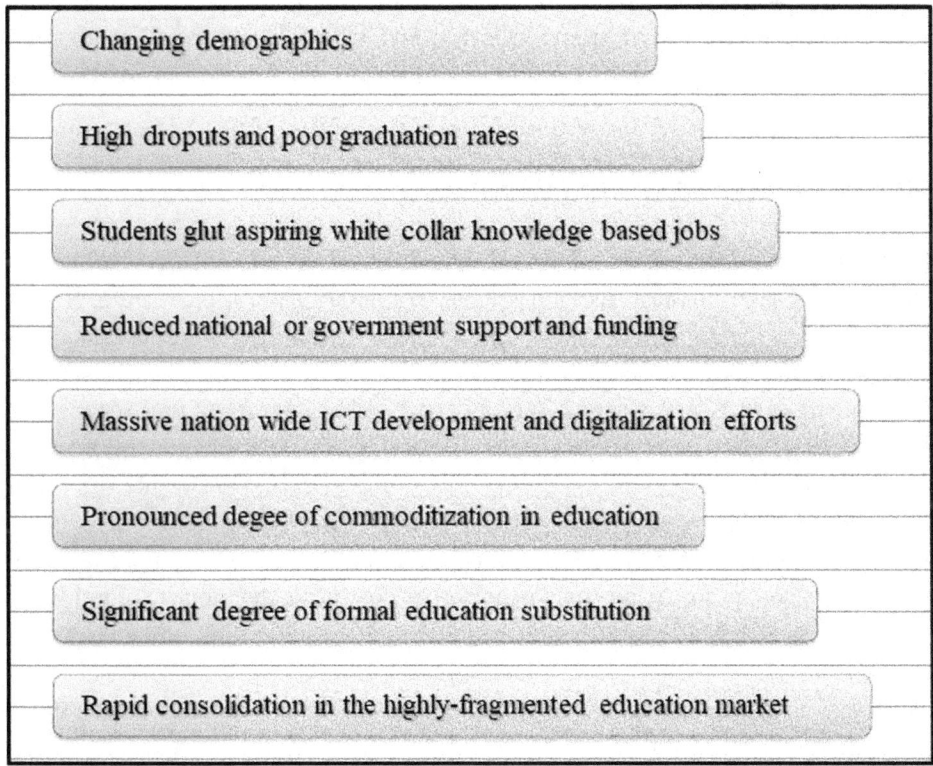

OPPORTUNITIES IN THE EMERGING MARKET

Despite the overall possible growth rate for Self-paced eLearning there are lucrative opportunities in particular verticals and for particular products which include healthcare industry, global market for digital English language learning is booming and there are significant revenue opportunities for suppliers. (Ambient, 2015)

Managed education services (also called online program management and edtech program management) in the higher education segments and managed training services in the corporate segments across the globe are bright spots for the eLearning industry. Example: India-based Nspira is an online education management firm serving the Indian higher education segment. They obtained $60 million in funding in January 2016, which is a very high amount for a learning technology supplier in India. Managed training and education services usually entail supporting very large numbers of users and very few suppliers can scale their offerings to that extent. The revenues are concentrated in a handful of companies that have the resources to scale their services for large numbers of users. Managed services (School-as-a-Service,) turnkey bundles that include content design, content development, cloud-based hosting and delivery, and most importantly, 24/7 technical support; all at a fraction of the cost that the institutions would spend if they did it themselves are few other emerging opportunities.

Solutions and Recommendations

There are major convergent inhibitors which do effect eLearning in emerging economies. Some of these include intense commoditization, eLearning product lifecycle is in the final stage and suppliers are diversifying beyond eLearning, breakdown of the global LMS market and profound degree of product substitution including the leapfrog effect in mobile-only approaches by some of these economies and countries. So what is needed is the makeup for the lack of Innovation which is the root cause of the issues and concerns in the eLearning. Despite the recent advances in learning research and technology in general, no significant innovations have been introduced in the last decade for eLearning. Courseware has not changed in decades. The only significant change in the LMS market is the move to cloud-based solutions, but that is a software industry trend and not something unique to LMS.

However, it is not clear what technology has done for education, learning and development (Baporikar, 2018). Fast changes in other are seen but there are not descriptive education variables whose curves are exponentially growing. All the corporations have recognized that knowledge and the ability to apply it on daily life activities represent a source of competitiveness and survival. Moreover, the rapid increase in the technological sophistication, diversity, and pervasiveness of 3D virtual learning environments, along with the proliferation of research on their effectiveness in educational settings, necessitates frequent systematic analytical syntheses of their effectiveness.

Sitzmann's (2011) finding that students learned better when simulations were used in the form of practice sessions than when they were used in a stand-alone format. This makes eLearning more relevant and useful for fostering deeper learning (Clark, Tanner-Smith & Killingsworth, 2016). According to Hattie and Timperley (2007), feedback has tremendous impact on learning gains, both positive and negative. Therefore, it is essential that teachers are made knowledgeable about the features and situations that make feedback effective (Merchant, Goetz, Cifuentes, Keeney-Kennicutt, & Davis, 2014). .

Further, many organizations have leaped on the possibilities offered by the deployment of educational training material over the World Wide Web. Universal access, continuous availability, and the potential for large cost savings have excited managers and training specialists alike. This has resulted in steep learning curves for setting up an e-learning infrastructure (Fallon & Brown, 2016). For medium-sized organizations, this is not very evident, and it is even less evident in small organizations. This is a serious issue because in this knowledge age; a person who has good knowledge at the right time will have a better chance to be successful. But if small organizations do not use the power of knowledge to compete with big companies, it will be a case of "tied sheep against a loose wolf" situation in terms of competitiveness and survival. In the face of the fierce competition in the increasingly global and demanding markets and with the understanding of the role of knowledge in the new productive processes (Baporikar, 2015), it is time to aggressive propagate for educating so as to create and transform knowledge based on e-Learning to become more competitive.

FUTURE RESEARCH DIRECTIONS

E-learning systems are emerging in many settings of our society. Schools, universities, and several others use these systems. E-learning systems allow learning anytime and anywhere (Aparicio, Bacao & Oliveira 2017). Thus it overcome these learning barriers and paved ways for inclusivity, but the effect of non-cognitive skills on the success of e-learning systems is yet to be explored. Organizations sometimes pay lip service to training, but intensifying competitive pressures are now forcing them to look hard at ways of having effective strategies for human resource development and training. Organizations will sooner or later have to relook at the existing strategies and work out for e-learning strategies to adapt to the borderless world (Baporikar, 2014). The areas where studies need to be undertaken include the matching and identification of training needs across the board and borders, understanding the cultural aspects of learning and integrating the cultural aspects of learning with technology apart from how to help individuals and learners to learn-delearn-relearn in an effective manner. Coomey and Stephenson (2001) found little if any definitive evidence of the overall effectiveness of 'e-learning' compared with more conventional methods. This is not to say that this medium is ineffective but rather to say that there is little systematic and empirical work to show evidence of its evaluation. The vast and growing bulk of information now available about e-learning, both in print and online has focused on the potential of technology or the enthusiasm of its users and lacked the pedagogical guidance stemming from research that would inform the processes of online course development, review and moderation. In accordance with this Goodyear (2001) noted: "the literature on learning in higher education is surprisingly quiet with respect to what both lay people and practitioners might expect to be a key construct". Steeples and Jones (2002) also reported: "the big lesson about technology and learning from the 20th century is that less is known about how people learn than many educational researchers are inclined to admit". Thus the key issues revolve around the nature and the components of effective teaching and learning and are pointing towards the need for establishing the pedagogies of e-learning or e-pedagogy and presenting research based recommendations for the e-pedagogues. It becomes more evident that there is a great need for a pedagogical assessment of online teaching and training. This dearth of content analysis is due to the time required to perform such analyses (Hara, Bonk and Angeli, 2000) and researchers still lack a reliable instrument or an analytical framework to analyze the online discussions. Goodyear (2001) noted: "Analyzing the content of networked learning discussions is a troublesome research area and several commentators have remarked on the difficulty of connecting online texts to discourse to learning"

CONCLUSION

The e-learning is a type of instruction has been using terms like computer assisted learning (CAL), computer based instruction (CBI) for over 30 years, along with other similar terms and abbreviations for the use of IT in education. Special progress in the use of computers in education was enabled by multimedia technology, and technological and pedagogical revolution in distance education happened with the development of World Wide Web. The subject of Electronic Learning (E-Learning) has become pertinent in the dynamic world of today which is driven by information technology. The global economy has not been left out of the positive impacts of e-learning especially in the corporate world where e-learning has reduced the cost of training of personnel. The basic concept of e-learning presupposes that electronic driven technologies can be used to facilitate and enhance learning process. E-learning has come to be a form of bridge for those who did not have the first time opportunity to formal education. Though there are some lapses associated with the full implementation of e-learning, the benefits derived from it far outweigh the challenges. Part of the core value of e-learning is that learning is a life-long process, important to successful participation in the social, cultural, civic, and economic life of the society (Baporikar, 2016a). There is an expectation of a significant consolidation in the e-learning market as large companies' increase their penetration and smaller ones are swallowed up or find the going too tough. Their success, whatever their size, will depend on how many companies can be persuaded not just to test the waters of the e-learning market but to take the plunge. Many of the developing economies are mobile-only countries and eLearning will never gain significant adoption in those countries. It is interesting that new learning technology companies are citing the lack of innovation in the eLearning industry in their marketing material. A company called Knowledge Avatars sells a product used to create digital tutors and even digital students. In their marketing material, they state that "Conventional e-learning is outdated! It does not meet students' individual needs. Conventional e-learning has a dropout rate of 50%! Students need help to learn in a format that they will enjoy using!"

A number of studies comparing eLearning to more traditional methods have been carried out. Based on these it can be concluded that it is another useful tool in the teaching toolbox Chumley-Jones, Dobbie and Alford (2002). It is not a panacea but neither should it be dismissed as a passing "fad". Just like non-electronic teaching methods it has its strengths and weaknesses (one would rarely use a lecture to teach a surgeon to operate or a number of parallel small group tutorials to give a standardised overview of a subject). Some learners find it useful, some less so, just as some learners enjoy interactivity and some prefer a more passive approach (Baporikar, 2016b). As with most teaching modalities, deep rather than superficial learners appear to enjoy the greatest benefit (Hahne, Benndorf, Fre and Herzig (2005). A number of studies show positive learner perceptions. Comparison with more "traditional" teaching is unhelpful. Further accessibility by way of internet access for low-income individuals is increasingly commonplace because of free Wi-Fi in many public spaces and smartphones (File, 2013). Hence, the future is to look at what eLearning can do and use it to its strengths; eLearning is good for just in time learning as per individual time and need assuming the learner finds it a medium from which learning takes place. It crosses geographical boundaries and time zones and provides access for the learner to a wealth of resources beyond individual, home or institution can access. The challenge now is for educators to fill data repositories with useful, and help learners access the full richness of the medium.

REFERENCES

Ambient. (2015). *The 2015-2020 Worldwide Digital English Language Learning Market Series*. Ambient Insight, LLC.

Aparicio, M., Bacao, F., & Oliveira, T. (2017). Grit in the path to e-learning success. *Computers in Human Behavior, 66*, 388–399. doi:10.1016/j.chb.2016.10.009

Baporikar, N. (2014). Effective E-Learning Strategies for a Borderless World. In J. Pelet (Ed.), *E-Learning 2.0 Technologies and Web Applications in Higher Education* (pp. 22–44). Hershey, PA: IGI Global; doi:10.4018/978-1-4666-4876-0.ch002

Baporikar, N. (2015). Knowledge Management in Small and Medium Enterprises. In J. Zhao, P. Ordóñez de Pablos, & R. Tennyson (Eds.), *Organizational Innovation and IT Governance in Emerging Economies* (pp. 1–20). Hershey, PA: IGI Global; doi:10.4018/978-1-4666-7332-8.ch001

Baporikar, N. (2016a). Lifelong Learning in Knowledge Society. In P. Ordóñez de Pablos & R. Tennyson (Eds.), *Impact of Economic Crisis on Education and the Next-Generation Workforce* (pp. 263–284). Hershey, PA: IGI Global; doi:10.4018/978-1-4666-9455-2.ch012

Baporikar, N. (2016b). Student Learning and Information Technology Nexus. [IJSSMET]. *International Journal of Service Science, Management, Engineering, and Technology, 7*(2), 34–45. doi:10.4018/IJSSMET.2016040103

Baporikar, N. (2017). *Innovation and Shifting Perspectives in Management Education* (pp. 1–352). Hershey, PA: IGI Global; doi:10.4018/978-1-5225-1019-2

Barron, A. E., & Ivers, K. W. (1996). *The Internet and Instruction: Ideas and Activities*. Englewood, CO: Libraries Unlimited.

Barron, A. E., & Orwig, G. W. (1997). *New Technologies for Education: A Beginner's Guide*. Englewood, CO: Libraries Unlimited.

Boettcher, J. (1997). *Florida State University*. Pedagogy and Learning.

Bukowitz, W. R., & Williams, R. L. (1999). *The Knowledge Management Fieldbook*. London: Prentice Hall.

Casey, P., Dager, N., & Magel, M. (1998). Emerging Technology: Tools for Today and Tomorrow. *AV Video Multimedia Producer., 20*(1), 44–53.

Chumley-Jones, H., Dobbie, A., & Alford, C. (2002). Web-based learning: Sound educational method or hype? A review of the educational literature. *Academic Medicine, 77*(10Supplement), S86–S93. doi:10.1097/00001888-200210001-00028 PMID:12377715

Clark, D. B., Tanner-Smith, E. E., & Killingsworth, S. S. (2016). Digital games, design, and learning: A systematic review and meta-analysis. *Review of Educational Research, 86*(1), 79–122. doi:10.3102/0034654315582065 PMID:26937054

Collis, B. (1996). *Tele-Learning in a Digital World*. London: International Thomson Computer Press.

Coomey, M., & Stephenson, J. (2001). Online Learning: it is all about dialogue, involvement, support and control—according to the research. In J. Stephenson (Ed.), *Teaching and Learning Online: Pedagogies for New Technologies*. London, UK: Kogan Page.

Distance Learning: A Primer. (1997). Retrieved from http://www.mountainlake. org/distance/primer.htm

Egan, M. W., Sebastian, J., & Welch, M. (1991, March). Effective Television Teaching: Perceptions of those that Count Most...Distance Learners. *Proceedings of the Rural Education Symposium* (ED 342 579).

Fallon, C., & Brown, S. (2016). *E-learning standards: a guide to purchasing, developing, and deploying standards-conformant e-learning*. CRC Press.

Feeley, J. (1997, August). Wideband Web. *Digital Video,* 42-48.

File, T. (2013). *Computer and internet use in the United States. Current population survey reports*. Retrieved from https://www. census.gov/history/ pdf/2013computeruse.pdf

Franklin, N., Yoakam, M., & Warren, R. (1996). *Distance Learning: A Guidebook for System Planning and Implementation*. Indiana University.

Giurgiu, L. (2017). Microlearning an evolving elearning trend. *Scientific Bulletin, 22*(1), 18–23. doi:10.1515/bsaft-2017-0003

Goodyear, P. (2001). Psychological Foundations of Networked Learning. In C. Jones & C. Steeples (Eds.), *Networked Learning: Perspectives and Issues. Springer*.

Hahne, A. K., Benndorf, R., Frey, P., & Herzig, S. (2005). Attitude towards computer-based learning: Determinants as revealed by a controlled interventional study. *Medical Education, 39*(9), 935–943. doi:10.1111/j.1365-2929.2005.02249.x PMID:16150034

Hansen, N. (1998). *Save the Beaches 1998: An International Project for Global Awareness*. Available at http://ednhp.hartford.edu/www/Nina/

Hara, N., Bonk, C. J., & Angeli, C. (2000). Content Analysis of Online Discussion in an Applied Educational Psychology Course. *Instructional Science, 28*(2), 115–152. doi:10.1023/A:1003764722829

Hattie, J., & Timperley, H. (2007). The power of feedback. *Review of Educational Research, 77*(1), 81–112. doi:10.3102/003465430298487

Hong, J. C., & Kuo, C. L. (1999). Knowledge Management in the Learning Organization. *Leadership and Organization Development Journal, 20*(4), 207–215. doi:10.1108/01437739910277019

Liu, Y., & Wang, H. (2009). A Comparative Study on E-learning Technologies and Products: From the East to the West. *Systems Research and Behavioral Science, 26*(2), 191–209. doi:10.1002res.959

Martensson, M. (2000). A Critical Review of Knowledge Management as a Tool. *Journal of Knowledge Management, 4*(3), 204–216. doi:10.1108/13673270010350002

Merchant, Z., Goetz, E. T., Cifuentes, L., Keeney-Kennicutt, W., & Davis, T. J. (2014). Effectiveness of virtual reality-based instruction on students' learning outcomes in K-12 and higher education: A meta-analysis. *Computers & Education, 70*, 29–40. doi:10.1016/j.compedu.2013.07.033

Minoli, D. (1996). *Distance Learning Technology and Applications*. Boston, MA: Artech House.

Moore, M. G., & Thompson, M. M. (1990). The Effects of Distance Learning: A Summary of the Literature. Research Monograph No. 2. University Park, The Pennsylvania State University: American Center for the Study of Distance Education (ED 330-321).

O'Neill, M., & McHugh, P. (Eds.). (1996). *Effective Distance Learning*. Alexandria, VA: American Society of Training and Development.

Parker, A. (1997). A Distance Education How-To Manual: Recommendations from the Field. *Educational Technology Review, 8*, 7–10.

Ponce, D. (2003). *What can E-learning Learn from Knowledge Management?* Paper presented in 3rd European Knowledge Management Summer School, San Sebastian, Spain. Retrieved from http://www.knowledgeboard.com

Porter, L. R. (1997). *Creating the Virtual Classroom: Distance Learning with the Internet*. John Wiley & Sons, Inc.

Roknuzzaman, M., Kanai, H., & Umemoto, K. (2009). Integration of Knowledge Management Process into Digital Library System: A Theoretical Perspective. *Library Review, 58*(5), 372–386. doi:10.1108/00242530910961792

Salvador, R. (1996). What's New in Net Connectivity? *Electronic Learning, 16*(1), 14.

Schutte, J. G. (1996). *Virtual Teaching in Higher Education: The New Intellectual Superhighway or Just another Traffic Jam?* Available at http://www.csun.edu/sociology/virexp.htm

Sitzmann, T. (2011). A meta-analytic examination of the instructional effectiveness of computer-based simulation games. *Personnel Psychology, 64*(2), 489–528. doi:10.1111/j.1744-6570.2011.01190.x

Steeples, C., & Jones, C. (2002). *Networked Learning: Perspectives and Issues*. London: Springer-Verlag London Limited. doi:10.1007/978-1-4471-0181-9

Stephenson, J. (2002). *Teaching & Learning Online: Pedagogies for New Technologies*. London: Kogan Page Limited.

Thornburg, D. D. (1995). Welcome to the Communication Age. *Internet Research, 5*(1), 64–70.

Verduin, J. R., & Clark, T. A. (1991). *Distance Education: The Foundations of Effective Practice*. San Francisco, CA: Jossey - Bass Publishers.

Violante, M. G., & Vezzetti, E. (2014). Implementing a new approach for the design of an e-learning platform in engineering education. *Computer Applications in Engineering Education, 22*(4), 708–727. doi:10.1002/cae.21564

Wild, R. H., Griggs, K. A., & Downing, T. (2002). A framework for e-learning as a tool for knowledge management. *Industrial Management & Data Systems, 102*(7), 371–380. doi:10.1108/02635570210439463

Willis, B. (1995, October). *Distance Learning at a Glance*. University of Idaho Engineering Outreach. Available at http://www.uidaho.edu/evo/distglan.html

KEY TERMS AND DEFINITIONS

E-Learning: Electronic learning (or e-learning or eLearning) is a type of education where the medium of instruction is computer technology. In some instances, no in-person interaction takes place. It can be defined as a planned teaching/learning experience that uses a wide spectrum of technologies, mainly internet or computer-based, to reach learners.

Knowledge: Acquaintance with facts, truths, or principles, as from study or investigation; general erudition, familiarity or conversance, as with a particular subject or branch of learning including acquaintance or familiarity gained by sight, experience, research or report.

Learning Management Systems: Learning management is the capacity to design pedagogic strategies that achieve learning outcomes in students, where the emphasis is placed on student learning rather than instructor preparation. A learning management system (LMS) is a software application or web-based technology used to plan, implement, and assess a specific learning process.

Strategies: A method or plan chosen to bring about a desired future, such as achievement of a goal or solution to a problem. Strategy is a result of choices made, on where to play and how to win, in business it has got to do maximize long-term value.

Training: Organized activity aimed at imparting information and/or instructions to improve the recipient's performance or to help him or her attain a required level of knowledge or skill.

Chapter 9
Advanced Human– Computer Interaction in E–Learning Systems for Handicapped People

Joanna Julia Zukowska
Warsaw School of Economics, Poland

Zdzisław Sroczyński
Silesian University of Technology, Poland

ABSTRACT

The chapter concerns the implementation of novel and advanced HCI (human-computer interaction) methods in the design of educational systems aimed at people with disabilities. E-learning applications can significantly improve the quality of life for handicapped students by increasing their self-reliance and adjusting the learning time frame. The structure and methods used to design the interaction applied in this kind of educational system varies significantly depending on the type of the user's disability. There are examples of the interaction developed with the needs of disabled students in mind discussed in the chapter. The main advantages of different solutions were identified and examined. The authors also try to recognize possible threats and suggest some solutions to avoid them.

DOI: 10.4018/978-1-5225-7435-4.ch009

E-LEARNING

The majority of contemporary organizations look for new methods of development focusing on cost reduction. The globalization of economy and development of telecommunication technologies increase the efficiency of communication, at the same time reducing its cost. There are more and more areas of life that demanded direct involvement until recently and now have become remotely accessible, enabling the users to break the distance and time barriers. These factors also bring about the development of new methods of education defined as e-learning (Debande, O., Ottersten, E.K. 2004.).

From entrepreneur's point of view, e-learning is one of outsourcing varieties, specifically developed by more and more businesses of IT, telecommunication, finance or training sectors. In some of them this kind of education comprises several dozen per cent of all personnel training courses (Żukowska, 2004).

E-learning means remote education with the use of the Internet, multimedia or even virtual reality. With the help of e-learning the student may acquire information, develop knowledge, check progress in learning and communicate with other participants of the process of education – without the necessity to travel from place to place (Costagliola, et al. 2008). This remote mode of learning also enables the selection of the most suitable path of education and then to follow it in convenient time and pace (Sandars, Langlois, 2005). The fundamental advantages of e-learning are particularly important for people with mobility issues, physically handicapped, requiring permanent medical care or forced to undergo regular medical procedures, for example as part of permanent dialysis therapy, complex oncological therapies or complex rehabilitation after various surgical operations (Baumann-Birkbeck, Karaksha, 2015; Cimmaruta, et al., 2017; Patel, et al., 2018).

The following basic types of e-learning can be distinguished:

- **Combined Education**: Consisting in implementation of the best characteristics of traditional forms of teaching into the electronic education process (Costagliola, et al. 2008),
- **Synchronous Learning:** In which a pupil (student) has an opportunity to participate in selected activities at the specific real-time hour. This type of conducting activities requires the participation of teacher (lecturer) – coordinator. Each participant of e-learning (training) may communicate with the virtual teacher via teleconference, virtual board, online chats or audio conversations (Dana, Darmawan, 2017),

- **Asynchronous Learning**: The most popular e-learning form, enabling individual selection of activity frequency, depending on the learner's capabilities. The basic media are in this case electronic documents, e-mail messages, message boards, groups and discussion forums (Olson, Codde, demaagd, et al., 2011; Islam, Beer, Slack, 2015),
- **Knowledge Bases:** Building databases by appropriate intermediation enabling efficient searches, cataloging and commenting on information (Suresh, Vishnu, Gayathri, 2018),
- **Online Support:** Real-time conversation with the teacher via e-mail messages, chat systems, discussion groups providing at the same time with opportunity to gain exact accurate information from reliable sources in a relatively short time (Sadikin, Purwanto, 2018).

It should be mentioned in this point that there is an immense technological chaos in the literature related to this subject. The term pupil is often identified with a student, trainee, educational process participant, similarly, the term 'teacher' is identified with lecturer, coach or training instructor. The same phenomenon occurs with the term 'training' identified lecture, workshop, lesson, development stage. Therefore, for the purposes of this paper, pairs of terms have been introduced: learner-student, teacher-lecturer, lecture-training.

Further, based on the literature studies, the basic functional modules of e-learning systems include:

- Learning Management System (LMS) enabling to manage virtual training organization. LMS provides information on subjects, courses and their participants. It is the means to build a knowledge base, enroll the participants, check the learners' progress, build statistics of using particular system modules (Yang, Hwang, et at. 2013).
- Learning Content Management System: (LCMS) enables the creation, edition and on-line publication of electronic documents composing the knowledge base of specific subjects. On principle, LCMS should not require special IT knowledge so that specialists in various sciences could use it. LCMS also stores all information about participants in the process of education, knowledge acquisition stages and its results, it also ensures communication and opportunity for providing feedback to the system administrators. The communication tools held by the LCMS module decide on the possibility and convenience of communication between learners and teachers as well as among groups of pupils (Rajper, Shaikh,2016).

- Content Management System (CMS) enables to build the content of specific subjects of training courses and other system elements, such as message boards or Internet service (Truong, 2016).
- Intelligent Learning System (ILS) manages individual data of the system users, stores statistics of materials use, test results, errors and frequently asked questions. Such information may be used for implementation of new system functionalities, to make it customized to individual user needs (Atman, Inceoğlu, et al., 2009; Ahmad, Tasir, et al.,2013).

The expert forum, mentor's personality, technical support and training base comprise additional significant e-learning system elements. The expert forum enables exchange of experiences with specialists, while the remote access substantially facilitates worldwide solicitation of experts to cooperate in this scope. A mentor is a virtual teacher whose task is to help and motivate the students. The mentor's virtuality consists in the possibility of cooperation between one teacher and numerous pupils in a way assuring apparently exclusive and individual contact with the teacher. The training base is a repository of all educational materials, training aids and technical infrastructure used for the organization of the educational process.

Publishing the contents of courses and training sessions online as well as the remote access to such materials and communication with the teachers demand permanent technical support. Any online educational system that does not function fluently and causes problems to the participants or offers lower work comfort than traditional forms of education, may only discourage the potential users.

E-Learning and Handicapped People

Richness of presentation methods of educational contents used in e-learning and, most of all, the easy way of selecting learning place and time, convenient for the pupil, are the characteristics particularly significant for disabled people. Physically handicapped people go through a nightmare of issues while moving and traveling, so the e-learning methods help them save time and reduce expenses. Certainly the factors restricting the use of remote education cannot be ignored, such as the costs of hardware and ICT connections or lack of direct contact with the living teacher or tutor, which to some people might become more important than the technological achievements or individual work opportunities.

The blind, in turn, suffer from deficiency of professionally prepared and accessible educational materials. Most of the books, exercise books with math problems or even online electronic documents are easily accessible to the sighted people only. The existing computer tools (OCR systems and systems assisting in creation and translation of electronic documents) provide conversion of averagely complex documents into audio or Braille formats, but they often require additional participation of the operator. The solutions available provide fully automated conversion of documents in a uniform format neither to the blind nor sighted people.

The most serious problems occur at the attempts of presentation of documents containing a complex mathematical, physical or chemical notation, i.e. all kinds of technical and scientific contents. In addition to deficiency of technical solutions in this scope, the multiplicity of standards actually differing almost from country to country brings about additional issues (for example the mathematical Braille dialect was codified separately in the USA, Germany and Poland). The use of solutions applied for ordinary documents, such as speech generators (successfully used by the blind for years), tone representations of multidimensional structures, high-definition point networks (used for presentation of documents consisting of text data and graphics) does not prove right for complex technical documents, particularly mathematical ones. All the methods are relatively expensive or restrict the scope of contents transmitted and, most importantly, require special preparation of the document directly by the author or later by appropriately trained operator (Karshmer A.I., Bledsoe Ch., 2002).

As part of the NCBiR project performed in Poland "INFOMAT-E Public information system for people with sight and hearing organ dysfunctions", surveys were made with the use of questionnaire on 96 people, of whom 77 were visually impaired, 29 had hearing disability and 10 had both disabilities (Piasecki, 2014).

The surveys show that 57% of all the respondents own or use computers, which means that the saturation is relatively high. Out of people who do not use computers, but declare the need to use it, the reason why they do not use it is the fact that it is difficult to operate and use. 42% respondents declare that they use the Internet. 34% respondents declare knowledge of software facilitating the use of computer by disabled people, however, 18% respondents use the software. The respondents specified the following programs (types of programs): increasing and reading the screen content: Jaws, Window-Eyes, SuperNova, Magic, Lunar Plus. 9% respondents declare the use of electronic devices (mainly GPS navigation). The group below 30 years of age with minimum secondary education intensively uses all technological novelties, telephones, computers and the Internet. These are undoubtedly potential students and e-learning system recipients. Among all the respondents the Internet is used mainly to acquire information (35%), maintain contacts (31%), have entertainment (21%), settle official matters (12%) and do shopping (9%) (Piasecki, 2014).

The statistical data of GUS (Chief Statistical Office) for Poland confirm that the percentage of pupils with special educational needs is growing, which includes without limitation pupils with sight dysfunction, in generally available and integration classes. In the school year 1995/1996 the total number of 6 thousand children attended such classes, while in the school year 2013/2014 – 35 thousand. Similar growing tendency was recorded in middle schools – in the school year 2000/2001 16,5 thousand pupils with special educational needs attended generally available and integration classes and in 2013/2014 – 21 thousand. According to the data of Polish Union of the Blind 109 blind pupils and 4690 visually impaired pupils attended generally available schools, while 246 blind and 903 visually impaired – at special institutions. The situation is the result of implementation of inclusive, open school model in Poland, considering the needs of every child educated in regional school (Rubin et al., 2015).

The aim of the surveys made in the first half of 2014 by TRAKT The Fund for Polish Blind and Visually Impaired People was recognition of the stage of computerization of teaching mathematics in special centers, schools with integration classes and at generally available schools attended by pupils with sight dysfunction. Another area included the needs declared by the respondents in the scope of ICT assistance technologies, supporting the didactic work of the teacher and parent with the pupil at school and at home. 142 respondents all over Poland participated in the tests, responded the surveys online or on the phone. Three groups of pupils were distinguished among the respondents: visually impaired pupils, their parents and their mathematics teachers. The tests were in the form of surveys containing three groups of questions: specific nature of teaching mathematics at school and at home; the use of ICT technologies the demand for functions supporting mathematical education of visually impaired pupils. Most of the teachers surveyed (58%) assessed the general level of mathematical efficiency of visually impaired pupils as lower or substantially lower than that of their fully able peers, whereas the pupils (40%), mostly visually impaired and educated at special institutions, assessed their level as equal to that of their fully able peers. Nevertheless, large group of pupils (38%) defined their level as lower or substantially lower even than that of their sighted peers (Rubin et al., 2015).

The test results indicated the lack of technological support of mathematics teaching process and market deficiency of state-of-the-art systems with user-friendly interface, functionally adapted to the needs of sighted, visually impaired and blind people – systems that would facilitate and accelerate the communication between such persons and increase the adaptability of mathematical knowledge. The fact that as many as 66 percent of the pupils tested do not use any electronic devices for learning mathematics, of which 73 per cent are blind pupils, confirms the impeded access to appropriate software that would be really helpful in recognition of the mathematical questions, both at school and at home and with the use of the Internet. This is of special importance in the context of readiness to take up new technological challenges responding to the needs of learning mathematics, in spite of simultaneous, noticed in both groups – of teachers and pupils – substantial ignorance of Braille writing system and Braille mathematical notation (Rubin et al., 2015).

The availability of appropriate library materials is an immensely significant element indicating efficient and effective didactic process. In the late 1980's the first attempts to implement integration teaching on university level appeared in Poland, while in the early 1990's integration studies were organized for the first 4 disabled persons. The number grew every year and later further institutions became committed in the process in which service centers were open or representatives for handicapped students were employed. The architectural availability of university buildings improved, the computer stations were furnished with new technologies to support handicapped people and governmental institutions opened target programs directed to handicapped students and alumni. The latest data indicate that in 2013/14 cal 29 thousand handicapped people studied in Poland. The largest group consists of motor organ and visually disabled people. In 2013 2638 visually disabled people studied at Polish higher schools. This is not a homogeneous group – it consists of blind and visually impaired persons (Fedorowicz-Kruszewska, 2015).

One of the key aspects of education including students with sight disabilities is to provide them with access to educational materials in the formats convenient to them. The analysis of websites of Polish tertiary education institutions showed that their most common measures taken for students with sight disabilities consist in furnishing computer stations with auxiliary technologies, arranging rental units of specialist equipment to facilitate the educational process, relevant entries in the library lending rules and scanning academic work books and other documents (Fedorowicz-Kruszewska, 2015).

E-Learning of General Science vs. the Needs of Blind People

The extensive overview of methods applied by teachers and students for recording mathematical notation in totally virtualized e-learning environment presented in the paper (Cuartero-Olivera et al., 2012) indicates that there is no significant difference between the knowledge and achievements of the students depending on the form they present their works in. Nevertheless, the elegant, elaborate electronic form usually gains higher marks due to the additional effort put in the appropriate preparation of documents including the answers and exercises.

Furthermore, there are no reasons to think that blind people may have lower abilities to general science subjects than sighted people (Edwards 1998). However, they have significantly more problems with communication by mathematical language, either with other people (e.g. the teacher) or for their own purposes (to record the interim results of transformation and calculations).

The overview of historic projects discussing this subject matter enables us to determine the achievements by date as well as the appropriate interpretation of blind students' needs in this scope.

The Maths project developed as part of the European Commission program represented an attempt to integrate speech and sound generators with the graphic screen, in order to support the creation and edition of algebraic expressions on the secondary school level. Unfortunately, the project did not go beyond the prototype stage (Edwards 1998, MATHS 2003).

The formats of recording mathematical notation presently used, such as LaTeX or MathML meet the basic assumption significant for a blind recipient, i.e. the record linearity, which enables the presentation of the record fragment on a Braille ruler or printing on a printer embossing Braille dot alphabet characters. Unfortunately, the formats are relatively complicated and require multiple characters to record simple expressions even – because they are intended to machine, rather than direct transformation by a human (Sroczyński, 2000). Works have been taken up on MathML document conversion tools into a form of selected Braille mathematical dialect (in this case SMFB - Stuttgart Mathematical Notation For the Blind). However, the results obtained do not assure either edition or interaction with the user, therefore, they do not enable bilateral information exchange, necessary in the process of education and at work (Rotard et al., 2003).

The set of tools enabling both blind and sighted people to work on the same documents has been developed in the State University of Oregon. It is composed of Tiger – Braille editor and convex graphics based on its own dialect called DotsPlus, AGC (Accessible Graphing Calculator) – a tool to calculate the value of function and draw graphs through tonal representation, WinTriangle – editor of mathematical expressions adapted to the needs of blind people, enabling to exchange the work results with others via standard formats. The tools are available in free-of-charge versions and have won interest and users among blind people (Gardner et al., 2002).

Some promising results can be gained when applying voice recognition. Some attempts to use such technology through adaptation of existing commercial applications (Dragon NaturallySpeaking, Scientific WorkPlace) have been made by Metroplex Voice Computing (McClellan, 2003) and Texthelp Ltd. (Texthelp, 2018) in the form of commercial, partly paid product called EquatIO.

Duxbury Braille Translator is an application supporting the creation and translation of documents into various Braille language versions, including the American mathematical dialect of Braille: Nemeth Code (Osterhaus, 2004). However, this is most of all a tool to prepare documents for publishing in Braille, most convenient for a sighted operator and not allowing for unrestricted document exchange between sighted and visually impaired people (Duxbury, 2004).

The MAVIS project enabled to present a hierarchical structure of a mathematical expression, enables to generate a Braille mathematical code on the fly and provides an extensive preview for the visually impaired people. Some special solutions were implemented in this system to reduce the ambiguity of the voice-activated formulas and bases for dictation by the user (Karshmer et al., 1999; Karshmer et al., 2002). MAVIS was also a base to develop a translator between varieties of Braille mathematical dialect to enable smooth document exchange between blind mathematicians worldwide.

Significant works related to automatic translation of mathematical notation from TeX/LaTeX language into Braille mathematical dialect were done in Poland. The TRANSLATOR Project (Kalbarczyk, 2002) assured the unification and expansion of the Braille language standard applicable in our country and preparation of tools enabling: printing of books with mathematical notation in dot writing, access to electronic publications by the blind people, preparation of school workbooks, facilitation of individual work of visually impaired people on technical and scientific document, support to interaction between a blind pupil and their teacher.

The codifications of Braille mathematical dialect used in Poland were presented in the papers (Świerczek, 2002; Kauba, 2011). The standards of encoding mathematical notation in Braille dot language are based on various assumptions, depending on a country or region of the world, they usually implement additional restrictions to notations, tags and key words. Braille dot system undergoes continuous development, which is confirmed by subsequent, significantly modified editions of specifications, so the analysis of mathematical expressions translation for publications accessible to visually impaired people represents a permanent challenge and requires the solution of numerous engineering and organizational issues. The measures are to provide legibility of transmission of the source, 2D and hierarchical visual notation encoded by means of linear dot writing, without forcing the author and reader to apply unnatural embedding of parentheses, disproportionately extending their record.

The Lambda Project is an alternative interesting proposal to expand the concept of Braille mathematical dialect (Edwards et al., 2006). It is an attempt of fresh and free of historical burdens or regionalisms approach to define the set of characters and key-words enabling to describe mathematical expressions by means of dot writing. An interesting characteristic suggested in this study is the possibility of temporary reduction of formulas to a specific level of detail (e.g. providing information on the existence of a fraction only, without details concerning the content of the numerator and the denominator), which corresponds to the natural way of reading or demonstration of the mathematical language by sighted people.

Whereas the experimental system described in the papers (Sroczyński, 2002; Sroczyński, 2003) through the integration of tools for creation, publishing and presentation of complex scientific, technical and mathematical documents meets the assumptions for making the same contents available to blind, visually impaired and sighted people. By detection of the software used by the recipient the system server may choose the most suitable form of document presentation and carry out its possible conversion into e.g. Braille dot language. The action is done in a totally transparent manner to the user and requires no special measures on the part of the publication author. Such approach provides a unique opportunity to build an e-learning system providing the same complex educational contents to disabled people as to all the other users. The server converting mathematical publications by type of browser used for viewing the documents uses an implementation of a translator enabling to convert mathematical expressions recorded in MathML into dot records in Braille language. Such solution is also an opportunity to develop a uniform, coherent publishing system, independent of the recipient's equipment or skills and available to a visually impaired recipient as well. So a possibility arises to build e-learning providing the disabled with the same complex educational contents as to all the users and a system of technical documentation exchange within an enterprise employing blind people working on common projects with sighted people. The expansion of this approach is the implementation of mathematical notation verbalization in order to integrate with the existing formats of audio-books and document readers, and web pages.

The preparation of mathematical and technical documents available to the blind people is undoubtedly a difficult process, full of new challenges. Thousands of printed books are still waiting for conversion into electronic form. They include numerous works containing mathematical notation, so the need arises to develop new methods of machine translation of such documents structure. Unfortunately, the development of practically useful and efficient algorithms of automatic mathematical notation recognition in the form of graphics still represents a serious design challenge (Sroczyński, 2003), because it requires the implementation of advanced graph algorithms, including numerous heuristic rules and integration of various computer systems (Sroczynski, 2010). All the above reasons contribute to the fact that development of e-learning and telework systems in science and engineering design is still restricted and preparation of materials for the blind people is immensely work-consuming and costly.

Publishing documents containing complex mathematical notation on the Internet represents a significant challenge for the authors and requires additional training by the recipients. The standards developed so far, such as MathML based on XML not always can be fully implemented, mainly because of such implementation impediments (Stevens 1996).

Not all the documents, however, can be prepared for appropriate processing on the server, because it requires significant work loads and hiring specially trained people for the typesetting process. The gigantic base of books, math problem workbooks and memos is available in black print version only, so the automatic preparation of publishing such items is necessary. The issue applies to ordinary text to a much lesser extent, because the contemporarily available Optical Character Recognition (OCR) systems enable highly automated conversion of documents into electronic form, as described in a paper (Brzoza, et al. 2003) based on the example of online library available to the blind people. It means that didactic materials containing no mathematical notation or other technical notations may be published within e-learning systems much more efficiently, without detriment to their quality. Moreover, whatever the publication format, such documents can be easily browsed and cataloged. If such materials are made available to visually impaired people, it usually is possible with the use of standard image acquisition devices or screen-reader software. The modern written text conversion systems into speech, the natural literary language causes no problems, so automatic reading a book is done with correct intonation and punctuation even.

For technical language, however, particularly mathematical notation, the task becomes by far more complex. Implementation of efficient automatic acquisition methods, selection and recognition of the nature of mathematical expressions occurring in the text would allow for building systems providing:

- Easy pre-processing of existing documents available in printed form only for publishing them in electronic form within online libraries or e-learning systems, document flow systems,
- Possibility to process mathematical printed or hand-written documents in real time, e.g. In didactic systems, such as electronic board, conference systems,
- Possibility to catalog and search for information in mathematical and technical documents recorded in various formats, including web pages using graphic files for processing mathematical expressions and technical and engineering documentation,
- Possibility to publish documents containing mathematical notation in a manner legible to visually impaired recipients, i.e. in the form of Braille mathematical dialect, directly on the Internet, by means of appropriately prepared www server (Sroczyńska et al., 2006).

It is worth emphasizing that the question of recognizing mathematical expressions is not restricted to making technical and mathematical publications available to the bling people only. Some other applications can also be indicated, such as implementation of hand-written mathematical expressions in educational applications and mobile devices, making printed works available in e-learning, interactive didactic systems or processing the existing WWW sites containing mathematical notation recorded as graphic files for cataloging and information search, particularly information stored in internal resources of such organizations as universities or colleges, enterprises or offices.

DESIGNING HUMAN-COMPUTER INTERACTIONS IN E-LEARNING SYSTEMS

The expression of the „IT revolution" observed for some time is dissemination of mobile devices and dedicated mobile applications and specially prepared web sites and applications along with them (Kapczyński, 2015). Designers of this class of software consider the specific needs of the recipients, resulting from the use of relatively small touch-screens. As a touch-screen, small to classic computer monitor, is the basic input-output device in contemporary mobile devices, it determines the scale of active driving elements used, such as keys, links or lists (Sroczyński, 2017). They must be positioned maintaining appropriate spaces and sizes to make finger pointing unambiguous. Most of user commands are transmitted through the touch-screen and appropriate gestures made by one or more fingers. Although the so-called screen-keyboard is available, the text commands are restricted to the minimum necessary (Nielsen et al., 2013).

It is worth emphasizing that touch-screens, an example of the use of natural human-computer interaction tools, may be successfully used in tasks related to indication. Whereas, when it is necessary to manipulate with objects accurately, for example in advanced graphic programs or as part of typesetting complex text documents, the touch intermediation is often disappointing (Sikorski, 2010). Due to the required accuracy of indications, the touch-screens cause problems to elderly and physically disabled people and for blind and visually impaired people their use is a serious challenge or requires the implementation of additional supportive solutions (Kocielinski, 2013).

The mobile devices, contrary to most of classic office or even mobile computers, have a set of additional embedded input devices, such as cameras, accelerometers, GPS signal sensors, compasses and in flag models also fingerprint readers, barometers or thermometers. With such a wide range of additional input devices, the application designer may create new data input methods, for example, shaking the device to start a particular procedure.

However, the growing computing efficiency of popular and widely available mobile devices from the economic point of view causes that the methods using human speech analysis and synthesis to drive a computer application become realistic. All the popular mobile operating systems presently have the option of dictating text and automatic recognition of words spoken. This open a path to designing usable intermediation of applications based on voice commands, which has been used, without limitation, in experimental, "smart" Google Glass glasses, which, due to their size, are obviously devoid of a touchscreen (Suresh, Vishnu, Gayathri, 2018).

The above considerations enable the formulation of some general observations. Firstly, the modern computer applications are designed with consideration to anticipated aspects of human-machine interaction. Secondly, however, designing of those interactions must consider the specific nature of popular mobile devices.

The subjective user's assessment of the usability of a specific solution is composed of numerous factors, regarded in the scope of human-computer interaction. The basic attributes describing the application's usability have been identified in a classic paper (Nielsen, 1994):

- **Efficiency**: Easy target reaching,
- **Satisfaction**: The lack of discomfort, positive attitude to the product,
- **Learnability**: Easy learning of rules of operation in order to start work promptly
- **Memorability**: Easy returning to work with the system after a break,
- **Faultlessness**: Restriction of the number of errors made and ability to resume operation after a failure.

Measuring the efficiency that in numerous situations can be expressed as time necessary for performance of a specific task is the easiest way. The other attributes are by far more abstract and, out of them, the largest load of subjective emotions is surely brought by the user's satisfaction. However, it is the satisfaction that decides on the success and dissemination of specific products. The significance of all the attributes mentioned above is the foundation for a correct design of usable intermediation of e-learning systems. The interaction built in this way must consider industry standards, assumptions made by the graphic designer and some social patterns, such as the commonly used symbolism (Sroczynski, 2014b).

An example of an industry standard, describing in a formal and detailed way all the aspects of correct application intermediation (called application interface) is „iOS Human Interface Guidelines" developed by Apple. Placing a mobile application in App Store requires obtaining a positive opinion in the review system composed of automatic tests and assessment made by an expert – corporation employee.

A thorough verification of the disseminated applications obviously is to provide safety to the users, because it allows for rejection of malware (viruses, Trojan horses, etc.), and simply underdeveloped, bringing about the risk of loss of data or other digital hazards. Such attitude introduces significant changes in comparison to software distribution systems for desktop computers dominated by wholesale distribution of "box" licenses or licenses customized to the recipient's needs directly by the manufacturer.

Similar sets of recommendations are also published by other manufacturers of mobile devices. Very detailed standards for the Android platform were developed at Google as "material design". Microsoft along with the premiere of Windows 10, promotes the "Universal Windows Platform (UWP)" representing without limitation the specification of standard human-computer intermediation for applications operating within the Windows ecosystem.

All the measures are to build a set of user-friendly applications, easily operated and inconsequence satisfying and useful (the economic factor obviously plays a significant role, because the store operators charge a commission on selling the applications via their infrastructure). Certain asymmetry in the operation of stores with applications from various manufacturers: the two largest companies, i.e. Apple and Google occupy almost the whole market of mobile applications, however, although the number of Google Play store users is the largest, the revenues generated by iOS App Store from Apple by far outstrip the competitors (Sroczyński, 2017). It is clear that the users of the said platforms differ by their preferences and wealth.

Mobile applications are by far a novel quality in the field of computer system designing, which forces their authors to intense redesign of the existing solutions so that they can meet the users' expectations. The characteristics of mobile devices define a significant set of such requirements, which may include (Żukowska et al., 2014):

- The use of small screens of various sizes and proportions,
- Touch gesture operation with the lack of physical keyboard and restricted use of the onscreen keyboard,
- Including large control elements ("too big finger" issue, covering the application use area),
- Division into forms always occupying the entire screen (activities, views),
- The use of cameras and sensors (accelerometer, compass, gps) as standard input devices,
- Restricted multitasking resulting from the tendency to maximize the efficiency with simultaneous saving of energy taken from the device battery and difficulty in presentation of multiple processes at the same time.

Consequently, the general indication concerning the human-computer interactions design for mobile devices is the implementation of similar functionality on various platforms and identical graphic motives, maintaining at the same time usable standards characteristic for a specific mobile operating system. For visually impaired people the interaction design, however, requires a lot more elaborated measures, going far beyond the common adaptation to the standards. Furthermore, the e-learning systems used in science and technology education force the use of advanced conversion procedures, considering the context of the message, knowledge category and frequently even the local mathematical notation dialect.

Conversion Into Braille Dot Writing: Implementation Details

The mathematical visual notation is most frequently recorded with the use of one of the so-called equation/formula editors and their subsequent exporting to binary formats, e.g. MathML or LaTeX, or it is directly created in the popular LaTeX format. The conversion of documents prepared this way into dot writing, however, is not a trivial task and in practical implementation requires definition of numerous additional assumptions, considering in particular the complexity of a formula fragments, which decides on the rules of the mathematical Braille language applied.

The advantage of automatic document conversion into the dot language is surely the option to resign from the assistance of a person fluently using such language, i.e. the expansion of the circle of teachers able to participate in the didactic process of a visually impaired person.

The materials converted into Braille language can be used in individual studying, so potentially they well fit in the e-learning systems requirements. However the technical devices used to present such documents have some disadvantages, significant, from the e-learning point of view. The most important one is the restriction of the number of symbols shown occurring in case of using Braille rulers (monitors). 40 up to 80 characters offered by the very expensive devices available on the market is by far too little to picture even medium sized mathematical expression without rewinding. Braille printers printing convex symbols on paper sheets are inconvenient and difficult to transport, while their cost exceeds what an individual user can afford. Therefore, they rather cannot be used in e-learning, because their use would force the pupil to give up individual learning and reduce the e-learning system to a form of support of stationary education at a didactic centre appropriately equipped.

Braille mathematical language is of linear nature and therefore, recording the expressions commonly appearing in mathematics, using spatial distribution of symbols, encounters some difficulties. In some cases, however, Braille record may also be done in a way corresponding to the black print appearance. For example this is the case of common fractions with the denominator usually written on a so-called lowered level, which reflects the visual nature of the mathematical record.

The Braille alphabet is restricted to 64 characters, therefore the necessity appears to use the same symbols combined with special characters to encode various characters. Thus, the meaning of Braille mathematical record strongly depends on the context.

The paper (Sroczyński, 2014a) presents a prototype of automatic translator of mathematical notation into Braille language made as a data exporting module from "Equation wizard" application developed for MS Windows operating system. The system built in such a way offers an option to construct human-computer interactions through publishing of documents in various types of media ("Equation wizard" operates on structural formats, such as LaTeX and MathML as well as graphic, e.g. PNG), which are simultaneously legible to visually impaired people, assuring a high level of support during translation and preparation of the didactic materials.

At present the translator, significantly expanded in comparison to the prototype, enables to develop and convert into Braille notation, compliant with the current Polish standards implemented in 2011, expressions containing:

Figure 1. A document containing a mathematical notation while being edited in "Equation wizard" application with Polish GUI mode: "Edytor wzorów" (top), visualization of printout from a Braille printer (bottom: simulation by means of Braille fonts)

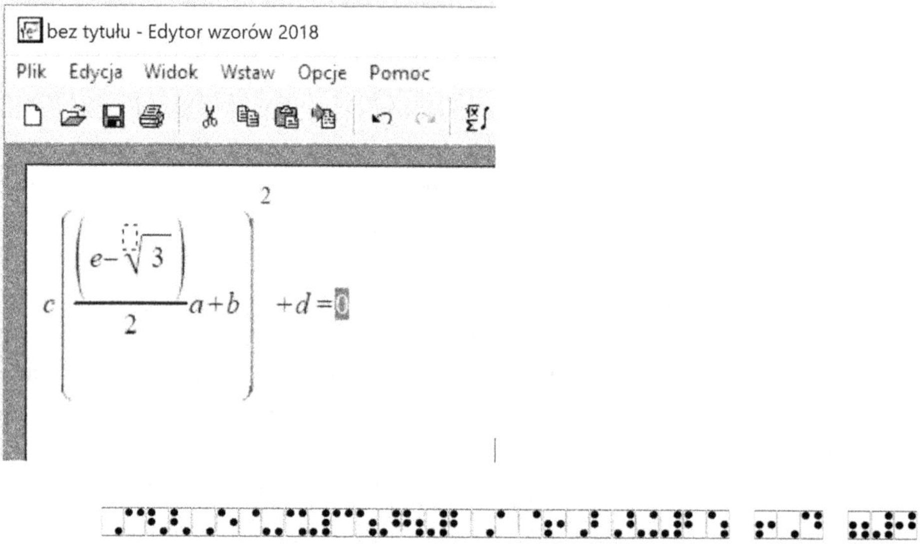

- Capital and lower case letters, variables and identifiers, lower case and capital letter characters,
- Integers and floating point numbers, numeric character
- Basic arithmetic and relational operators, equations,
- Brackets, distinguishing their type,
- Fractions noted with the use of continuity mark,
- Simple expressions with subscript,
- Simple expressions with integral power,
- Square roots,
- Roots with integer coefficient,
- Simple equations with summation,
- Definite and indefinite integrals.

A sample translation result is presented in Figure 1.

The translator module in some cases exports embedded formulas with the use of bracket notation, which is permitted by the standard, but in the future it may be replaced by equivalent more concise notation with the use of level characters. Such context approach was actually implemented in the verbalization module, available in the same typesetting system.

Verbalization of Mathematical Notation

An alternative potential method of providing information contained in the didactic materials is their acoustic version. The conversion of mathematical notation into speech (in other words verbalization, math-to-speech) would enable avoidance of some issues characteristic for the use of Braille. In the easiest cases there is even no need to implement any additional principles to the conventions customarily used. Mathematical expressions, physical or chemical formulas are read during didactic activities, after all. Moreover, the teacher often dictates the pupil a problem to be noted and solved on the board during traditional classes. We must remember that a visually impaired person has no opportunity to interact with partial graphic notation of a formula discussed verbally, thus, while preparing the verbal notation to them we must particularly ensure that any ambiguities are avoided. For example an overt definition of beginning and end of fraction and the fractional hyphen or marking the beginning and end of the numerator and denominator are used.

Notably, the use of text-to-speech (TTS) techniques also permits for resignation form the costly equipment through the use of standards sound options offered by computers, laptops, tablets or even smartphones. All the devices enable browsing through websites that can be presented in sound version and thus made available to the visually impaired people, and in the case of mobile devices, some dedicated applications may also be developed. Whether such sound version will be carried out by arduous manual conversion of subsequent expressions into their verbal representation, or rather the sound version will be the effect o automatic conversion, is in turn the factor conditioning the promptness and adequacy of the didactic materials properly prepared to the needs of blind people.

The correct structure of human-computer interaction as part of automation of conversion of complex mathematical notation into its verbal version depends on consideration to numerous customary standards and personal habits of the authors. Similarly to the graphic record of mathematical notation, the verbal version often differs from country to country or language, particularly from a research centre even. In other words, several soft criteria are related to it, often used by the author's intuition. Thus, verbal mathematical notation may be defined as natural language, i.e. not formally determined and based on traditional rules, frequently creating numerous dialects. These varieties, differing by pronunciation principles on the one hand and interpretation of some expressions, on the other, cause that correct and efficient understanding of dictated mathematical notation requires intense exercise and practice as a minimum. Detailed analyses of data on spaces between the symbols verbalized by people reading the formulas loud indicate the potential possibilities of statistical distinction between expression sounding similarly, but differing semantically (Wigmore et al. 2009). On the other hand, however, such parameters of verbal expression strongly depend on a particular author, their physical condition, experience and habits.

Therefore, in spite of the existing implementations of such solutions for English – for example in MathPlayer plugin from Design Science, matching of the algorithms used is immensely important – generally defined as math-to-speech – to the specific nature of native languages (for example, Polish with implementation details presented further in this chapter). Notably, however, the English version even is not free from imperfections related to operation of brackets, superscripts and subscripts, and complex component made from fractions (Design Science, 2018). The complete publishing process in Greek, encoded by means of DAISY format supplemented with verbalization of mathematical expressions, developed with the use of MathType commercial software, was presented in the papers (Brzoza, 2008) and (Riga, 2016). An important achievement of the latter project („DAISY Digital Talking Math Books") is the analysis of error made by the recipients, carried out on relatively numerous sample documents by sighted users. Unfortunately, as mentioned before, the involvement of blind people in such tests, particularly carried out on university course level, is really impeded, due to the restricted logistic capacities provided for such experiments.

Whatever the native language to ultimately express a specific mathematical expression, it should be encoded in a certain structural format. For this purpose a notation considering the appearance of the formula may only be used or, alternatively, a notation taking into the consideration the semantics of the expression processed. The most popular system of typesetting mathematical documents – LaTeX, principally enables to describe the graphic arrangement of an expression only, in addition it provides the possibility to achieve similar visual effects by various methods (through the use of different commands and their sequence). Direct verbalization of LaTeX notation, although meeting the necessary linearity condition, would be at least partially difficult to understand by the listener without contextualization. It refers to the simplest expressions even containing symbols, Greek letters or fractions, in which the analysis of the whole expression is necessary in order to supplement the missing information on the meaning of the verbalized formula.

The more recent MathML, designed on the basis of XML and used for processing of mathematical formulas in web environment, two layers have been projected: the presentation layer used for visualization only and structural layer used for the interpretation of the meaning of a mathematical notation. The use of the structural layer enables the correct definition, for example, of the numbers in superscript and subscript of the symbols, particularly, if such symbols represent names of functions. The certainty about the range of functions, encoded in LaTeX, do not have to be in brackets, is obtained in a similar way. Unfortunately, the direct export to the structural layer of MathML is only possible from typical algebraic and mathematical programs, while the vast majority of formulas are set in formula editors using the presentation layer or a LaTeX code only. The presentation layer also is more popular in the online publications presently available.

Similarly to LaTeX, MathML cannot be read directly either, both in the presentation and structural layer, as it contains long tag names, surrounding the basic symbols of arithmetic operations. The length of transcription in this language largely exceeds the expressions commonly used in didactics of general science.

Basing on the above consideration, in order to voice read a mathematical formula correctly, such formula recorded in one of the structural languages (LaTeX, MathML, formats of popular programs supporting computation, such as Mathematica) should be transformed into a hierarchical form, tree data structure, corresponding to the structure of a mathematical expression, Within the next step it is possible to estimate certain characteristics of subsequent fragments of the transformed expression, such as the complexity defined by the number of characters and other symbols, distinction between alphabetic characters and digits, etc. Afterwards, according to the rules of reading mathematical expressions, so including the operation sequence, brackets and expression embedding, using the recurrence top-bottom approach – the further sub-expressions should be converted into text, traversing the structural tree of a mathematical expression. The last stage is the possible activation of a text-to-speech available in the operating system or fitting the verbalized expression in an online document or other didactic materials prepared within the e-learning system.

The existing e-learning systems, such as the 4Math platform (Brzoza et al., 2012) the sets of interactive exercises are saved, transformed and visualized by means of dedicated proprietary translators of domain languages (in this case the superset of LaTeX language). The supplementation of information, in turn, used by the readers applied by visually impaired people is part of manual translation made by the authors of specific problems (Maćkowski et al., 2017). Obviously, the base of problems adapted to the needs of blind people is restricted in comparison to all the didactic materials.

In this point it is notable that the possibly detailed definition of mathematical formula presentation rules facilitates the performance of a reverse task, i.e. the recognition of a mathematical expression structure spoken loud (Fateman, 2004). Dictating mathematical formulas including their entire potential complexity and richness of notations would enable a fluent interaction between the visually impaired people and the machine. The formula spoken through the automatic converted transforming structural formats can be modified, transformed by a blind person by means of verbal commands and its new fragments may be interpreted in virtue of recognition of definitions also provided in sound form by the disabled user. The comparison of efficiency for this class system called TalkMaths (Attanayake, 2015) indicates that this mode of mathematical expression edition may give results of comparable quality (both in terms of implementation time and notation correctness) to standard visual editors, such as the popular MathType.

The efficient recognition of single words and sentences is in the field of well evidenced and implemented solutions in commercial application and even in the popular Windows family operating systems (Baker et al., 2009). Therefore the principal challenge is the proper interpretation of the semantics of the message provided, demanding definition of rules, assumptions and restrictions of the language used, like in case of automatic analysis of mathematical expressions recorded in a graphic form (Sroczyński, 2012). Thus, putting the natural language of mathematical notation in formal frames, the bilateral human-computer communication facilitating the e-learning system operation can be assured to the visually impaired people.

The way of speaking mathematical expressions and their dictation for machine recognition is often deliberately modified in comparison to standard, everyday pronunciation sued by mathematicians in education. To reduce the extent of errors while recognizing single letter, the spelling similar to the one used in the military sector (Fateman, 2013), moreover, the additional conventions used in order to obtain a compact and at the same time clear and unambiguous form are applied.

As a result, the literature sources contain examples in which the simplest formulas, such as the sample expression in Figure 2, are recorded by totally different methods.

For the native language, the specific nature and national conventions typical for the given country should be additionally taken into the consideration. Such requirements after all build the common communication platform for disabled people and other pupils: the formulas spoken are understandable to everyone and do not require the teachers to learn any new notation.

Figure 2. Sample mathematical expression in standard 2D graphic notation (top), verbalized version according to (Elliot et al., 2007) (center), verbalized version according to (Fateman, 2013) (bottom)

$$\frac{-b+\sqrt{b^2-4ac}}{2a}$$

„fraction minus bravo plus or minus square root bravo squared minus four alpha charlie down two alpha"

„the quantity minus b plus or minus the square-root of the quantity b squared minus 4 a c end all over the quantity 2 a end"

The detailed analysis of verbalization principles for mathematical notation was carried out as part of „PlatMat" educational platform, for which the Polish language rules have been determined on a secondary school level. The translation uses the context enabling distinction of sub-expressions of identical position, but different meaning. The input format used for this system is MathML (Salamonczyk, 2015). Similar approach for the same input language was earlier verbalized for books.

The possible issues resulting from ambiguity of linear record devoid of supplementation with additional definitions of sub-expression endings were presented in the paper (Ferreira et al., 2004). The risk ob misinterpretation of the sub-expression range is usually neglected for 2D graphic presentation of mathematical notation, however, in case of dictating expressions of medium length even, the number of such errors grows significantly and their restriction is among the greatest challenges of verbalization.

As part of the tests carried out an automatic translator of mathematical expressions was implemented for the "Equation wizard" editor, used in the experiments discussed earlier with export to Braille language. For mathematical formula transformation sets of contextual rules was used, considering, without limitation, the complexity of sub-expressions. The translator performs the concept of math-to-speech in Polish and English for formulas containing elementary arithmetic operations, fractions, roots, superscripts (powers), subscripts, integrals, brackets, summations, products and limits (Bier et al., 2015). The full mode is available, assuring unambiguity of verbal record and simplified mode, consisting in implementation of heuristic rules, optimizing the verbalization by shortening the resulting record. The evaluation of the verbal descriptions generated proved that the solution developed was practically useful and conforming with the common conventions in the environment of academic teachers. The expansion of the translator by further mathematical notation elements will allow for its application to the education of disabled people as part of elementary courses of analysis and algebra within engineering studies.

The engine used in the test and performing the human-computer interaction for presentation and transformation of mathematical formulas (cf. Figure 3), was supplemented with the option of importing data from LaTeX, which enabled loading the most popular mathematical notation. The internal structure of data is performed via extended tree of objects, which facilitates the adaptation of new methods of transformation, conversion and publication of formulas. Adding the option of formula description in a verbal manner is a good way to supplement the existing option of data exporting to mathematical Braille dialect.

Figure 3. Graphic user interface of verbalization module of mathematical formulas in the "Equation wizard" editor

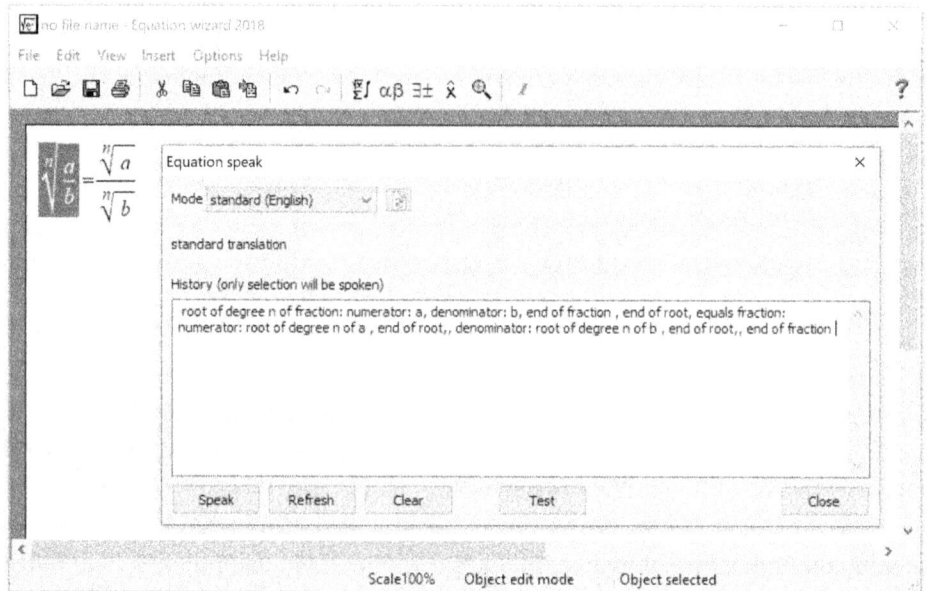

SUMMARY

This chapter presents an overview of questions related to publishing documents within e-learning systems with particular consideration to the materials containing complex mathematical notation, adapted to the needs of visually disabled people. The disadvantages and advantages of the available conversion methods have been presented, part of which still being at the experimental stage. Descriptions of various implementations have been offered concerning standard descriptive languages, such as MathML and LaTeX, in the mathematical Braille language and verbal description to be expressed by computer system by appropriate speech synthesizer. The human-computer interaction tools designed in this way, supporting the process of mathematical expressions translation may become the foundation for further research, concerning in particular the unwritten standards of expressing mathematics and expanding the syntactic potentials by further structures used in mathematical notation. Due to the relatively low number of disabled students in tertiary education system, the subsequent stages of implementation of the said systems require the coordination of numerous entities involved in various fields, from health services, through the sector of education and up to the businesses and scientific research institutions of the IT sector.

The detailed analysis of the opportunities offered by the described tools leads to a conclusion that they may represent a mutual supplementation. Depending on the situation, needs and capabilities of the user, in some application Braille dot writing may become more effective, while in other situation the direct speech analysis as the source of input data may appear immensely productive for interactions operating on mathematical notation.

At present, in the world full of very fast civilization progress, with the rapid life, environment, richness of changes and news, e-learning appears as the valuable answer to the challenges posed to enterprises and individuals. The education institutions and many other organizations will be forced to implement and use this kind of education in the near future. Global Internet, network databases and search engines, remote multimedia systems are becoming the most popular source of information and knowledge, especially for the handicapped people. They are able to achieve better education and fight unemployment problems thanks to main advantages of e-learning: a freedom of choice of time and frequency of the lectures, independence from the physical classroom, the availability of well-prepared multimodal educational content and individual partnership between students and their mentors during the learning process. E-learning will also give one more advantage to students educated in this way–they will be well prepared to compete in the future world of e-work.

REFERENCES

Ahmad, N., Tasir, Z., Kasim, J., & Sahat, H. (2013). Automatic detection of learning styles in learning management systems by using literature-based method. *Procedia: Social and Behavioral Sciences, 103*, 181–189. doi:10.1016/j.sbspro.2013.10.324

Atman, N., & Inceoğlu, M. M. (2009). Learning styles diagnosis based on learner behaviors in web based learning. In Computational Science and Its Applications–ICCSA 2009. Springer. doi:10.1007/978-3-642-02457-3_73

Attanayake, D., Denholm-Price, J., Hunter, G., Pfluegel, E., & Wigmore, A. (2015). Speech interfaces for mathematics: opportunities and limitations for visually impaired learners. *IMA International Conference on Barriers and Enablers to Learning Maths: Enhancing Learning and Teaching for All Learners.*

Baker, J.M., Deng, L., Glass, J., Khudanpur, S., Lee, C., Morgan, N., O'Shaughnessy D. (2009). Research Developments and Directions in Speech Recognition and Understanding, Part 1. *IEEE Signal Processing Magazine, 75.*

Baumann-Birkbeck, L., Karaksha, A., Anoopkumar-Dukie, S., Grant, G., Davey, A., Nirthanan, S., & Owen, S. (2015). Benefits of e-learning in chemotherapy pharmacology education. *Curr Pharm Teach Learn., 7*(1), 106–111. doi:10.1016/j.cptl.2014.09.014

Bier, A., & Sroczyński, Z. (2015, June). Adaptive math-to-speech interface. In *Proceedings of the Mulitimedia, Interaction, Design and Innovation* (p. 7). ACM. 10.1145/2814464.2814471

Brzoza, P. (2008, July). Multimedia MathReader for Daisy Books. In *International Conference on Computers for Handicapped Persons* (pp. 875-878). Springer.

Brzoza, P., Lobos, E., Macura, J., Sikora, B., & Zabka, M. (2012). ForMath-Intelligent Tutoring System in Mathematics. CSEDU, (1), 118-122.

Brzoza, P., & Skurowski, P. (2003). Biblioteka internetowa dostępna dla osób niewidomych. [Online Library available to the blind people]. Studia Informatica, 24(3).

Cimmaruta, Ch., Liguori, L., Monticelli, M., Andreotti, G., & Citro, V. (2017, October). E-Learning for Rare Diseases: An Example Using Fabry Disease. *International Journal of Molecular Sciences, 18*(10), 1–15. doi:10.3390/ijms18102049 PMID:28946642

Costagliola, G., De Lucia, A., Ferrucci, F., Gravino, C., & Scanniello, G. (2008, December). Assessing the usability of a visual tool for the definition of e-learning processes. *Journal of Visual Languages and Computing*, *19*(6), 721–737. doi:10.1016/j.jvlc.2008.01.003

Cuartero-Olivera, J., Hunter, G., & Pérez-Navarro, A. (2012). Reading and writing mathematical notation in e-learning environments. *eLearn Center Research Paper Series*, (4).

Dana, I. S., & Darmawan, N. (2017). The Study of User Acceptance toward E-Learning System in Higher Education. *Indonesian Journal of Electrical Engineering and Computer Science*, *7*, 514–523.

Debande, O., & Ottersten, E. K. (2004). Information and Communication Technologies: A Tool Empowering and Developing the Horizon of the Learner. *Higher Education Management and Policy*, *16*(2), 31–61. doi:10.1787/hemp-v16-art15-en

Design Science (2018). *MathPlayer Can Speak!* Retrieved from http://www.dessci.com/en/products/mathplayer/tech/accessibility.htm

Duxbury. (2004). Retrieved from http://www.duxburysystems.com/

Edwards, A. (1998). *Access to Mathematics for blind people: The Maths Project, CTI Mathematics*. The University of Birmingham.

Edwards, A. D. N., McCartney, H., & Fogarolo, F. (2006). Lambda: A multimodal approach to making mathematics accessible to blind students. *Proceedings of the 8th international ACM SIGACCESS Conference on Computers and Accessibility*, 48–54.

Elliott, C., & Bilmes, J. (2007). Computer Based Mathematics Using Continuous Speech Recognition. In Striking a Chord: Vocal Interaction in Assistive Technologies, Games, and More: CHI 2007 workshop on non-verbal acoustic interaction. San Jose, CA: ACM.

Fateman, R. (2004). Handwriting + Speech for Computer Entry of Mathematics. Work in progress NSF grant CCR-9901933, Computer Science Division, EECS Department, University of California at Berkeley.

Fateman, R. (2013). *How can we speak math?* (Unpublished). Computer Science Division, EECS Department, University of California at Berkeley.

Fedorowicz-Kruszewska, M. (2015). Biblioteczne zasoby cyfrowe jako niezbędny element współczesnego środowiska edukacyjnego studentów z niepełnosprawnością wzroku. *E-mentor*, *3*, 48–53. doi:10.15219/em60.1186

Ferreira, H., & Freitas, D. (2004, July). Enhancing the accessibility of mathematics for blind people: The AudioMath project. In *International Conference on Computers for Handicapped Persons* (pp. 678-685). Springer. 10.1007/978-3-540-27817-7_101

Gardner, J. A., Stewart, R., Francioni, J., & Smith, A. (2002). *Tiger, AGC, and Win-Triangle, removing the barrier to sem education*. Center On Disabilities Technology And Persons With Disabilities Conference 2002, California State University.

Islam, N., Beer, M., & Slack, F. (2015). E-Learning Challenges Faced by Academics in Higher Education: A Literature Review. *Journal of Education and Training Studies*, *3*(5), 102–112. doi:10.11114/jets.v3i5.947

Kalbarczyk, M. (2002). Translator - przekształcanie tekstu na system punktowy Braille'a. Translator – transformation of text into Braille dot system. Informatyka w Szkole XVIII, Toruń 2002.

Kapczyński, A. (2015). Inżynierowie zarządzania w świecie pełnym cyfrowych możliwości. Engineers of Management in the world full of digital opportunities. Zeszyty Naukowe Politechniki Śląskiej Seria Zarządzanie z. 80/Nr kol. 1933, Gliwice 2015.

Karshmer, A.I., & Bledsoe, C. (2002). *Access to Mathematics by Blind Students, Books and electronic school bags for inclusive education of young visually impaired people*. BrailleNet 2002.

Karshmer, A.I., Gupta, G., Geiger, S., & Weaver, C. (1999). The MAVIS Project. *Journal of Behavior and Information Technology, 18*(1).

Kauba, K. (Ed.). (2011). Brajlowska notacja matematyczna, fizyczna, chemiczna. Braille mathematical, physical, chemical notation, wydanie II, Kraków, Laski, Łódź 2011.

Kocielinski, D., & Brzostek-Pawlowska, J. (2013, September). Improving the accessibility of touchscreen-based mobile devices: Integrating Android-based devices and Braille notetakers. In *Computer Science and Information Systems (FedCSIS), 2013 Federated Conference on* (pp. 655-658). IEEE.

Maćkowski, M., Brzoza, P., Żabka, M., & Spinczyk, D. (2017). Multimedia platform for mathematics' interactive learning accessible to blind people. *Multimedia Tools and Applications, 77*(5), 6191–6208. doi:10.100711042-017-4526-z

MATHS. (2003). *Mathematical Access for Technology and Science for Visually Disabled People*. Retrieved from http://www.cs.york.ac.uk/maths/

McClellan, N. (2003). *Speech Recognition + Mathematics = OPPORTUNITY!* Center On Disabilities Technology And Persons With Disabilities Conference 2003, California State University.

Miesenberger, K., Klaus, J., & Zagler, W. L. (Eds.). (2002). Computers Helping People with Special Needs. *8th International Conference, ICCHP 2002, Linz, Austria, Proceedings.*

Nielsen, J. (1994). *Usability engineering*. Elsevier.

Nielsen, J., & Budiu, R. (2013). *Mobile usability*. MITP-Verlags GmbH & Co. KG.

Olson, J., Codde, J., & DeMaagd, K. (2011). An Analysis of e-Learning Impacts & Best Practices in Developing Countries. Michigan State Univ.

Osterhaus, S. (2004). *Texas School for the Blind and Visually Impaired*. Retrieved from http://www.tsbvi.edu/math/

Patel, P.B., Patel, T., Saurabh, M.K., & Thakkar, S. (2018). Perceptions and Effectiveness of Use of E-Learning in Pharmacology Education. *Journal of Clinical & Diagnostic Research, 12*(7), 12-16.

Piasecki, A. (2014). Wykorzystanie technologii komunikacyjnych przez osoby z dysfunkcjami narządów wzroku i słuchu. *The Use of communication technologies by people with sight and hearing organ dysfunctions. Studia Ekonomiczne, 199*, 240–248.

Rajper, S., & Shaikh, A. W. (2016, June). Personalized e-learning systems: A user modeling technique. *Pakistan Journal of Science, 68*(2), 239–243.

Riga, P., Kouroupetroglou, G., & Ioannidou, P. P. (2016, July). An Evaluation Methodology of Math-to-Speech in Non-English DAISY Digital Talking Books. In *International Conference on Computers Helping People with Special Needs* (pp. 27-34). Springer. 10.1007/978-3-319-41264-1_4

Rotard, M., Bosse, K., Schweikhardt, W., & Ertl, T. (2003). Access to Mathematical Expressions in MathML for the Blind. In Universal Access in HCI (vol. 4, pp. 1325-1329). Lawrence Erlbaum Associates.

Rubin, M., Faderewski, M., & Mikułowski, D. (2015). Badania stanu i potrzeb informatyzacji edukacji matematycznej uczniów niewidomych i słabowidzących w Polsce. Testing the condition and needs of computerization of mathematical education for the blind and visually impaired pupils in Poland. *E-mentor, 1*(58), 34-40.

Sadikin, M., & Purwanto, S. K. (2018, June). The Implementation of E-learning System Governance to Deal With User Need, Institution Objective, and Regulation Compliance. *Telkomnika.*, *16*(3), 1332–1344. doi:10.12928/telkomnika.v16i3.8699

Salamonczyk, A., & Brzostek-Pawlowska, J. (2015, June). Translation of MathML formulas to Polish text, example applications in teaching the blind. In *Cybernetics (CYBCONF), 2015 IEEE 2nd International Conference on* (pp. 240-244). IEEE. 10.1109/CYBConf.2015.7175939

Sandars, J., & Langlois, M. (2005, March). E-learning and the educator in primary care: Responding to the challenge. *Education for Primary Care, 16*(2), 129–133.

Sikorski, M. (2010). Interakcja człowiek-komputer [Wydawnictwo Polsko-Japońska Wyższa Szkoła Technik Komputerowych.]. *Human-Computer Interaction*, 1–345.

Sroczyńska, A., & Sroczyński, Z. (2006). Telepraca i zdalna edukacja osób niepełnosprawnych wzrokowo [Telework and e-learning of visually impaired and blind people]. *Zeszyty Naukowe. Organizacja i Zarządzanie/Politechnika Śląska*, 183-192.

Sroczyński, Z. (2000). MathML – język opisu wyrażeń matematycznych w dokumentach internetowych [MathML – language of description of mathematical expressions in online documents]. *Studia Informatica, 21*(41), 125-145.

Sroczyński, Z. (2002). Serwer WWW jako serwer dokumentów zawierających złożoną notację matematyczną [WWW server as server of documents containing complex mathematical notation]. *Studia Informatica, 23*(49), 103-111.

Sroczyński, Z. (2003). Prezentacja dokumentów internetowych zawierających złożoną notację matematyczną dla potrzeb osób niewidomych [Presentation of online documents containing complex mathematical notation for blind people]. *Studia Informatica, 24*(55), 179-187.

Sroczynski, Z. (2010). Priority levels and heuristic rules in the structural recognition of mathematical formulae. *Theoretical and Applied Informatics*, *22*(4), 273. doi:10.2478/v10179-010-0014-0

Sroczyński, Z. (2012). Analiza struktury złożonych wyrażeń matematycznych dla potrzeb prezentacji dokumentów w Internecie [The analysis of the structure of complex mathematical expressions for the purposes of online presentation]. Zastosowania Internetu, Dąbrowa Górnicza.

Sroczyński, Z. (2014a). Interakcja człowiek-komputer w systemach e-learningu dostępnych dla osób niepełnosprawnych wzrokowo [The human-computer interaction in e-learning systems available to the visually handicapped people]. *The Role of Informatics in Economic and Social Sciences. Innovations and Interdisciplinary Implications, 39.*

Sroczynski, Z. (2014b). Human-computer interaction on mobile devices with the FM application platform. Internet in the Information Society. In *Insights on the Information Systems, Structures and Applications*. Academy of Business in Dabrowa Gornicza Press.

Sroczyński, Z. (2017). Jakość interakcji człowiek-komputer czynnikiem decydującym o popularności aplikacji mobilnych. *The quality of human-computer interactions as a factor deciding on the popularity of mobile applications. Studia Ekonomiczne, 317*, 106–117.

Stevens, R. D. (1996). *Principles for the Design of Auditory Interfaces to Present Complex Information to Blind People*. Praca doktorska. The University of York, Department of Computer Science.

Suresh, M., Vishnu, P., & Gayathri, R. (2018, September). Effect of e-learning on academic performance of undergraduate students. *Drug Invention Today.*, *10*(9), 1797–1800.

Świerczek, J. (Ed.). (2002). Brajlowska notacja matematyczna, fizyczna, chemiczna. Braille mathematical, physical, chemical notation.

Texthelp. (2018). Retrieved from https://www.texthelp.com/en-us/products/equatio/

Truong, H. M. (2016). Integrating learning styles and adaptive e-learning system: Current developments, problems and opportunities. *Computers in Human Behavior, 55*, 1185-1193.

Wigmore, A. M., Hunter, G. J. A., Pfluegel, E., & Denholm-Price, J. C. W. (2009). *TalkMaths: A speech user interface for dictating mathematical expressions into electronic documents.* In *2nd ISCA Workshop of Speech and Language Technology in Education (SLaTE 2009)*, Wroxall, UK.

Yang, T. C., & Hwang, G. J. (2013). Development of an adaptive learning system with multiple perspectives based on students' learning styles and cognitive styles. *Journal of Educational Technology & Society*, *16*(4), 185.

Żukowska, J. (2004). E-learning jako skuteczne narzędzie e-business wykorzystywane w przedsiębiorstwie dążącym do sukcesu [E-learning as an effective e-business tool used in a success oriented enterprise]. *Konferencja Instrumenty i formy organizacyjne procesów zarządzania w społeczeństwie informacyjnym.*

Żukowska, J., & Sroczyński, Z. (2014). Internetowe aplikacje mobilne narzędziem budowania przewagi konkurencyjnej przedsiębiorstw [Online mobile application as a tool in building the competitive advantage of enterprises]. In *Internet w społeczeństwie informacyjnym. Nowoczesne systemy informatyczne i ich bezpieczeństwo* [The Internet in information society. Modern IT systems and their safety]. Wydawnictwo Wyższej Szkoły Biznesu w Dąbrowie Górniczej, Dąbrowa Górnicza.

Compilation of References

Abedalaziz, N., Jamaluddin, S., & Leng, C. H. (2013). Measuring attitudes toward computer and internet usage among postgraduate students in Malaysia. *TOJET: The Turkish Online Journal of Educational Technology*, *12*(2), 200–216.

Abedalaziz, N., & Muaidi, H. (2012). Attitudes towards Internet-Based Distance Education Among Academic Staff of Malaysian Universities. *OIDA International Journal of Sustainable Development*, *5*(1), 81–90.

Abt, C. C. (1987). *Serious Games*. University Press of America.

Acquatella, F. (2017). MOOC as an organizational learning process. *Question(s) de management,* (2), 21-34.

Agamben, G. (2006). *Qu'est ce qu'un dispositif? (Payot & Rivages)*. Paris: Editions Payot & Rivages.

Ahmad, N., Tasir, Z., Kasim, J., & Sahat, H. (2013). Automatic detection of learning styles in learning management systems by using literature-based method. *Procedia: Social and Behavioral Sciences*, *103*, 181–189. doi:10.1016/j.sbspro.2013.10.324

Ajjan, H., & Hartshorne, R. (2008). Investigating faculty decisions to adopt Web 2.0 technologies: Theory and empirical tests. *The Internet and Higher Education*, *11*(2), 71–80. doi:10.1016/j.iheduc.2008.05.002

Akrich, M., Callon, M., & Latour, B. (2006). *Sociologie de la traduction: textes fondateurs*. Paris, France: Presses de l'École des Mines.

Al Mahmud, A. (2011). Students' Attitudes towards Internet: A study on Private Universities of Bangladesh. *European Journal of Business and Management*, *3*(6), 9–19.

Al Otaibi, K. N. (2012). Attitudes towards the use of the internet. *Psychological Research, 2*(3), 151–159.

Albion, P. R. (2008). Web 2.0 in Teacher Education: Two Imperatives for Action. *Computers in the Schools, 24*(3-4), 181–198. doi:10.1080/07380560802368173

Aleem, S., Capretz, L. F., & Ahmed, F. (2016). Game development software engineering process life cycle: A systematic review. *Journal of Software Engineering Research and Development, 4*(6), 1–30.

Alemi, M., & Tavakoli, E. (2016). Audio lingual method. *3rd International Conference on Applied Research in Language Studies*, Tehran, Iran.

Alexander, B. (2006). A new way of innovation for teaching and learning. *EDUCAUSE Review, 41*(2), 32–44.

Alfadly, A. A. (2013). The efficiency of the "Learning Management System (LMS)" in AOU, Kuwait, as a communication tool in an E-learning system. *International Journal of Educational Management, 27*(2), 157–169. doi:10.1108/09513541311297577

Ali, Z. S. (2014). Pakistani Students' Perceptions about Use of the Internet in their Academic Activities. *E-Learning and Digital Media, 11*(3), 222–230. doi:10.2304/elea.2014.11.3.222

Almarabeh, T., Majdalawi, Y. Kh., & Mohammad, H. (2016). Internet Usage, Challenges, and Attitudes among University Students: Case Study of the University of Jordan. *Journal of Software Engineering and Applications, 9*(12), 577–587. doi:10.4236/jsea.2016.912039

Amato, S., & Boutin, É. (2013). Rites d'interaction et forums de discussion en ligne : Une approche nethnospective de comportements de déférence et de civilité. *Les Cahiers du numérique, 9*(3), 135-159. doi:10.3166/LCN.9.1.25-38

Ambient. (2015). *The 2015-2020 Worldwide Digital English Language Learning Market Series*. Ambient Insight, LLC.

Amoia, M., Bretaudiere, T., Denis, A., Gardent, C., & Perez-Beltrachini, L. (2012). A serious game for second language acquisition in a virtual environment. *Systemics. Cybernetics and Informatics, 10*(1), 24–34.

Amundson, L. (2017). Web 2.0 Technologies: The Best-Fit Model for Preservice Teachers. *Journal of Technology and Teacher Education, 25*(2), 131–154.

Anafi, F. O., Obada, D. O., & Samotu, I. A. (2015). Integrating Internet into Engineering Education: A Case Study of Students' Usage and Attitudes in Faculty of Engineering, Ahmadu Bello University. *Bulgarian Journal of Science and Education Policy*, *9*(1), 129–147.

Anderson, A. (2001). Internet use among college students: An exploratory study. *Journal of American College Health*, *50*(1), 21–26. doi:10.1080/07448480109595707 PMID:11534747

Anderson, D. K., & Reed, W. M. (1998). The effects of Internet instruction, prior computer experience, and learning style on teachers' Internet attitudes and knowledge. *Journal of Educational Computing Research*, *19*(3), 227–246. doi:10.2190/8WX1-5Q3J-P3BW-JD61

Angadi, G. R. (2012). Post graduate students attitude towards the use of the internet. *International Journal of Education and Psychological Research*, *1*(1), 30–37.

An, Y.-J., & Williams, K. (2010). Teaching with Web 2.0 technologies: Benefits, barriers and lessons learned. *International Journal of Instructional Technology and Distance Learning*, *7*(3), 41–48.

Aparicio, M., Bacao, F., & Oliveira, T. (2017). Grit in the path to e-learning success. *Computers in Human Behavior*, *66*, 388–399. doi:10.1016/j.chb.2016.10.009

Archambault, L., Wetzel, K., Foulger, T. S., & Williams, M. K. (2010). Professional development 2.0. *Journal of Digital Learning in Teacher Education*, *27*(1), 4–11. doi:10.1080/21532974.2010.10784651

Atman, N., & Inceoğlu, M. M. (2009). Learning styles diagnosis based on learner behaviors in web based learning. In Computational Science and Its Applications–ICCSA 2009. Springer. doi:10.1007/978-3-642-02457-3_73

Attanayake, D., Denholm-Price, J., Hunter, G., Pfluegel, E., & Wigmore, A. (2015). Speech interfaces for mathematics: opportunities and limitations for visually impaired learners. *IMA International Conference on Barriers and Enablers to Learning Maths: Enhancing Learning and Teaching for All Learners*.

Ayaz, Y., & Genc, Z. S. (2016). Digital game-based language learning in foreign language teacher education. *Turkish Online Journal of Distance Education*, *17*(4), 130–146.

Aydin, S. (2007). Attitudes of EFL Learners towards the Internet. *The Turkish Online Journal of Educational Technology, 6*(3), 18-26.

Baker, J.M., Deng, L., Glass, J., Khudanpur, S., Lee, C., Morgan, N., O'Shaughnessy D. (2009). Research Developments and Directions in Speech Recognition and Understanding, Part 1. *IEEE Signal Processing Magazine, 75*.

Baltodano, M. M. (2016). ICT Training Requirements in Higher Education: Case Study of Training Programme for the Didactical Use of Web 2.0 Applications. *Educational Excellence, 2*(1), 15–27. doi:10.18562/IJEE.2015.0011

Balubaid, M. A. (2013). Using Web 2.0 Technology to Enhance Knowledge Sharing in an Academic Department. *Procedia: Social and Behavioral Sciences, 102*, 406–420. doi:10.1016/j.sbspro.2013.10.756

Baporikar, N. (2014). Effective E-Learning Strategies for a Borderless World. In J. Pelet (Ed.), *E-Learning 2.0 Technologies and Web Applications in Higher Education* (pp. 22–44). Hershey, PA: IGI Global; doi:10.4018/978-1-4666-4876-0.ch002

Baporikar, N. (2015). Knowledge Management in Small and Medium Enterprises. In J. Zhao, P. Ordóñez de Pablos, & R. Tennyson (Eds.), *Organizational Innovation and IT Governance in Emerging Economies* (pp. 1–20). Hershey, PA: IGI Global; doi:10.4018/978-1-4666-7332-8.ch001

Baporikar, N. (2016a). Lifelong Learning in Knowledge Society. In P. Ordóñez de Pablos & R. Tennyson (Eds.), *Impact of Economic Crisis on Education and the Next-Generation Workforce* (pp. 263–284). Hershey, PA: IGI Global; doi:10.4018/978-1-4666-9455-2.ch012

Baporikar, N. (2016b). Student Learning and Information Technology Nexus. [IJSSMET]. *International Journal of Service Science, Management, Engineering, and Technology, 7*(2), 34–45. doi:10.4018/IJSSMET.2016040103

Baporikar, N. (2017). *Innovation and Shifting Perspectives in Management Education* (pp. 1–352). Hershey, PA: IGI Global; doi:10.4018/978-1-5225-1019-2

Barron, A. E., & Ivers, K. W. (1996). *The Internet and Instruction: Ideas and Activities*. Englewood, CO: Libraries Unlimited.

Barron, A. E., & Orwig, G. W. (1997). *New Technologies for Education: A Beginner's Guide*. Englewood, CO: Libraries Unlimited.

Bashir, S., Mahmood, K., & Shafiq, F. (2008). Internet Use among University Students: A Survey in University of the Punjab, Lahore. *Pakistan Journal of Library & Information Science*, *9*, 49–65.

Bates, T. (2011). Understanding Web 2.0 and its implications for e-learning. In M. Lee & C. McLoughlin (Eds.), *Web 2.0-Based E-Learning: Applying Social Informatics for Tertiary Teaching* (pp. 21–42). Hershey, PA: IGI Global. doi:10.4018/978-1-60566-294-7.ch002

Baumann-Birkbeck, L., Karaksha, A., Anoopkumar-Dukie, S., Grant, G., Davey, A., Nirthanan, S., & Owen, S. (2015). Benefits of e-learning in chemotherapy pharmacology education. *Curr Pharm Teach Learn.*, *7*(1), 106–111. doi:10.1016/j.cptl.2014.09.014

Bautier, É., Crinon, J., Eloy, F., Joigneaux, C., Kakpo, S., Rayou, P., & Rochex, J.-Y. (2015). Supports pédagogiques et inégalités scolaires: études sociologiques (S. A. Bonnéry, Éd.). Paris, France: la Dispute.

Baxter, G. J., Connolly, T. M., Stansfield, M. H., Tsvetkova, N., & Stoimenova, B. (2011). Introducing Web 2.0 in education: A structured approach adopting a Web 2.0 implementation framework. In *Proceedings of the 7th International Conference on Next Generation Web Services Practices (NWeSP)* (pp. 499-504). IEEE. 10.1109/NWeSP.2011.6088230

Beetham, H., & Sharpe, R. (2007). *Rethinking pedagogy for a digital age: designing and delivering e-learning*. London: Routledge. doi:10.4324/9780203961681

Bellon, J., Bellon, E., & Blank, M. A. (1991). *Teaching from a Research Knowledge Base: A Development and Renewal Process*. New York, NY: Macmillan Publishing Company.

Benghozi, P.-J., Bitouzet, C., Soulier, E., & Zacklad, M. (2001). *Le mode communautaire: vers une nouvelle forme d'organisation*. Retrieved from http://hal.archives-ouvertes.fr/hal-00262785

Benito-Ruiz, E. (2009). Infoxication 2.0. Handbook of research on Web, 2, 60-79.

Bernard, F., & Durampart, M. (2013). *Savoirs en action: culture et réseaux méditerranéens* (Vol. 1). Paris, France: CNRS.

Bier, A., & Sroczyński, Z. (2015, June). Adaptive math-to-speech interface. In *Proceedings of the Mulitimedia, Interaction, Design and Innovation* (p. 7). ACM. 10.1145/2814464.2814471

Biggs, J. B. (1999). *Teaching for Quality Learning at University*. Buckingham, UK: SRHE & Open University Press.

Blanchard, M. R., LePrevost, C. E., Tolin, A. D., & Gutierrez, K. S. (2016). Investigating Technology-Enhanced Teacher Professional Development in Rural, High-Poverty Middle Schools. *Educational Researcher*, *45*(3), 207–220. doi:10.3102/0013189X16644602

Bloor, M., & Wood, F. (2006). *Keywords in Qualitative Methods:A Vocabulary of Research Concepts* (1st ed.). London: SAGE Publications. doi:10.4135/9781849209403

Boettcher, J. (1997). *Florida State University*. Pedagogy and Learning.

Bower, M. (2015). A typology of Web 2.0 learning technologies. *EDUCAUSE, 8*.

Bower, M. (2016). Deriving a typology of Web 2.0 learning technologies. *British Journal of Educational Technology*, *47*(4), 763–777. doi:10.1111/bjet.12344

Brandon, J. (2008). Web 2.0 definition for non-techies. *Computer World*. Retrieved from. http://blogs.computerworld.com/web_2_0_define_2_0

Braun, V., & Clarke, V. (2006). Using thematic analysis in psychology. *Qualitative Research in Psychology*, *3*(2), 77–101. doi:10.1191/1478088706qp063oa

Brengarth, L. B., & Mujkic, E. (2016). WEB 2.0: How social media applications leverage nonprofit responses during a wildfire crisis. *Computers in Human Behavior*, *54*, 589–596. doi:10.1016/j.chb.2015.07.010

Brzoza, P., & Skurowski, P. (2003). Biblioteka internetowa dostępna dla osób niewidomych. [Online Library available to the blind people]. Studia Informatica, 24(3).

Brzoza, P., Lobos, E., Macura, J., Sikora, B., & Zabka, M. (2012). ForMath-Intelligent Tutoring System in Mathematics. CSEDU, (1), 118-122.

Brzoza, P. (2008, July). Multimedia MathReader for Daisy Books. In *International Conference on Computers for Handicapped Persons* (pp. 875-878). Springer.

Bubas, G., Coric, A., & Orehovacki, T. (2011). Strategies for implementation of Web 2.0 tools in academic education. *Proceedings of the 17th European University Information Systems International Congress.*

Buchem, I., & Hamelmann, H. (2011). Developing 21st century skills: Web 2.0 in Higher Education-A case study. *Elearning Papers, 24*, 1-5.

Budiman, A. (2017). Behaviorism in foreign language teaching methodology. *English Franca, 1*(2), 101–114.

Bukowitz, W. R., & Williams, R. L. (1999). *The Knowledge Management Fieldbook.* London: Prentice Hall.

Cantu, D. A. (2000). Technology integration in preservice history teacher education. *Journal of the Association for History and Computing, 3*(2), 1–19.

Caron-Fasan, M.L, Channal V. (2008). Scenarios for exploring business models. *Expansion Management Review, 128.*

Casey, P., Dager, N., & Magel, M. (1998). Emerging Technology: Tools for Today and Tomorrow. *AV Video Multimedia Producer., 20*(1), 44–53.

CAST. (2011). Universal Design for Learning Guidelines version 2.0. Wakefield, MA: CAST.

CAST. (2018). *Universal Design for Learning Guidelines version 2.2.* Retrieved from http://udlguidelines.cast.org

Cazan, A. M., Cocoradă, E., & Maican, C. I. (2016). Computer anxiety and attitudes towards the computer and the internet with Romanian high-school and university students. *Computers in Human Behavior, 55*, 258–267. doi:10.1016/j.chb.2015.09.001

Chapman, A., & Russell, R. (2009). *Shared Infrastructure Services Landscape Study: A survey of the use of Web 2.0 tools and services in the UK HE sector.*

Cheek, H. N., & Castle, K. (1981). The Effects of Back-to-Basics on Mathematics Education. *Contemporary Educational Psychology, 6*(3), 263–277. doi:10.1016/0361-476X(81)90008-4

Chen, S.-C., Yen, D. C., & Hwang, M. I. (2012). Factors influencing the continuance intention to the usage of Web 2.0: An empirical study. *Computers in Human Behavior, 28*(3), 933–941. doi:10.1016/j.chb.2011.12.014

Chia, H. P., & Pritchard, A. (2014). Using a virtual learning community (VLC) to facilitate a cross-national science research collaboration between secondary school students. *Computers & Education*, *79*, 1–15. doi:10.1016/j.compedu.2014.07.005

Chicoine, D. (2004). Ignoring the Obvious: A Constructivist Critique of a Traditional Teacher Education Program. Educational Studies. *Journal of the American Educational Studies Association*, *36*(3), 245–263.

Chou, H.-C. (2016). Strategies for teaching indigenous languages to preschoolers in Taiwan: A case of language immersion. *International Journal of Humanities and Social Science Invention*, *5*(9), 57–62.

Christensen, C. M. (1997). *The Innovator's Dilemma: When New Technologies Cause Great Firms to Fail*. Boston Harvard Business School Press.

Chua, A. Y. K., & Goh, D. H. (2010). A study of Web 2.0 applications in library websites. *Library & Information Science Research*, *32*(3), 203–211. doi:10.1016/j.lisr.2010.01.002

Chumley-Jones, H., Dobbie, A., & Alford, C. (2002). Web-based learning: Sound educational method or hype? A review of the educational literature. *Academic Medicine*, *77*(10Supplement), S86–S93. doi:10.1097/00001888-200210001-00028 PMID:12377715

Cimmaruta, Ch., Liguori, L., Monticelli, M., Andreotti, G., & Citro, V. (2017, October). E-Learning for Rare Diseases: An Example Using Fabry Disease. *International Journal of Molecular Sciences*, *18*(10), 1–15. doi:10.3390/ijms18102049 PMID:28946642

Clark, D. B., Tanner-Smith, E. E., & Killingsworth, S. S. (2016). Digital games, design, and learning: A systematic review and meta-analysis. *Review of Educational Research*, *86*(1), 79–122. doi:10.3102/0034654315582065 PMID:26937054

Clarke, R. (2008). Web 2.0 as syndication. *Journal of Theoretical and Applied Electronic Commerce Research*, *3*(2), 30–43. doi:10.4067/S0718-18762008000100004

Cobb, P. (2000). Constructivism. In A. E. Kazdin (Ed.), *Encyclopedia of Psychology* (Vol. 2, pp. 277–279). New York: American Psychological Association and Oxford University Press, Inc.

Cocoradă, E. (2016). The internet attitude with socio-humanities high-school and university students. *Romanian Journal of Experimental Applied Psychology*, *6*(1), 21–30.

Coffin, R. J., & MacIntyre, P. D. (1999). Motivational influences on computer-related affective states. *Computers in Human Behavior*, *15*(5), 549–569. doi:10.1016/S0747-5632(99)00036-9

Cole, M. (2009). Using Wiki technology to support student engagement: Lessons from the trenches. *Computers & Education*, *52*(1), 141–146. doi:10.1016/j.compedu.2008.07.003

Collis, B. (1996). *Tele-Learning in a Digital World*. London: International Thomson Computer Press.

Constantinides, E., & Fountain, S. J. (2008). Web 2.0: Conceptual foundations and marketing issues. *Journal of Direct. Data and Digital Marketing Practice*, *9*(3), 231–244. doi:10.1057/palgrave.dddmp.4350098

Coomey, M., & Stephenson, J. (2001). Online Learning: it is all about dialogue, involvement, support and control—according to the research. In J. Stephenson (Ed.), *Teaching and Learning Online: Pedagogies for New Technologies*. London, UK: Kogan Page.

Correa Ferreira, G., Ortiz Torres, E. M., Vargas Garcia, M., Lemos Vasconcellos, S. J., Schopf Frizzo, N., & Julio Costa, M. (2018). The effect of bilingualism on cognitive and auditory abilities in normal hearing adults. *Revista CEFAC*, *20*(1), 21–28. doi:10.1590/1982-0216201820112417

Corrocher, N. (2011). The adoption of Web 2.0 services: An empirical investigation. *Technological Forecasting and Social Change*, *78*(4), 547–558. doi:10.1016/j.techfore.2010.10.006

Costagliola, G., De Lucia, A., Ferrucci, F., Gravino, C., & Scanniello, G. (2008, December). Assessing the usability of a visual tool for the definition of e-learning processes. *Journal of Visual Languages and Computing*, *19*(6), 721–737. doi:10.1016/j.jvlc.2008.01.003

Cross, S. (2013). *Evaluation of the OLDS MOOC curriculum design course: participant perspectives, expectations and experiences.* Milton Keynes, UK: OLDS MOOC Project.

Cuartero-Olivera, J., Hunter, G., & Pérez-Navarro, A. (2012). Reading and writing mathematical notation in e-learning environments. *eLearn Center Research Paper Series*, (4).

Dahiya, S., & Verma, C. (2014). Analysis of student's attitude regarding internet in relation to study level and stream. *International Journal of Science and Research*, 447-452.

Dana, I. S., & Darmawan, N. (2017). The Study of User Acceptance toward E-Learning System in Higher Education. *Indonesian Journal of Electrical Engineering and Computer Science*, *7*, 514–523.

Danciu, L., & Grosseck, G. (2011). Social aspects of web 2.0 technologies: Teaching or teachers' challenges? *Procedia: Social and Behavioral Sciences*, *15*, 3768–3773. doi:10.1016/j.sbspro.2011.04.371

Daniel, L. E., & Daniel, L. E. (2012). Internet History (Web and Browser Caching). In L. E. Daniel & L. E. Daniel (Eds.), *Digital Forensics for Legal Professionals* (pp. 213–218). Boston: Syngress. doi:10.1016/B978-1-59749-643-8.00031-6

Daunert, A.L. & Harteis. (2014). Pre-service teachers' perspectives and practices in utilizing ubiquitous technologies for academic-oriented learning and knowledge management. In J. Pelet (Ed.), *E-Learning 2.0 Technologies and Web Applications in Higher Education* (pp. 254-272). Hershey, PA: Information Science Reference. doi:10.4018/978-1-4666-4876-0.ch013

De Gloria, A., Bellotti, F., & Berta, R. (2014). Serious games for education and training. *International Journal of Serious Games*, *1*(1), 1–15. doi:10.17083/ijsg.v1i1.11

Dearstyne, B. W. (2007). Blogs, mashups, and wikis: Oh my! *Information Management Journal*, *41*(4), 24–33.

Debande, O., & Ottersten, E. K. (2004). Information and Communication Technologies: A Tool Empowering and Developing the Horizon of the Learner. *Higher Education Management and Policy*, *16*(2), 31–61. doi:10.1787/hemp-v16-art15-en

Demirdag, S. (2016). Examining the Computer Attitudes and Internet Attitudes of Substitute Teachers: Self-Confidence towards ICT. *International Journal of Psycho-Educational Sciences*, 5(2), 89–100.

Demirezen, M. (1988). Behaviorist theory and language learning. *Journal of Hacettepe University Faculty of Education*, 3, 135–140.

DePietro, P. (2013). *Transforming Education with New Media: Participatory Pedagogy, Interactive Learning and Web 2.0*. New York: Peter Lang. doi:10.3726/978-1-4539-0831-0

Depover, C. (2014). Economic and pedagogical models for MOOCs? *Distance and Mediation of Knowledge, 2*(5).

Depover, C., Deschryver, N., & Monasta, A. (1999). *Guide de soutien aux projets de formation en alternance*. Mons, Belgique: Université de Mons-Hainaut, Unité de technologie de l'éducation.

Design Science (2018). *MathPlayer Can Speak!* Retrieved from http://www.dessci.com/en/products/mathplayer/tech/accessibility.htm

Dias, S. B., Hadjileontiadou, S. J., Diniz, J. A., & Hadjileontiadis, L. J. (2017). Computer-based concept mapping combined with learning management system use: An explorative study under the self- and collaborative-mode. *Computers & Education*, 107, 127–146. doi:10.1016/j.compedu.2017.01.009

Distance Learning: A Primer. (1997). Retrieved from http://www.mountainlake.org/distance/primer.htm

Dlab, M. H., Candrlic, S., & Sabranovic, S. (2016). Criteria for Selection of a Web 2.0 Tool for Process Modeling Education. In M. Auer, D. Guralnick, & J. Uhomoibhi (Eds.), *Interactive Collaborative Learning. ICL 2016. Advances in Intelligent Systems and Computing* (Vol. 544). Cham: Springer.

Dohn, N. (2009). Web 2.0: Inherent tensions and evident challenges for education. *Computer-Supported Collaborative Learning*, 4(3), 343–363. doi:10.100711412-009-9066-8

Domenget, J.-C., Larroche, V., Peyrelong, M.-F., & Merzeau, L. (2015). *Reconnaissance et temporalités: une approche info-communicationnelle*. Paris, France: l'Harmattan.

Dongyu, Z., Fanyu, & Wanyi, D. (2013). Sociocultural theory applied to second language learning: Collaborative learning with reference to the Chinese context. *International Education Studies*, *6*(9), 165–174.

Duggan, A., Hess, B., Morgan, D., Kim, S., & Wilson, K. (2001). Measuring Students' Attitudes toward Educational Use of The Internet. *Journal of Educational Computing Research*, *25*(3), 267–281. doi:10.2190/GTFB-4D6U-YCAX-UV91

Durndell, A., & Haag, Z. (2002). Computer self efficacy, computer anxiety, attitudes towards the Internet and reported experience with the Internet, by gender, in an East European sample. *Computers in Human Behavior*, *18*(5), 521–535. doi:10.1016/S0747-5632(02)00006-7

Duxbury. (2004). Retrieved from http://www.duxburysystems.com/

Eaton, S. E. (2010). *Formal, non-formal and informal learning: The case of literacy, essential skills, and language learning in Canada*. Eaton International Consulting Inc.

Echeng, R., Usoro, A., & Ewuzie, I. (2016). *Factors to Consider when Enhancing the Use of Web 2.0 Technologies in Higher Education: Students' and Lectures' Views for Quality Use*. Academic Press.

Echeng, R., & Usoro, A. (2016). Enhancing the use of Web 2.0 Technologies in Higher Education: Students' and Lectures' Views. *Journal of International Technology and Information Management*, *25*(1), 6.

Eduljee, N. B., & Kumar, S. S. (2017). Exploring Attitudes Towards the Internet: A Study of Indian College Students. *International Research Journal of Multidisciplinary Studies*, *3*(1), 1–12.

Edwards, A. D. N., McCartney, H., & Fogarolo, F. (2006). Lambda: A multimodal approach to making mathematics accessible to blind students. *Proceedings of the 8th international ACM SIGACCESS Conference on Computers and Accessibility*, 48–54.

Edwards, A. (1998). *Access to Mathematics for blind people: The Maths Project, CTI Mathematics*. The University of Birmingham.

Egan, M. W., Sebastian, J., & Welch, M. (1991, March). Effective Television Teaching: Perceptions of those that Count Most...Distance Learners. *Proceedings of the Rural Education Symposium* (ED 342 579).

Elliott, C., & Bilmes, J. (2007). Computer Based Mathematics Using Continuous Speech Recognition. In Striking a Chord: Vocal Interaction in Assistive Technologies, Games, and More: CHI 2007 workshop on non-verbal acoustic interaction. San Jose, CA: ACM.

Elman, J. (1991). Distributed representations, simple recurrent networks, and grammatical structure. *Machine Learning*, 7(2-3), 195–225. doi:10.1007/BF00114844

Englund, C., Olofsson, A. D., & Price, L. (2017). Teaching with technology in higher education: Understanding conceptual change and development in practice. *Higher Education Research & Development*, 36(1), 73–87. doi:10.1080/0729436 0.2016.1171300

Eren, O. (2015). Vocabulary learning on learner-created content by using web 2.0 tools. *Contemporary Educational Technology*, 6(4), 281–300.

Ertmer, P. A., Newby, T. J., Yu, J. H., Liu, W., Tomory, A., Lee, Y. M., ... Sendurur, P. (2011). Facilitating students' global perspectives: Collaborating with international partners using Web 2.0 technologies. *Internet and Higher Education*, 14(4), 251–261. doi:10.1016/j.iheduc.2011.05.005

Evans, M. A., & Powell, A. (2007). Conceptual and practical issues related to the design for and sustainability of communities of practice: The case of e-portfolio use in preservice teacher training. *Technology, Pedagogy and Education*, 16(2), 199–214. doi:10.1080/14759390701406810

Ewing, T. (2008). Participation cycles and emergent cultures in an online community. *International Journal of Market Research*, 50(5), 575–590. doi:10.2501/S1470785308200043

Fallon, C., & Brown, S. (2016). *E-learning standards: a guide to purchasing, developing, and deploying standards-conformant e-learning*. CRC Press.

Fan, S., Radford, J., & Fabian, D. (2016). A mixed-method research to investigate the adoption of mobile devices and Web2.0 technologies among medical students and educators. *BMC Medical Informatics and Decision Making*, 16(1), 43. doi:10.1186/2911-016-0283-6 PMID:27094813

Fateman, R. (2004). Handwriting + Speech for Computer Entry of Mathematics. Work in progress NSF grant CCR-9901933, Computer Science Division, EECS Department, University of California at Berkeley.

Fateman, R. (2013). *How can we speak math?* (Unpublished). Computer Science Division, EECS Department, University of California at Berkeley.

Fedorowicz-Kruszewska, M. (2015). Biblioteczne zasoby cyfrowe jako niezbędny element współczesnego środowiska edukacyjnego studentów z niepełnosprawnością wzroku. *E-mentor, 3*, 48–53. doi:10.15219/em60.1186

Feeley, J. (1997, August). Wideband Web. *Digital Video, 42-48.*

Feldmann, B. (2014). Two decades of e-learning in distance teaching–from Web 1.0 to Web 2.0 at the University of Hagen. In L. Uden, J. Sinclair, Y.-H. Tao & D. Liberona (Eds.), *Learning Technology for Education in Cloud. MOOC and Big Data: Proceedings of theThird International Workshop* (pp. 163-172). Cham: Springer International Publishing. 10.1007/978-3-319-10671-7_16

Ferdig, R. (2007). Examining social software in teacher education. *Journal of Technology and Teacher Education, 15*(1), 5–10.

Ferreira, H., & Freitas, D. (2004, July). Enhancing the accessibility of mathematics for blind people: The AudioMath project. In *International Conference on Computers for Handicapped Persons* (pp. 678-685). Springer. 10.1007/978-3-540-27817-7_101

File, T. (2013). *Computer and internet use in the United States. Current population survey reports.* Retrieved from https://www. census.gov/history/pdf/2013computeruse.pdf

Firat, E. A., & Koksal, M. S. (2017). The relationship between use of Web 2.0 tools by prospective science teachers and their biotechnology literacy. *Computers in Human Behavior, 70*, 44–50. doi:10.1016/j.chb.2016.12.067

Flichy, P. (2004). L'individualisme connecté entre la technique numérique et la société. *Reseaux, 124*(2), 17–51. doi:10.3917/res.124.0017

Franklin, N., Yoakam, M., & Warren, R. (1996). *Distance Learning: A Guidebook for System Planning and Implementation.* Indiana University.

Frank, M. L. (1990). What Myths about Mathematics Are Held and Conveyed by Teachers? *The Arithmetic Teacher, 37*(5), 10–12.

Furniss, E. (2014). *Perspectives on policy and practice: indigenous language and education*. EAC.

Gagné, R. M. (1977). *The Conditions of Learning*. New York: Holt, Rinehart & Winston.

Gagné, R. M. (1985). *The Conditions of Learning (4ᵗʰ ed.)*. New York: Holt, Rinehart & Winston.

Gagné, R. M., Wager, W. W., Golas, K., & Keller, J. M. (2005). *Principles of Instructional Design* (5th ed.). Belmont, CA: Wadsworth/Thomson Learning Inc.

Gall, M. D., Gall, J. P., & Borg, W. R. (2007). *Educational Research: an Introduction*. Boston: Pearson Education, Inc.

Gardner, J. A., Stewart, R., Francioni, J., & Smith, A. (2002). *Tiger, AGC, and Win-Triangle, removing the barrier to sem education*. Center On Disabilities Technology And Persons With Disabilities Conference 2002, California State University.

Garfinkel, H., Barthélemy, M. T., & Quéré, L. T. (2007). *Recherches en ethnométhodologie* (B. Dupret & J.-M. de Queiroz, Trans.). Paris, France: Presses universitaires de France.

Gbrich, C. (2007). *Qualitative Data Analysis: An Introduction* (1st ed.). London: Sage Publications.

Ghalem, A. (2017). Teachers' Perceptions of the Use of The Internet-Assisted Language Learning in Solving Medical Students' English Language Problems. *Asian Journal of Educational Research*, *5*(4), 30–42.

Giurgiu, L. (2017). Microlearning an evolving elearning trend. *Scientific Bulletin*, *22*(1), 18–23. doi:10.1515/bsaft-2017-0003

Glaser, R. (1990). Toward new models for assessment. *International Journal of Educational Research*, *14*, 475–483.

Godwin-Jone, R. (2016). Augmented reality and language learning: From annotated vocabulary to place-based mobiles games. *Language Learning & Technology*, *20*(3), 9–19.

Goodlad, J. I. (1982). Response: Let's Get on with the Reconstruction. *Phi Delta Kappan*, *64*(1), 19–20.

Goodyear, P. (2001). Psychological Foundations of Networked Learning. In C. Jones & C. Steeples (Eds.), *Networked Learning: Perspectives and Issues. Springer.*

Gregory, M. S.-J., & Lodge, J. M. (2015). Academic workload: The silent barrier to the implementation of technology-enhanced learning strategies in higher education. *Distance Education, 36*(2), 210–230. doi:10.1080/01587919.2015.1055056

Grosseck, G. (2009). To use or not to use web 2.0 in higher education? *Procedia: Social and Behavioral Sciences, 1*(1), 478–482. doi:10.1016/j.sbspro.2009.01.087

Gutiérrez, R. T. (2018). Understanding the role of digital commons in the web; The making of HTML5. *Telematics and Informatics, 35*(5), 1438–1449. doi:10.1016/j.tele.2018.03.013

Hagiu, A., & Wright, J. (2015). Multi-sided platforms. *International Journal of Industrial Organization, 43*, 162–174. doi:10.1016/j.ijindorg.2015.03.003

Hahne, A. K., Benndorf, R., Frey, P., & Herzig, S. (2005). Attitude towards computer-based learning: Determinants as revealed by a controlled interventional study. *Medical Education, 39*(9), 935–943. doi:10.1111/j.1365-2929.2005.02249.x PMID:16150034

Hamel, G. P., & Prahalad, C. K. (1989). Strategic intent. *Harvard Business Review*, 3. PMID:10303477

Han, O. B., Halim, N. D. B. A., Shariffuddin, R. S. B., & Abdullah, Z. B. (2013). Computer Based Courseware in Learning Mathematics: Potentials and Constrains. *Procedia: Social and Behavioral Sciences, 103*, 238–244. doi:10.1016/j.sbspro.2013.10.331

Hansen, N. (1998). *Save the Beaches 1998: An International Project for Global Awareness.* Available at http://ednhp.hartford.edu/www/Nina/

Hara, N., Bonk, C. J., & Angeli, C. (2000). Content Analysis of Online Discussion in an Applied Educational Psychology Course. *Instructional Science, 28*(2), 115–152. doi:10.1023/A:1003764722829

Hartshorne, R., & Ajjan, H. (2009). Examining student decisions to adopt web 2.0 technologies: Theory and empirical tests. *Journal of Computing in Higher Education, 21*(3), 183–198. doi:10.100712528-009-9023-6

Hattie, J., & Timperley, H. (2007). The power of feedback. *Review of Educational Research, 77*(1), 81–112. doi:10.3102/003465430298487

Henri, F., & Rigault, C. R. (1996). Collaborative Distance Learning and Computer Conferencing. In T. T. Liao (Éd.), *Advanced Educational Technology: Research Issues and Future Potential* (pp. 45-76). Springer Berlin Heidelberg. Retrieved from http://link.springer.com/chapter/10.1007/978-3-642-60968-8_3

Herrington, T., Sparrow, L., & Herrington, J. (1999). Investigating mathematics education using multimedia. *Journal of Technology and Teacher Education, 7*(3), 175–186.

Holenko Dlab, M., Candrlic, S., & Sabranovic, S. (2016). Criteria for Selection of a Web 2.0 Tool for Process Modeling Education. In M. E. Auer, D. Guralnick & J. Uhomoibhi (Eds.), *Interactive Collaborative Learning: Proceedings of the 19th ICL Conference* (vol. 1, pp. 88-96). Cham: Springer International Publishing.

Homola, M., & Kubincová, Z. (2009). Taking advantage of Web 2.0 in organized education (a survey). In M. Auer (Ed.), *Proceedings of the Interactive Computer aided Learning (ICL) International Conference* (pp. 741-752). Kassel, Germany: Kassel University Press.

Hong, J. C., & Kuo, C. L. (1999). Knowledge Management in the Learning Organization. *Leadership and Organization Development Journal, 20*(4), 207–215. doi:10.1108/01437739910277019

Hong, J. C., Tai, K. H., Hwang, M. Y., Kuo, Y. C., & Chen, J. S. (2017). Internet cognitive failure relevant to users' satisfaction with content and interface design to reflect continuance intention to use a government e-learning system. *Computers in Human Behavior, 66*, 353–362. doi:10.1016/j.chb.2016.08.044

Hong, K. S., Ridzuan, A. A., & Kuek, M. K. (2003). Students' attitudes towards the use of the Internet for learning: A study at a university in Malaysia. *Journal of Educational Technology & Society, 6*(2), 45–49.

Honneth, A. (2013). *La lutte pour la reconnaissance* (P. Rusch, Trans.). Paris, France: Gallimard, impr.

Hopson, M. H., Simms, R. L., & Knezek, G. A. (2002). Using a technologically enriched environment to improve higher-order thinking skills. *Journal of Research on Technology in Education, 34*(2), 109–119. doi:10.1080/15391523.2001.10782338

Hornbach, C. (2004). Response to Masafumi Ogawa, "Music Teacher Education in Japan: Structure, Problems, and Perspectives. *Philosophy of Music Education Review, 12*(2), 201–204. doi:10.1353/pme.2005.0005

Howard, S. K., Yang, J., Ma, J., Maton, K., & Rennie, E. (2018). App clusters: Exploring patterns of multiple app use in primary learning contexts. *Computers & Education, 127*, 154–164. doi:10.1016/j.compedu.2018.08.021

Huang, H. M. (2002). Toward constructivism for adult learners in online learning environments. *British Journal of Educational Technology, 33*(1), 27–37. doi:10.1111/1467-8535.00236

Huang, H. M., & Liaw, S. S. (2005). Exploring user's attitudes and intentions toward the web as a survey tool. *Computers in Human Behavior, 21*(5), 729–743. doi:10.1016/j.chb.2004.02.020

Huet, J.-M., & Simon, A. (2018). The new digital horizons: What are the digital revolution trends? In *Coll. Management in action* (p. 119). Pearson.

Hulin, R., & Na, X. (2014). A study of Chomsky's universal grammar in second language acquisition. *International Journal on Studies in English Language and Literature, 2*(12), 1–7.

Isaias, P., Miranda, P., & Pifano, S. (2017). Model for The Effective Implementation of Web 2.0 In Higher Education from The Viewpoint of the Teachers. *Proceedings of the 10Th International Conference of Education, Research and Innovation (ICERI 2017)*.

Isaias, P., Miranda, P., & Pífano, S. (2009). Towards An Effective E-Learning 2.0. In *Proceedings of the 1st International Conference on Education and New Learning Technologies (EDULEARN 09)* (pp. 4997-5004). Barcelona, Spain: IATED.

Islam, N., Beer, M., & Slack, F. (2015). E-Learning Challenges Faced by Academics in Higher Education: A Literature Review. *Journal of Education and Training Studies, 3*(5), 102–112. doi:10.11114/jets.v3i5.947

Isman, A., & Dabaj, F. (2004). Attitudes of Students Towards Internet. *Turkish Online Journal of Distance Education, 5*(4). Retrieved from https://pdfs.semanticscholar.org/a5c7/3921b2e7b656deeb6116088bb484e730915c.pdf

Israel, O. (2013). Attitude of undergraduates towards educational usage of the Internet: A case of library schools in Delta and Edo States of Nigeria. *International Journal of Science and Technology Educational Research, 4*(4), 57–62.

Jacob, W. J., Cheng, S. Y., & Porter, M. K. (2015). Global review of indigenous educations: issues of identity, culture, and language. In W. Jacob, S. Cheng, & M. Porter (Eds.), *Indigenous Education: Language, Culture, and Identity*. Springer.

Jacquinot, G. (1993). Apprivoiser la distance et supprimer l'absence? ou les défis de la formation à distance. *Revue française de pédagogie*, 55–67. Retrieved from http://www.jstor.org/stable/41200347

Jain, N., Patidar, P. C., & Malviya, R. (2011). Internet as learning tool: Indian engineering student's perception. *Indian Journal of Computer Science and Engineering, 2*(2), 244–247.

Jakobson, R., & Vine, B. (1985). Verbal art, verbal sign, verbal time (K. Pomorska & S. Rudy, Éd.). Oxford, UK: Blackwell.

Jimoyiannis, A. (2015). TPACK 2.0: Towards a Framework Guiding Web 2.0 Integration in Educational Practice. In M. S. Khine (Ed.), *New Directions in Technological Pedagogical Content Knowledge Research Multiple Perspectives* (pp. 83–108). Charlotte, NC: Information Age Publishing.

Jimoyiannis, A., Tsiotakis, P., & Roussinos, D. (2012). Blogs in higher education: Analysing students' participation and presence in a community of blogging. In M. B. Nunes, & P. Isaías (Eds.), *Proceedings of the IADIS International Conference on e-Learning* (pp. 228-235). Lisbon, Portugal: IADIS Press.

Jimoyiannis, A., Tsiotakis, P., Roussinos, D., & Siorenta, A. (2013). Preparing teachers to integrate Web 2.0 in school practice: Toward a framework for Pedagogy 2.0. *Australasian Journal of Educational Technology, 29*(2), 248–267. doi:10.14742/ajet.157

Joanisse, M. F., & McClelland, J. L. (2015). Connectionist perspectives on language learning, representation and processing. *Wiley Interdisciplinary Reviews: Cognitive Science, 2015*. doi:10.1002/wcs.1340 PMID:26263227

Johnson, L., Adams Becker, S., Estrada, V., & Freeman, A. (2014). *Horizon Report: 2014 Higher Education Edition*. Austin, Texas: The New Media Consortium. Retrieved from http://www.nmc.org/pdf/2014-nmc-horizon-report-he-EN.pdf

Josèphe, P. (2008). *La société immédiate: essai* (Vol. 1). Paris, France: Calmann-Lévy.

Jouët, J. (2000). Retour critique sur la sociologie des usages. *Reseaux, 18*(100), 487–521. doi:10.3406/reso.2000.2235

Joyce, M., & Kirakowski, J. (2013). Development of a general internet attitude scale. In *Design, User Experience, and Usability. Design Philosophy, Methods, and Tools* (pp. 250-260). Academic Press. 10.1007/978-3-642-39229-0_33

Kalbarczyk, M. (2002). Translator - przekształcanie tekstu na system punktowy Braille'a. Translator – transformation of text into Braille dot system. Informatyka w Szkole XVIII, Toruń 2002.

Kapczyński, A. (2015). Inżynierowie zarządzania w świecie pełnym cyfrowych możliwości. Engineers of Management in the world full of digital opportunities. Zeszyty Naukowe Politechniki Śląskiej Seria Zarządzanie z. 80/Nr kol. 1933, Gliwice 2015.

Kapenieks, J. (2013). User-friendly e-learning Environment for Educational Action Research. *Procedia Computer Science, 26*, 121–142. doi:10.1016/j.procs.2013.12.012

Karakaya, A. F., & Demirkan, H. (2015). Collaborative digital environments to enhance the creativity of designers. *Computers in Human Behavior, 42*, 176–186. doi:10.1016/j.chb.2014.03.029

Karshmer, A.I., & Bledsoe, C. (2002). *Access to Mathematics by Blind Students, Books and electronic school bags for inclusive education of young visually impaired people*. BrailleNet 2002.

Karshmer, A.I., Gupta, G., Geiger, S., & Weaver, C. (1999). The MAVIS Project. *Journal of Behavior and Information Technology, 18*(1).

Karvounidis, T., Chimos, K., Bersimis, S., & Douligeris, C. (2014). Evaluating Web 2.0 technologies in higher education using students' perceptions and performance. *Journal of Computer Assisted Learning, 30*(6), 577–596. doi:10.1111/jcal.12069

Karvounidis, T., Chimos, K., Bersimis, S., & Douligeris, C. (2018). Factors, issues and interdependencies in the incorporation of a Web 2.0 based learning environment in higher education. *Education and Information Technologies, 23*(2), 935–955. doi:10.100710639-017-9644-8

Kauba, K. (Ed.). (2011). Brajlowska notacja matematyczna, fizyczna, chemiczna. Braille mathematical, physical, chemical notation, wydanie II, Kraków, Laski, Łódź 2011.

Kim, W. C., & Mauborgne, R. (2005). Blue ocean strategy: From theory to practice. *California Management Review, 47*(3), 105–121. doi:10.1177/000812560504700301

King, L., & Schielmann, S. (2004). *The challenge of Indigenous Education: Practice and Perspectives*. UNESCO.

Kirkwood, A. & Price, L. (2016). *Technology-Enabled Learning: Handbook*. Commonwealth of Learning.

Kirkwood, A., & Price, L. (2016). *Technology Enabled Learning: Handbook*. Commonwealth of Learning.

Kirkwood, A., & Price, L. (2005). Learners and Learning in the Twenty-first Century: What do we know about students' attitudes towards and experiences of information and communication technologies that will help us design courses? *Studies in Higher Education, 30*(3), 257–274. doi:10.1080/03075070500095689

Kirkwood, A., & Price, L. (2008). Assessment and student learning: A fundamental relationship and the role of information and communication technologies. *Open Learning: The Journal of Open and Distance Learning, 23*(1), 5–16. doi:10.1080/02680510701815160

Knowles, J. G. (1988). A Beginning Teacher's Experience: Reflections on Becoming a Teacher. *Language Arts, 65*(7), 702–712.

Kocielinski, D., & Brzostek-Pawlowska, J. (2013, September). Improving the accessibility of touchscreen-based mobile devices: Integrating Android-based devices and Braille notetakers. In *Computer Science and Information Systems (FedCSIS), 2013 Federated Conference on* (pp. 655-658). IEEE.

Kramanski, B., & Michalsky, T. (2010). Preparing preservice teachers for self-regulated learning in the context of technological pedagogical content knowledge. *Learning and Instruction, 20*(5), 434–447. doi:10.1016/j.learninstruc.2009.05.003

Krashen, S. D. (1983). Bilingual education and second language acquisition theory. In C. F. Leyba (Ed.), *Schooling and Language Minority Students: A Theoretical Framework* (2nd ed.). Legal Books Distributing.

Krashen, S. D. (2018). *The conduit hypothesis: how reading leads to academic language competence*. Language Magazine.

Kregor, G., Breslin, M., & Fountain, W. (2012). Experience and beliefs of technology users at an Australian university: Keys to maximising e-learning potential. *Australasian Journal of Educational Technology, 28*(8). doi:10.14742/ajet.777

Kumar, S. (2009). Undergraduate perceptions of the usefulness of Web 2.0 in higher education: Survey development. *Proceedings of the 8th European Conference on e-Learning*, 308-314.

Lai, L. S. L., & Turban, E. (2008). Group formation and operations in the Web 2.0 environment and social networks. *Group Decision and Negotiation, 17*(5), 387–402. doi:10.100710726-008-9113-2

Lai, Y. C., & Ng, E. M. (2011). Using wikis to develop student teachers' learning, teaching, and assessment capabilities. *The Internet and Higher Education, 14*(1), 15–26. doi:10.1016/j.iheduc.2010.06.001

Lan, Y. J. (2015). Contextual EFL learning in a 3d virtual environment. *Language Learning & Technology, 19*(2), 16–31.

Lau, K. H., Lam, T., Kam, B. H., Nkhoma, M., Richardson, J., & Thomas, S. (2018). The role of textbook learning resources in e-learning: A taxonomic study. *Computers & Education, 118*, 10–24. doi:10.1016/j.compedu.2017.11.005

Lazar, I. M. (2018). *Investigations on the relationship between the aspirational level and the acceptance of modern technology in education by learners* (Unpublished doctoral dissertation). University of Bucharest, Bucharest, Romania.

Lee, M. K. O., Cheung, C. M. K., & Chen, Z. (2005). Acceptance of Internet-based Learning Medium: The role of extrinsic and intrinsic motivation. *Information & Management, 42*(8), 1095–1104. doi:10.1016/j.im.2003.10.007

Lehmann-Ortega, L., & Roy, P. (2009). Disruptive strategies. *Revue française de gestion,* (7), 113-126.

Liaw, S. S., & Huang, H. M. (2006). Information retrieval from the World Wide Web: A user-focused approach based on individual experience with search engines. *Computers in Human Behavior, 22*(3), 501–517. doi:10.1016/j.chb.2004.10.007

Licoppe, C. (Ed.). (2009). L'évolution des cultures numériques: de la mutation du lien social à l'organisation du travail. Limoges, France: Fyp éd.

Li, N., & Kirkup, G. (2007). Gender and cultural differences in Internet use: A study of China and the UK. *Computers & Education*, *48*(12), 301–317. doi:10.1016/j.compedu.2005.01.007

Liu, Y., & Wang, H. (2009). A Comparative Study on E-learning Technologies and Products: From the East to the West. *Systems Research and Behavioral Science*, *26*(2), 191–209. doi:10.1002res.959

Lock, A., & Strong, T. (2010). *Social Constructionism. Sources and stirrings in theory and practice*. Cambridge, UK: Cambridge University Press. doi:10.1017/CBO9780511815454

Löfström, E., & Nevgi, A. (2007). From strategic planning to meaningful learning: Diverse perspectives on the development of web-based teaching and learning in higher education. *British Journal of Educational Technology*, *38*(2), 312–324. doi:10.1111/j.1467-8535.2006.00625.x

Luan, W. S., Fung, N. G., Nawawi, M., & Hong, T. S. (2005). Experienced and inexperienced Internet users among pre-service teachers: Their use and attitudes toward the Internet. *Journal of Educational Technology & Society*, *8*(1), 90–103.

Macaskill, W., & Owen, D. (2006). Web 2.0 to go. *Proceedings of LIANZA Conference 2006*.

Maćkowski, M., Brzoza, P., Żabka, M., & Spinczyk, D. (2017). Multimedia platform for mathematics' interactive learning accessible to blind people. *Multimedia Tools and Applications*, *77*(5), 6191–6208. doi:10.100711042-017-4526-z

Madden, A., Ford, N., Miller, D., & Levy, P. (2005). Using the internet in teaching:the views of practitioners –asurvey of the views of secondary school teacher in Sheffield, UK. *British Journal of Educational Technology*, *36*(2), 255–280. doi:10.1111/j.1467-8535.2005.00456.x

Maican, C. I., & Cocoradă, E. (2017). Computers, Internet and Smartphone Attitudes Among Romanian University Students. *European Journal of Multidisciplinary Studies*, *5*(1), 85–92. doi:10.26417/ejms.v5i1.p85-92

Maloney, E. (2007). What Web 2.0 can teach us about learning. *The Chronicle of Higher Education*, *25*(18), B26.

Markides, C. (2006). Disruptive Innovation; In need of Better Theory. *Journal of Product Innovation Management*, *23*(1), 19–25. doi:10.1111/j.1540-5885.2005.00177.x

Marosan, Z., Josanov, B., & Savic, N. (2015). Technology leaders of computer and Web 2.0 usage in higher education: Case study. *Skola biznisa,* (2), 32-48.

Martensson, M. (2000). A Critical Review of Knowledge Management as a Tool. *Journal of Knowledge Management, 4*(3), 204–216. doi:10.1108/13673270010350002

Martin, A. (2006). Literacies for the digital age. In A. Martin & D. Madigan (Eds.), *Digital Literacies for Learning* (pp. 3–25). London: Facet Publications.

MATHS. (2003). *Mathematical Access for Technology and Science for Visually Disabled People.* Retrieved from http://www.cs.york.ac.uk/maths/

McClellan, N. (2003). *Speech Recognition + Mathematics = OPPORTUNITY!* Center On Disabilities Technology And Persons With Disabilities Conference 2003, California State University.

McLean, R., Richards, B. H., & Wardman, J. I. (2007). The effect of Web 2.0 on the future of medical practice and education: Darwikinian evolution of folksonomic revolution? *The Medical Journal of Australia, 187*(3), 174–177. PMID:17680746

McLoughlin, C., & Alam, S. L. (2014). A case study of instructor scaffolding using Web 2.0 tools to teach social informatics. *Journal of Information Systems Education, 25*(2), 125.

McLoughlin, C., & Lee, M. J. (2010). Personalised and self regulated learning in the Web 2.0 era: International exemplars of innovative pedagogy using social software. *Australasian Journal of Educational Technology, 26*(1). doi:10.14742/ajet.1100

Menezes, V. (2013). Second language acquisition: reconciling theories. *Open Journal of Applied Sciences, 2013*(3), 404-412. Doi:10.4236/ojapps.2013.37050

Merchant, Z., Goetz, E. T., Cifuentes, L., Keeney-Kennicutt, W., & Davis, T. J. (2014). Effectiveness of virtual reality-based instruction on students' learning outcomes in K-12 and higher education: A meta-analysis. *Computers & Education, 70*, 29–40. doi:10.1016/j.compedu.2013.07.033

Metzger, J.-P., Badillo, Y., Chabot, E., Chevalier, Y., & Collectif. (2004). *Médiation et représentation des savoirs.* Editions L'Harmattan.

Miesenberger, K., Klaus, J., & Zagler, W. L. (Eds.). (2002). Computers Helping People with Special Needs. *8th International Conference, ICCHP 2002, Linz, Austria, Proceedings.*

Minoli, D. (1996). *Distance Learning Technology and Applications*. Boston, MA: Artech House.

Miranda, P., Isaias, P., & Pífano, S. (2016). *Higher Education Students' Perceptions of Positive and Negative Effects of Social Networking in Portugal. In Social Networking and Education* (pp. 111–127). Springer.

Moore, M. G., & Thompson, M. M. (1990). The Effects of Distance Learning: A Summary of the Literature. Research Monograph No. 2. University Park, The Pennsylvania State University: American Center for the Study of Distance Education (ED 330-321).

Morse, B. J., Gullekson, N. L., Morris, S. A., & Popovich, P. M. (2011). The development of a general Internet attitudes scale. *Computers in Human Behavior*, *27*(1), 480–489. doi:10.1016/j.chb.2010.09.016

Mozhaeva, G., Feshchenko, A., & Kulikov, I. (2014). E-learning in the Evaluation of Students and Teachers: LMS or Social Networks? *Procedia: Social and Behavioral Sciences*, *152*, 127–130. doi:10.1016/j.sbspro.2014.09.168

Muldner, K., & Burleson, W. (2015). Utilizing sensor data to model students' creativity in a digital environment. *Computers in Human Behavior*, *42*, 127–137. doi:10.1016/j.chb.2013.10.060

Musso, P., Ponthou, L., Seulliet, E., Viginier, P., & Charlès, B. (2007). *Fabriquer le futur 2: l'imaginaire au service de l'innovation*. Paris, France: Village mondial : Pearson education France.

Newland, B., & Byles, L. (2014). Changing academic teaching with Web 2.0 technologies. *Innovations in Education and Teaching International*, *51*(3), 315–325. doi:10.1080/14703297.2013.796727

Newman, R., Chang, V., Walters, R. J., & Wills, G. B. (2016). Web 2.0 - The past and the future. *International Journal of Information Management*, *36*(4), 591–598. doi:10.1016/j.ijinfomgt.2016.03.010

Nielsen, J. (1994). *Usability engineering*. Elsevier.

Nielsen, J., & Budiu, R. (2013). *Mobile usability*. MITP-Verlags GmbH & Co. KG.

Noor ul Amin, S. (2017). Internet-users and Internet Non-users Attitude towards Research: A Comparative Study on Post-Graduate Students. *Journal of Education and Practice, 8*(1), 1-9.

Northern Territory Government of Australia. (2017). *Guidelines for the Implementation of Indigenous Languages and Cultures Programs in Schools.* Department of Education.

Nowell, L. S., Norris, J. M., White, D. E., & Moules, N. J. (2017). Thematic Analysis: Striving to Meet the Trustworthiness Criteria. *International Journal of Qualitative Methods, 16*(1), 1–13. doi:10.1177/1609406917733847

Nugultham, K. (2012). Using Web 2.0 for Innovation and Information Technology in Education Course. *Procedia: Social and Behavioral Sciences, 46*, 4607–4610. doi:10.1016/j.sbspro.2012.06.305

O'Neill, M., & McHugh, P. (Eds.). (1996). *Effective Distance Learning.* Alexandria, VA: American Society of Training and Development.

O'Reilly, T. (2007). What is web 2.0, design patterns and business models for the next generation of software. *Communications & Stratégies, 65*, 17–37.

O'Reilly, T. (2007). What is Web 2.0: Design patterns and business models for the next generation of software. *Communications & Stratégies, 65*, 17–37.

Okello-Obura, C., & Ssekitto, F. (2015). WEB 2.0 technologies application in teaching and learning by makerere university academic staff. *Library Philosophy and Practice (e-journal)*, 24.

Olaniran, B. A., Burley, H., & Chang, M. (2010). Social Issues and Web 2.0: A Closer Look at Culture in E-Learning. In S. Murugesan (Ed.), *Handbook of Research on Web 2.0, 3.0, and X.0: Technologies, Business, and Social Applications* (pp. 613–629). Hershey, PA: IGI Global. doi:10.4018/978-1-60566-384-5.ch034

Olson, J., Codde, J., & DeMaagd, K. (2011). An Analysis of e-Learning Impacts & Best Practices in Developing Countries. Michigan State Univ.

Osterhaus, S. (2004). *Texas School for the Blind and Visually Impaired.* Retrieved from http://www.tsbvi.edu/math/

Ovelar, R. (2010). Exploring how faculties use and rate Web 2.0 for teaching and learning purposes. *Proceedings of the 5th Doctoral Consortium at the European Conference on Technology Enhanced Learning, CEUR Workshop Proceedings 709.*

Ozfidan, B., & Aydin, H. (2017). Curriculum related issues in bilingual education. *Higher Education Studies*, *7*(4), 25–34. doi:10.5539/hes.v7n4p25

Paiva, V. L. M. O. (2014). Main second language acquisition theories: From structuralism to complexity. *Revista Contexturas*, *23*, 112–124.

Palesh, O., Saltzman, K., & Koopman, C. (2004). Internet use and attitudes towards illicit internet use behavior in a sample of Russian college students. *Cyberpsychology & Behavior*, *7*(5), 553–558. doi:10.1089/cpb.2004.7.553 PMID:15667050

Panisoara, G., Duta, N., & Panisoara, I.-O. (2015). The Influence of Reasons Approving on Student Motivation for Learning. *Procedia: Social and Behavioral Sciences*, *197*, 1215–1222. doi:10.1016/j.sbspro.2015.07.382

Pânişoară, G., Sandu, C., Pânişoară, I.-O., & Duţă, N. (2015). Comparative Study Regarding Communication Styles of The Students. *Procedia: Social and Behavioral Sciences*, *186*, 202–208. doi:10.1016/j.sbspro.2015.04.066

Parker, A. (1997). A Distance Education How-To Manual: Recommendations from the Field. *Educational Technology Review*, *8*, 7–10.

Patel, P.B., Patel, T., Saurabh, M.K., & Thakkar, S. (2018). Perceptions and Effectiveness of Use of E-Learning in Pharmacology Education. *Journal of Clinical & Diagnostic Research*, *12*(7), 12-16.

Pathan, H., Memon, R. A., Memon, S., Khoso, A. R., & Bux, I. (2018). A critical review of Vygotsky's socio-cultural theory in second language acquisition. *International Journal of English Linguistics*, *8*(4), 232–236. doi:10.5539/ijel.v8n4p232

Pelet, J.-É., Pratt, M.A., & Fauvy, S. (2017). MOOCs: curating the web and using social media to enhance e-learning. In Mobile Platforms, Design, and Apps for Social Commerce. IGI Global.

Pelet, J.-É., & Papadopoulou, P. (2010). *Investigating the effect of color on memorization and trust in e-learning. In Impact of E-Business Technologies on Public and Private Organizations: Industry Comparisons and Perspectives* (pp. 52–78). IGI Global. doi:10.4018/978-1-60960-501-8.ch004

Pence, H. E. (2007). Preparing for the real web generation. *Journal of Educational Technology Systems*, *35*(3), 347–356. doi:10.2190/7116-G776-7P42-V110

Peng, H., Tsai, C.-C., & Wu, Y.-T. (2006). University Students' Self-efficacy and their Attitudes toward the Internet: The role of students' perceptions of the Internet. *Educational Studies*, *32*(1), 73–86. doi:10.1080/03055690500416025

Peraya, D. (2017). Au centre des Mooc, les capsules vidéo: un renouveau de la télévision éducative? *Distance and Mediation of Knowledge*, (17).

Petare, P. A., & Mohite, P. V. (2016). An empirical study on measuring attitude towards enjoyment and usefulness of internet among management students. *Imperial Journal of Interdisciplinary Studies*, *2*(6), 250–252.

Peterson-Ahmad, M. B., Stepp, J. B., & Somerville, K. (2018). Teaching Pre-Service Teachers How to Utilize Web 2.0 Platforms to Support the Educational Needs of Students with Disabilities in General Education Classrooms. *Education in Science*, *8*(2), 1–9. doi:10.3390/educsci8020080

Piasecki, A. (2014). Wykorzystanie technologii komunikacyjnych przez osoby z dysfunkcjami narządów wzroku i słuchu. *The Use of communication technologies by people with sight and hearing organ dysfunctions. Studia Ekonomiczne*, *199*, 240–248.

Pieri, M., & Diamantini, D. (2014). An e-learning web 2.0 experience. *Procedia: Social and Behavioral Sciences*, *116*, 1217–1221. doi:10.1016/j.sbspro.2014.01.371

Ponce, D. (2003). *What can E-learning Learn from Knowledge Management?* Paper presented in 3rd European Knowledge Management Summer School, San Sebastian, Spain. Retrieved from http://www.knowledgeboard.com

Porter, L. R. (1997). *Creating the Virtual Classroom: Distance Learning with the Internet*. John Wiley & Sons, Inc.

Powell, A. L. (2013). Computer anxiety: Comparison of research from the 1990s and 2000s. *Computers in Human Behavior*, *29*(6), 2337–2381. doi:10.1016/j.chb.2013.05.012

Prensky, M. (2007). *Digital game-based learning*. Paragon House.

Prensky, M. (2010). *Teaching Digital Natives: Partnering for Real Learning*. Corwin Press.

Price, L., & Kirkwood, A. (2008). Technology in the United Kingdom's higher education context. In S. Scott & K. Dixon (Eds.), *The 21st century, globalised university: Trends and development in teaching and learning* (pp. 83–113). Perth, Australia: Black Swan.

Pringle, R. M. (2006). Preservice Teachers' Exploration of Children's Alternative Conceptions: Cornerstone for Planning to Teach Science. *Journal of Science Teacher Education, 17*(3), 291–307. doi:10.100710972-006-9017-4

Proulx, S., & Vitalis, A. (1999). *Vers une citoyenneté simulée: médias, réseaux et mondialisation*. Rennes, France: Apogée.

Quéré, L. (2005). Les « dispositifs de confiance » dans l'espace public. *Reseaux, 132*(4), 185. doi:10.3917/res.132.0185

Rabin, S. (2010). *Introduction to Game Development* (2nd ed.). Boston, MA: Course Technology.

Rahimi, E., van den Berg, J., & Veen, W. (2013). A roadmap for building web2. 0-based personal learning environments in educational settings. In I. Buchem, G. Attwell, & G. Tur (Eds.), *Proceedings of the 4th International conference on Personal Learning Environments (The PLE Conference 2013)*. Berlin: Academic Press.

Rajper, S., & Shaikh, A. W. (2016, June). Personalized e-learning systems: A user modeling technique. *Pakistan Journal of Science, 68*(2), 239–243.

Ramadan, R., & Widyani, Y. (2013). Game development life cycle guidelines. *2013 International Conference on Advanced Computer Science and Information Systems*, 95-100.

Reddy, P. R., & Karthik, E. K. (2013). A study on students attitudes towards internet. *International Journal of Electronic Marketing and Retailing, 3*(1), 1–9.

Reed, P. (2014). Staff experience and attitudes towards technology-enhanced learning initiatives in one Faculty of Health and Life Sciences. *Research in Learning Technology, 22*.

Rhoads, R. A., Berdan, J., & Toven-Lindsey, B. (2013). The open courseware movement in higher Education: Unmasking power and raising questions about the Movement's democratic potential. *Educational Theory, 63*(1), 87-109.

Ricœur, P. (2006). *Parcours de la reconnaissance: trois études*. Paris, France: Stock.

Riga, P., Kouroupetroglou, G., & Ioannidou, P. P. (2016, July). An Evaluation Methodology of Math-to-Speech in Non-English DAISY Digital Talking Books. In *International Conference on Computers Helping People with Special Needs* (pp. 27-34). Springer. 10.1007/978-3-319-41264-1_4

Riva, G. (2001). From real to Virtual Communities: Cognition, Knowledge, and Intention in the World Wide Web. In C. R. Wolfe (Ed.), *Learning and Teaching on the World Wide Web* (pp. 131–151). San Diego, CA: Academic Press. doi:10.1016/B978-012761891-3/50010-2

Rogers-Estable, M. (2014). Web 2.0 use in higher education. *European Journal of Open, Distance and e-Learning, 17*(2), 130-142.

Roknuzzaman, M., Kanai, H., & Umemoto, K. (2009). Integration of Knowledge Management Process into Digital Library System: A Theoretical Perspective. *Library Review, 58*(5), 372–386. doi:10.1108/00242530910961792

Rosa, H. (2010). *Accélération: une critique sociale du temps* (D. Renault, Trans.). Paris, France: La Découverte, impr. 2010.

Rotard, M., Bosse, K., Schweikhardt, W., & Ertl, T. (2003). Access to Mathematical Expressions in MathML for the Blind. In Universal Access in HCI (vol. 4, pp. 1325-1329). Lawrence Erlbaum Associates.

Rothwell, W. J., & Kazanas, H. C. (2008). *Mastering the instructional design process. A systematic approach* (4th ed.). San Francisco: Wiley.

Rubin, M., Faderewski, M., & Mikułowski, D. (2015). Badania stanu i potrzeb informatyzacji edukacji matematycznej uczniów niewidomych i słabowidzących w Polsce. Testing the condition and needs of computerization of mathematical education for the blind and visually impaired pupils in Poland. *E-mentor, 1*(58), 34-40.

Sadaf, A., Newby, T. J., & Ertmer, P. A. (2012). Exploring Factors that Predict Preservice Teachers' Intentions to Use Web 2.0 Technologies Using Decomposed Theory of Planned Behavior. *Journal of Research on Technology in Education, 45*(2), 171–196. doi:10.1080/15391523.2012.10782602

Sadikin, M., & Purwanto, S. K. (2018, June). The Implementation of E-learning System Governance to Deal With User Need, Institution Objective, and Regulation Compliance. *Telkomnika., 16*(3), 1332–1344. doi:10.12928/telkomnika.v16i3.8699

Safran, C., Helic, D., & Gütl, C. (2007). E-Learning practices and Web 2.0. *Proceedings of the Conference ICL2007*. Kassel, Germany: Kassel University Press.

Salamonczyk, A., & Brzostek-Pawlowska, J. (2015, June). Translation of MathML formulas to Polish text, example applications in teaching the blind. In *Cybernetics (CYBCONF), 2015 IEEE 2nd International Conference on* (pp. 240-244). IEEE. 10.1109/CYBConf.2015.7175939

Salamon, L. M. (2003). *The resilient sector: The state of nonprofit America.* Washington, DC: Brookings Institution Press.

Salmon, G. (2005). Flying not flapping: A strategic framework for e-learning and pedagogical innovation in higher education institutions. *ALT-J*, *13*(3), 201–218. doi:10.3402/rlt.v13i3.11218

Salvador, R. (1996). What's New in Net Connectivity? *Electronic Learning*, *16*(1), 14.

Sam, H. K., Othman, A. E. A., & Nordin, Z. S. (2005). Computer Self-Efficacy, Computer Anxiety, and Attitudes toward the Internet: A Study among Undergraduates in Unimas. *Journal of Educational Technology & Society*, *8*(4), 205–219.

Sandars, J., & Langlois, M. (2005, March). E-learning and the educator in primary care: Responding to the challenge. *Education for Primary Care*, *16*(2), 129–133.

Sapountzi, A., & Psannis, K. E. (2018). Social networking data analysis tools & challenges. *Future Generation Computer Systems*, *86*, 893–913. doi:10.1016/j.future.2016.10.019

Sarasvathy, S. D., Dew, N., Velamuri, S. R., & Venkataraman, S. (2003). Three views of entrepreneurial opportunity. Handbook of entrepreneurship research, 141-160.

Schaeffert, S., & Ebner, M. (2010). New Forms of and Tools for Cooperative Learning with Social Software in Higher Education. In B. A. Morris & G. M. Ferguson (Eds.), *Computer-Assisted Teaching: New Developments* (pp. 151–156). Nova Publishing.

Schumann, J. H. (1986). Research on the acculturation model for second language acquisition. *Journal of Multilingual and Multicultural Development*, *7*(5), 379–392. doi:10.1080/01434632.1986.9994254

Schutte, J. G. (1996). *Virtual Teaching in Higher Education: The New Intellectual Superhighway or Just another Traffic Jam?* Available at http://www.csun.edu/sociology/virexp.htm

Seel, N. (2003). Psychologie des Lernens (2. Auflage). München: Ernst Reinhardt (UTB).

Selwyn, N., Marriott, N., & Marriott, P. (2000). Net gains or net pains? Business students' use of the Internet. *Higher Education Quarterly*, *54*(2), 166–186. doi:10.1111/1468-2273.00153

Sepahpanah, M., Movahedi, R., & Farani, A. Y. (2015). The Study of Students' Attitudes towards the Use of Internet in Education (Case Study: Kermanshah Azad University). Magazine of E-learning Distribution in Academy, 6(3), 40-50.

Shang, S. S. C., Li, E. Y., Wu, Y.-L., & Hou, O. C. L. (2011). Understanding Web 2.0 service models: A knowledge-creating perspective. *Information & Management*, *48*(4–5), 178–184. doi:10.1016/j.im.2011.01.005

Sharma, A. K., Pyase, R., & Jain, S. (2014). A study & survey of B. Ed students' attitudes towards using internet. *International Journal of Science and Research*, *4*(12), 1155–1158.

Shneiderman, B. (1998). *Designing the User Interface: strategies for effective human–computer interaction* (3rd ed.). Boston, MA: Addison-Wesley Longman.

Siemens, G. (2006). *Knowing Knowledge*. Lulu.com.

Sikorski, M. (2010). Interakcja człowiek-komputer [Wydawnictwo Polsko-Japońska Wyższa Szkoła Technik Komputerowych.]. *Human-Computer Interaction*, 1–345.

Sitzmann, T. (2011). A meta-analytic examination of the instructional effectiveness of computer-based simulation games. *Personnel Psychology*, *64*(2), 489–528. doi:10.1111/j.1744-6570.2011.01190.x

Smith, B., Caputi, P., & Rawstone, L. (2000). Differentiating computer experience and attitude towards computers: An empirical investigation. *Computers in Human Behavior*, *16*(1), 59–81. doi:10.1016/S0747-5632(99)00052-7

Song, S. (2018). *Second language acquisition as a mode-switching process – an empirical analysis of Korean Learners of English*. Palgrave Macmillan UK. Doi:10.1057/978-1-137-52436-2

Soomro, K. A., Zai, S. Y., & Jafri, I. H. (2015). Competence and usage of Web 2.0 technologies by higher education faculty. *Educational Media International, 52*(4), 284–295. doi:10.1080/09523987.2015.1095522

Srinidhi, N. N., Dilip Kumar, S. M., & Venugopal, K. R. (2018). Network optimizations in the Internet of Things: A review. *Engineering Science and Technology, an International Journal*. doi:10.1016/j.jestch.2018.09.003

Sroczyńska, A., & Sroczyński, Z. (2006). Telepraca i zdalna edukacja osób niepełnosprawnych wzrokowo [Telework and e-learning of visually impaired and blind people]. *Zeszyty Naukowe. Organizacja i Zarządzanie/Politechnika Śląska*, 183-192.

Sroczyński, Z. (2000). MathML – język opisu wyrażeń matematycznych w dokumentach internetowych [MathML – language of description of mathematical expressions in online documents]. *Studia Informatica, 21*(41), 125-145.

Sroczyński, Z. (2002). Serwer WWW jako serwer dokumentów zawierających złożoną notację matematyczną [WWW server as server of documents containing complex mathematical notation]. *Studia Informatica, 23*(49), 103-111.

Sroczyński, Z. (2003). Prezentacja dokumentów internetowych zawierających złożoną notację matematyczną dla potrzeb osób niewidomych [Presentation of online documents containing complex mathematical notation for blind people]. *Studia Informatica, 24*(55), 179-187.

Sroczyński, Z. (2012). Analiza struktury złożonych wyrażeń matematycznych dla potrzeb prezentacji dokumentów w Internecie [The analysis of the structure of complex mathematical expressions for the purposes of online presentation]. Zastosowania Internetu, Dąbrowa Górnicza.

Sroczyński, Z. (2014a). Interakcja człowiek-komputer w systemach e-learningu dostępnych dla osób niepełnosprawnych wzrokowo [The human-computer interaction in e-learning systems available to the visually handicapped people]. *The Role of Informatics in Economic and Social Sciences. Innovations and Interdisciplinary Implications, 39.*

Sroczynski, Z. (2014b). Human-computer interaction on mobile devices with the FM application platform. Internet in the Information Society. In *Insights on the Information Systems, Structures and Applications*. Academy of Business in Dabrowa Gornicza Press.

Sroczynski, Z. (2010). Priority levels and heuristic rules in the structural recognition of mathematical formulae. *Theoretical and Applied Informatics*, *22*(4), 273. doi:10.2478/v10179-010-0014-0

Sroczyński, Z. (2017). Jakość interakcji człowiek-komputer czynnikiem decydującym o popularności aplikacji mobilnych. *The quality of human-computer interactions as a factor deciding on the popularity of mobile applications. Studia Ekonomiczne*, *317*, 106–117.

Statista. (2016, December). *Number of video gamers worldwide in 2016, by region (in millions)*. Retrieved from https://www.statista.com/statistics/293304/number-video-gamers/

Steeples, C., & Jones, C. (2002). *Networked Learning: Perspectives and Issues*. London: Springer-Verlag London Limited. doi:10.1007/978-1-4471-0181-9

Stephenson, J. (2002). *Teaching & Learning Online: Pedagogies for New Technologies*. London: Kogan Page Limited.

Stevens, R. D. (1996). *Principles for the Design of Auditory Interfaces to Present Complex Information to Blind People*. Praca doktorska. The University of York, Department of Computer Science.

Stoney, S., & Wild, M. (1998). Motivation and interface design: Maximizing learning opportunities. *Journal of Computer Assisted Learning*, *14*(1), 40–50. doi:10.1046/j.1365-2729.1998.1410040.x

Sugiharto, S. (2010). The robustness of the comprehension hypothesis: A review of current research and implications for the teaching of writing. *Journal of Social Sciences and Humanities*, *18*(2), 417–425.

Suresh, M., Vishnu, P., & Gayathri, R. (2018, September). Effect of e-learning on academic performance of undergraduate students. *Drug Invention Today.*, *10*(9), 1797–1800.

Świerczek, J. (Ed.). (2002). Brajlowska notacja matematyczna, fizyczna, chemiczna. Braille mathematical, physical, chemical notation.

Teece, D. J. (2010). Business models, business strategy and innovation. *Long Range Planning*, *43*(2), 172–194. doi:10.1016/j.lrp.2009.07.003

Tétard, F., Patokorpi, E., & Packalén, K. (2009). Using wikis to support constructivist learning: a case study in university education settings. In *HICSS '09 Proceedings of the 42nd Hawaii International Conference on System Sciences* (pp. 1-10). IEEE Computer Society.

Texthelp. (2018). Retrieved from https://www.texthelp.com/en-us/products/equatio/

Thornburg, D. D. (1995). Welcome to the Communication Age. *Internet Research*, *5*(1), 64–70.

Tinto, V. (1997). Classrooms as communities. Exploring the educational character of student persistence. *The Journal of Higher Education*, *68*(6), 600–623.

Tinto, V. (1998). Colleges as communities. Taking research on student persistence seriously. *Review of Higher Education*, *21*(2), 167–177.

Tisseron, S. (2007). *L'intimité surexposée*. Paris.

Tlili, A., Essalmi, F., Jemni, M., Kinshuk, & Chen, N.-S. (2016). Role of personality in computer based learning. *Computers in Human Behavior*, *64*, 805–813. doi:10.1016/j.chb.2016.07.043

Tobias, S., & Fletcher, D. (2011). Learning from computer games: a research review. In S. D. Wannemacker, S. Vandercruysse, & G. Clarebout (Eds.), *Serious Games: The Challenge*. Springer.

Truong, H. M. (2016). Integrating learning styles and adaptive e-learning system: Current developments, problems and opportunities. *Computers in Human Behavior*, *55*, 1185-1193.

Tsai, C.-C., Lin, S., & Tsai, M.-J. (2001). Developing an Internet Attitude Scale for high school students. *Computers & Education*, *37*(1), 41–51. doi:10.1016/S0360-1315(01)00033-1

Tsalapatas, H., Heidmann, O., Alimisi, D., & Houstis, E. (2013). A serious game-based approach for situated learning of vehicular languages addressing work needs and cultural aspects. In *proceedings of the 7th International Technology, Education and Development Conference* (pp. 5059-5065). Valencia, Spain: IATED.

Tsvyatkova, D., & Storni, C. (2018). *Designing an educational interactive eBook for newly diagnosed children with type 1 diabetes: Mapping a new design space. International Journal of Child-Computer Interaction.* doi:10.1016/j.ijcci.2018.10.001

Tuncer, M., Dogan, Y., & Tanaș, R. (2013). Vocational School Students' Attitudes Towards Internet. *Procedia: Social and Behavioral Sciences, 103*, 1303–1308. doi:10.1016/j.sbspro.2013.10.460

Turcq, D. (2013). *Le management augmenté: faire face à la complexité.* Paris: Boostzone éd.

UNESCO. (2015). *Multilingualism in cyberspace: indigenous languages for empowerment.* San José, Costa Rica: UNESCO Regional Conference for Central America.

United Nations. (2018). *Indigenous languages. The united nations permanent forum on indigenous issues.* UN Department of Public Information.

Usun, S. (2003). Undergraduate Students Attitudes towards Educational Uses of Internet. *Interactive Educational Multimedia, 7*, 46–62.

Valente, A., Johnson, W. L., & Vilhjálmsson, H. H. (2006). The tactical language and culture training system: a demonstration. *Proceedings of The Twenty-First National Conference on Artificial Intelligence and Eighteenth Innovative Applications of Artificial Intelligence Conference*, 1955-1956.

Verduin, J. R., & Clark, T. A. (1991). *Distance Education: The Foundations of Effective Practice.* San Francisco, CA: Jossey - Bass Publishers.

Vetter, E. (2014). Combining formal and non-formal foreign language learning: First insights into a German-Spanish experiment at university level. *Studies in Applied Linguistics, 2014*, 39–50.

Vidal, M., Grandbastien, M., & Moeglin, P. (Eds.). (2010). Formation à distance : principe de provocation et innovations: Vol. 8. Cachan, France: Lavoisier.

Violante, M. G., & Vezzetti, E. (2014). Implementing a new approach for the design of an e-learning platform in engineering education. *Computer Applications in Engineering Education, 22*(4), 708–727. doi:10.1002/cae.21564

Virilio, P. (2010). *Le grand accélérateur.* Paris, France: Galilée.

Virtanen, J., & Rasi, P. (2017). Integrating Web 2.0 Technologies into Face-to-Face PBL to Support Producing, Storing, and Sharing Content in a Higher Education Course. *Interdisciplinary Journal of Problem-Based Learning, 11*(1).

Vitalis, A. (1994). *Médias et nouvelles technologies: pour une socio-politique des usages*. Rennes, France: Apogée.

Vitiello, M., Walk, S., Helic, D., Chang, V., & Guetl, C. (2018). User Behavioral Patterns and Early Dropouts Detection: Improved Users Profiling through Analysis of Successive Offering of MOOC. *Journal of Universal Computer Science, 24*(8), 1131–1150.

Viveret, P., & Le Doze, C. (2014). *Vivre à la bonne heure*. Paris, France: les Presses d'Ile-de-France.

Voithofer, R. (2007). *Web 2.0: What is it and how can it apply to teaching and teacher preparation?* Paper presented at the American Educational Research Association Conference. Retrieved from http://education.osu.edu/rvoithofer/papers/web2paper. pdf

Vygotskij, L. S., Sève, F., Sève, F., & Clot, Y. (1985). Pensée et langage. Ed. sociales.

Wan, S., & Niu, Z. (2018). An e-learning recommendation approach based on the self-organization of learning resource. *Knowledge-Based Systems, 160*, 71–87. doi:10.1016/j.knosys.2018.06.014

Wattanasoontorn, V., García-Hernández, R. J., & Sbert, M. (2012). Serious games for e-health care. In Y. Cai & S. L. Goei (Eds.), *Simulations, Serious Games and Their Applications*. Springer.

Watty, K., McKay, J., & Ngo, L. (2016). Innovators or inhibitors? Accounting faculty resistance to new educational technologies in higher education. *Journal of Accounting Education, 36*, 1–15. doi:10.1016/j.jaccedu.2016.03.003

Waycott, J., Sheard, J., Thompson, C., & Clerehan, R. (2013). Making students' work visible on the social web: A blessing or a curse? *Computers & Education, 68*, 86–95. doi:10.1016/j.compedu.2013.04.026

Wee Sing Sim, J., & Foon Hew, K. (2010). The use of weblogs in higher education settings: A review of empirical research. *Educational Research Review, 5*(2), 151–163. doi:10.1016/j.edurev.2010.01.001

Wertsch, J. V. (2010). Vygotsky and recent developments. In P. Peterson, E. Baker, & B. McGaw (Eds.), *International Encyclopedia of Education* (Vol. 3, pp. 231–236). Academic Press. doi:10.1016/B978-0-08-044894-7.00490-5

Wigmore, A. M., Hunter, G. J. A., Pfluegel, E., & Denholm-Price, J. C. W. (2009). *TalkMaths: A speech user interface for dictating mathematical expressions into electronic documents.* In *2nd ISCA Workshop of Speech and Language Technology in Education (SLaTE 2009)*, Wroxall, UK.

Wild, R. H., Griggs, K. A., & Downing, T. (2002). A framework for e-learning as a tool for knowledge management. *Industrial Management & Data Systems*, *102*(7), 371–380. doi:10.1108/02635570210439463

Wilkinson, P. (2016). A brief history of serious games. In *Entertainment Computing and Serious Games, LNCS 9970* (pp. 17–41). Springer. doi:10.1007/978-3-319-46152-6_2

Willis, B. (1995, October). *Distance Learning at a Glance.* University of Idaho Engineering Outreach. Available at http://www.uidaho.edu/evo/distglan.html

Woodrow, J. J. (1991). A comparison of four computer attitudes scales. *Journal of Educational Computing Research*, *7*(2), 165–187. doi:10.2190/WLAM-P42V-12A3-4LLQ

Wright, K. B. (2005). Researching Internet-based populations: Advantages and disadvantages of online survey research, online questionnaire authoring software packages, and web survey services. *Journal of Computer-Mediated Communication, 10*(3).

Wu, Y. T., & Tsai, C. C. (2006). University Students' Internet Attitudes and Internet Self-Efficacy: A Study at Three Universities in Taiwan. *Cyberpsychology & Behavior*, *9*(4), 441–450. doi:10.1089/cpb.2006.9.441 PMID:16901248

Yang, T. C., & Hwang, G. J. (2013). Development of an adaptive learning system with multiple perspectives based on students' learning styles and cognitive styles. *Journal of Educational Technology & Society*, *16*(4), 185.

Yuen, S. C.-Y., Yaoyuneyong, G., & Yuen, P. K. (2011). Perceptions, interest, and use: Teachers and web 2.0 tools in education. *International Journal of Technology in Teaching and Learning*, *7*(2), 109–123.

Zelick, S. A. (2013). The perception of Web 2.0 technologies on teaching and learning in higher education: A case study. *Creative Education*, *4*(07), 53–93. doi:10.4236/ce.2013.47A2010

Zhang, X., de Pablos, P. O., & Xu, Q. (2014). Culture effects on the knowledge sharing in multi-national virtual classes: A mixed method. *Computers in Human Behavior*, *31*, 491–498. doi:10.1016/j.chb.2013.04.021

Żukowska, J. (2004). E-learning jako skuteczne narzędzie e-business wykorzystywane w przedsiębiorstwie dążącym do sukcesu [E-learning as an effective e-business tool used in a success oriented enterprise]. *Konferencja Instrumenty i formy organizacyjne procesów zarządzania w społeczeństwie informacyjnym.*

Żukowska, J., & Sroczyński, Z. (2014). Internetowe aplikacje mobilne narzędziem budowania przewagi konkurencyjnej przedsiębiorstw [Online mobile application as a tool in building the competitive advantage of enterprises]. In *Internet w społeczeństwie informacyjnym. Nowoczesne systemy informatyczne i ich bezpieczeństwo* [The Internet in information society. Modern IT systems and their safety]. Wydawnictwo Wyższej Szkoły Biznesu w Dąbrowie Górniczej, Dąbrowa Górnicza.

Related References

To continue our tradition of advancing academic research, we have compiled a list of recommended IGI Global readings. These references will provide additional information and guidance to further enrich your knowledge and assist you with your own research and future publications.

Aburezeq, I. M., & Dweikat, F. F. (2017). Cloud Applications in Language Teaching: Examining Pre-Service Teachers' Expertise, Perceptions and Integration. *International Journal of Distance Education Technologies*, *15*(4), 39–60. doi:10.4018/IJDET.2017100103

Adera, B. (2017). Supporting Language and Literacy Development for English Language Learners. In J. Keengwe (Ed.), *Handbook of Research on Promoting Cross-Cultural Competence and Social Justice in Teacher Education* (pp. 339–354). Hershey, PA: IGI Global. doi:10.4018/978-1-5225-0897-7.ch018

Ahamer, G. (2011). How Technologies Can Localize Learners in Multicultural Space: A Newly Developed "Global Studies" Curriculum. *International Journal of Technology and Educational Marketing*, *1*(2), 1–24. doi:10.4018/ijtem.2011070101

Ahamer, G. (2015). Conclusions from Social Dynamics in Collaborative Environmental Didactics. *International Journal of Technology and Educational Marketing*, *5*(2), 68–92. doi:10.4018/IJTEM.2015070105

Ahamer, G. (2015). Designing and Analyzing Social Dynamics for Collaborative: Environmental Didactics. *International Journal of Technology and Educational Marketing*, *5*(2), 46–67. doi:10.4018/IJTEM.2015070104

Ahamer, G. (2017). Quality Assurance for a Developmental "Global Studies" (GS) Curriculum. In I. Management Association (Ed.), Educational Leadership and Administration: Concepts, Methodologies, Tools, and Applications (pp. 438-477). Hershey, PA: IGI Global. doi:10.4018/978-1-5225-1624-8.ch023

Ahamer, G. (2017). Quality Assurance for a Developmental "Global Studies" (GS) Curriculum. In I. Management Association (Ed.), Educational Leadership and Administration: Concepts, Methodologies, Tools, and Applications (pp. 438-477). Hershey, PA: IGI Global. doi:10.4018/978-1-5225-1624-8.ch023

Alegre de la Rosa, O. M., & Angulo, L. M. (2017). Social Inclusion and Intercultural Values in a School of Education. In S. Mukerji & P. Tripathi (Eds.), *Handbook of Research on Administration, Policy, and Leadership in Higher Education* (pp. 518–531). Hershey, PA: IGI Global. doi:10.4018/978-1-5225-0672-0.ch020

Ambikairajah, E., Sethu, V., Eaton, R., & Sheng, M. (2014). Evolving Use of Educational Technologies: Enhancing Lectures. In F. Alam (Ed.), *Using Technology Tools to Innovate Assessment, Reporting, and Teaching Practices in Engineering Education* (pp. 241–258). Hershey, PA: IGI Global. doi:10.4018/978-1-4666-5011-4.ch018

Anderson, K. M. (2017). Preparing Teachers in the Age of Equity and Inclusion. In I. Management Association (Ed.), Medical Education and Ethics: Concepts, Methodologies, Tools, and Applications (pp. 1532-1554). Hershey, PA: IGI Global. doi:10.4018/978-1-5225-0978-3.ch069

Awdziej, M. (2017). Case Study as a Teaching Method in Marketing. In D. Latusek (Ed.), *Case Studies as a Teaching Tool in Management Education* (pp. 244–263). Hershey, PA: IGI Global. doi:10.4018/978-1-5225-0770-3.ch013

Bain, B. (2014). Exploring Assessment of Critical Thinking Learning Outcomes in Online Higher Education. In V. Wang (Ed.), *Handbook of Research on Education and Technology in a Changing Society* (pp. 1191–1202). Hershey, PA: IGI Global. doi:10.4018/978-1-4666-6046-5.ch089

Banas, J. R., & York, C. S. (2017). Pre-Service Teachers' Motivation to Use Technology and the Impact of Authentic Learning Exercises. In L. Tomei (Ed.), *Exploring the New Era of Technology-Infused Education* (pp. 121–140). Hershey, PA: IGI Global. doi:10.4018/978-1-5225-1709-2.ch008

Bariso, E. U. (2015). Educational Policy Analysis Debates and New Learning Technologies in England. In M. Khosrow-Pour (Ed.), *Encyclopedia of Information Science and Technology* (3rd ed.; pp. 2371–2378). Hershey, PA: IGI Global. doi:10.4018/978-1-4666-5888-2.ch230

Beycioglu, K., & Wildy, H. (2015). Principal Preparation: The Case of Novice Principals in Turkey. In K. Beycioglu & P. Pashiardis (Eds.), *Multidimensional Perspectives on Principal Leadership Effectiveness* (pp. 1–17). Hershey, PA: IGI Global. doi:10.4018/978-1-4666-6591-0.ch001

Beycioglu, K., & Wildy, H. (2017). Principal Preparation: The Case of Novice Principals in Turkey. In I. Management Association (Ed.), Educational Leadership and Administration: Concepts, Methodologies, Tools, and Applications (pp. 1152-1169). Hershey, PA: IGI Global. doi:10.4018/978-1-5225-1624-8.ch054

Bharwani, S., & Musunuri, D. (2018). Reflection as a Process From Theory to Practice. In M. Khosrow-Pour, D.B.A. (Ed.), Encyclopedia of Information Science and Technology, Fourth Edition (pp. 1529-1539). Hershey, PA: IGI Global. doi:10.4018/978-1-5225-2255-3.ch132

Bisschoff, T., & Rhodes, C. (2011). Transformation through Marketing: A Case of a Secondary School in South Africa. In P. Tripathi & S. Mukerji (Eds.), *Cases on Innovations in Educational Marketing: Transnational and Technological Strategies* (pp. 263–272). Hershey, PA: IGI Global. doi:10.4018/978-1-60960-599-5.ch016

Bodomo, A. B. (2010). Educational Technologies (WebCT): Creating Constructivist and Interactive Learning Communities. In A. Bodomo (Ed.), *Computer-Mediated Communication for Linguistics and Literacy: Technology and Natural Language Education* (pp. 252–290). Hershey, PA: IGI Global. doi:10.4018/978-1-60566-868-0.ch010

Bohjanen, S. L., Cameron-Standerford, A., & Meidl, T. D. (2018). Capacity Building Pedagogy for Diverse Learners. In J. Keengwe (Ed.), *Handbook of Research on Pedagogical Models for Next-Generation Teaching and Learning* (pp. 195–212). Hershey, PA: IGI Global. doi:10.4018/978-1-5225-3873-8.ch011

Brewer, J. C. (2018). Measuring Text Readability Using Reading Level. In M. Khosrow-Pour, D.B.A. (Ed.), Encyclopedia of Information Science and Technology, Fourth Edition (pp. 1499-1507). Hershey, PA: IGI Global. doi:10.4018/978-1-5225-2255-3.ch129

Brown, S. L. (2017). A Case Study of Strategic Leadership and Research in Practice: Principal Preparation Programs that Work – An Educational Administration Perspective of Best Practices for Master's Degree Programs for Principal Preparation. In V. Wang (Ed.), *Encyclopedia of Strategic Leadership and Management* (pp. 1226–1244). Hershey, PA: IGI Global. doi:10.4018/978-1-5225-1049-9.ch086

Brzozowski, M., & Ferster, I. (2017). Educational Management Leadership: High School Principal's Management Style and Parental Involvement in School Management in Israel. In V. Potocan, M. Üngan, & Z. Nedelko (Eds.), *Handbook of Research on Managerial Solutions in Non-Profit Organizations* (pp. 55–74). Hershey, PA: IGI Global. doi:10.4018/978-1-5225-0731-4.ch003

Cannaday, J. (2017). The Masking Effect: Hidden Gifts and Disabilities of 2e Students. In P. Dickenson, P. Keough, & J. Courduff (Eds.), *Preparing Pre-Service Teachers for the Inclusive Classroom* (pp. 220–231). Hershey, PA: IGI Global. doi:10.4018/978-1-5225-1753-5.ch011

Capobianco, B. M., & Lehman, J. D. (2010). Fostering Educational Technology Integration in Science Teacher Education: Issues of Teacher Identity Development. In J. Yamamoto, J. Kush, R. Lombard, & C. Hertzog (Eds.), *Technology Implementation and Teacher Education: Reflective Models* (pp. 245–257). Hershey, PA: IGI Global. doi:10.4018/978-1-61520-897-5.ch014

Chao, G. H., Hsu, M. K., & Scovotti, C. (2013). Predicting Donations from a Cohort Group of Donors to Charities: A Direct Marketing Case Study. In J. Wang (Ed.), *Optimizing, Innovating, and Capitalizing on Information Systems for Operations* (pp. 196–214). Hershey, PA: IGI Global. doi:10.4018/978-1-4666-2925-7.ch010

Chauhan, A. (2015). Beyond the Phenomenon: Assessment in Massive Open Online Courses (MOOCs). In E. McKay & J. Lenarcic (Eds.), *Macro-Level Learning through Massive Open Online Courses (MOOCs): Strategies and Predictions for the Future* (pp. 119–140). Hershey, PA: IGI Global. doi:10.4018/978-1-4666-8324-2.ch007

Coffman, T. L., & Klinger, M. B. (2013). Managing Quality in Online Education. In G. Kurubacak & T. Yuzer (Eds.), *Project Management Approaches for Online Learning Design* (pp. 220–233). Hershey, PA: IGI Global. doi:10.4018/978-1-4666-2830-4.ch011

Contreras, E. C., & Contreras, I. I. (2018). Development of Communication Skills through Auditory Training Software in Special Education. In M. Khosrow-Pour, D.B.A. (Ed.), Encyclopedia of Information Science and Technology, Fourth Edition (pp. 2431-2441). Hershey, PA: IGI Global. doi:10.4018/978-1-5225-2255-3.ch212

Cook, R. G. (2011). Educational Marketing: Coming Down from the Cloud Using Landing Gear. In U. Demiray & S. Sever (Eds.), *Marketing Online Education Programs: Frameworks for Promotion and Communication* (pp. 26–31). Hershey, PA: IGI Global. doi:10.4018/978-1-60960-074-7.ch003

Cook, R. G., & Ley, K. (2015). Past, Future and Presents: Meeting New Online Challenges with Primal Marketing Solutions. *International Journal of Technology and Educational Marketing*, *5*(2), 19–33. doi:10.4018/IJTEM.2015070102

Cooley, D., & Whitten, E. (2017). Special Education Leadership and the Implementation of Response to Intervention. In F. Topor (Ed.), *Handbook of Research on Individualism and Identity in the Globalized Digital Age* (pp. 265–286). Hershey, PA: IGI Global. doi:10.4018/978-1-5225-0522-8.ch012

Cosner, S., Tozer, S., & Zavitkovsky, P. (2017). Enacting a Cycle of Inquiry Capstone Research Project in Doctoral-Level Leadership Preparation. In I. Management Association (Ed.), Educational Leadership and Administration: Concepts, Methodologies, Tools, and Applications (pp. 1460-1481). Hershey, PA: IGI Global. doi:10.4018/978-1-5225-1624-8.ch067

Crawford, C. M. (2018). Instructional Real World Community Engagement. In M. Khosrow-Pour, D.B.A. (Ed.), Encyclopedia of Information Science and Technology, Fourth Edition (pp. 1474-1486). Hershey, PA: IGI Global. doi:10.4018/978-1-5225-2255-3.ch127

Crosby-Cooper, T., & Pacis, D. (2017). Implementing Effective Student Support Teams. In P. Dickenson, P. Keough, & J. Courduff (Eds.), *Preparing Pre-Service Teachers for the Inclusive Classroom* (pp. 248–262). Hershey, PA: IGI Global. doi:10.4018/978-1-5225-1753-5.ch013

Curran, C. M., & Hawbaker, B. W. (2017). Cultivating Communities of Inclusive Practice: Professional Development for Educators – Research and Practice. In C. Curran & A. Petersen (Eds.), *Handbook of Research on Classroom Diversity and Inclusive Education Practice* (pp. 120–153). Hershey, PA: IGI Global. doi:10.4018/978-1-5225-2520-2.ch006

Dass, S., & Dabbagh, N. (2018). Faculty Adoption of 3D Avatar-Based Virtual World Learning Environments: An Exploratory Case Study. In I. Management Association (Ed.), Technology Adoption and Social Issues: Concepts, Methodologies, Tools, and Applications (pp. 1000-1033). Hershey, PA: IGI Global. doi:10.4018/978-1-5225-5201-7.ch045

Davison, A. M., & Scholl, K. G. (2017). Inclusive Recreation as Part of the IEP Process. In C. Curran & A. Petersen (Eds.), *Handbook of Research on Classroom Diversity and Inclusive Education Practice* (pp. 311–330). Hershey, PA: IGI Global. doi:10.4018/978-1-5225-2520-2.ch013

DeCoito, I. (2018). Addressing Digital Competencies, Curriculum Development, and Instructional Design in Science Teacher Education. In M. Khosrow-Pour, D.B.A. (Ed.), Encyclopedia of Information Science and Technology, Fourth Edition (pp. 1420-1431). Hershey, PA: IGI Global. doi:10.4018/978-1-5225-2255-3.ch122

DeCoito, I., & Richardson, T. (2017). Beyond Angry Birds™: Using Web-Based Tools to Engage Learners and Promote Inquiry in STEM Learning. In I. Levin & D. Tsybulsky (Eds.), *Digital Tools and Solutions for Inquiry-Based STEM Learning* (pp. 166–196). Hershey, PA: IGI Global. doi:10.4018/978-1-5225-2525-7.ch007

Delmas, P. M. (2017). Research-Based Leadership for Next-Generation Leaders. In R. Styron Jr & J. Styron (Eds.), *Comprehensive Problem-Solving and Skill Development for Next-Generation Leaders* (pp. 1–39). Hershey, PA: IGI Global. doi:10.4018/978-1-5225-1968-3.ch001

Demiray, U., & Ekren, G. (2018). Administrative-Related Evaluation for Distance Education Institutions in Turkey. In K. Buyuk, S. Kocdar, & A. Bozkurt (Eds.), *Administrative Leadership in Open and Distance Learning Programs* (pp. 263–288). Hershey, PA: IGI Global. doi:10.4018/978-1-5225-2645-2.ch011

Dickenson, P. (2017). What do we Know and Where Can We Grow?: Teachers Preparation for the Inclusive Classroom. In P. Dickenson, P. Keough, & J. Courduff (Eds.), *Preparing Pre-Service Teachers for the Inclusive Classroom* (pp. 1–22). Hershey, PA: IGI Global. doi:10.4018/978-1-5225-1753-5.ch001

Dickerson, J., & Coleman, H. V. (2012). Technology, E-Leadership and Educational Administration in Schools: Integrating Standards with Context and Guiding Questions. In V. Wang (Ed.), *Encyclopedia of E-Leadership, Counseling and Training* (pp. 408–422). Hershey, PA: IGI Global. doi:10.4018/978-1-61350-068-2.ch030

Dickerson, J., Coleman, H. V., & Geer, G. (2012). Thinking like a School Technology Leader. In V. Wang (Ed.), *Technology and Its Impact on Educational Leadership: Innovation and Change* (pp. 53–63). Hershey, PA: IGI Global. doi:10.4018/978-1-4666-0062-1.ch005

Donne, V., & Hansen, M. (2017). Teachers' Use of Assistive Technologies in Education. In L. Tomei (Ed.), *Exploring the New Era of Technology-Infused Education* (pp. 86–101). Hershey, PA: IGI Global. doi:10.4018/978-1-5225-1709-2.ch006

Donne, V., & Hansen, M. A. (2018). Business and Technology Educators: Practices for Inclusion. In I. Management Association (Ed.), Business Education and Ethics: Concepts, Methodologies, Tools, and Applications (pp. 471-484). Hershey, PA: IGI Global. doi:10.4018/978-1-5225-3153-1.ch026

Dreon, O., Shettel, J., & Bower, K. M. (2017). Preparing Next Generation Elementary Teachers for the Tools of Tomorrow. In M. Grassetti & S. Brookby (Eds.), *Advancing Next-Generation Teacher Education through Digital Tools and Applications* (pp. 143–159). Hershey, PA: IGI Global. doi:10.4018/978-1-5225-0965-3.ch008

Drinka, D., Voge, K., & Yen, M. Y. (2005). From Principles to Practice: Analyzing a Student Learning Outcomes Assessment System. *Journal of Cases on Information Technology*, 7(3), 37–56. doi:10.4018/jcit.2005070103

Durak, H. Y., & Güyer, T. (2018). Design and Development of an Instructional Program for Teaching Programming Processes to Gifted Students Using Scratch. In J. Cannaday (Ed.), *Curriculum Development for Gifted Education Programs* (pp. 61–99). Hershey, PA: IGI Global. doi:10.4018/978-1-5225-3041-1.ch004

Egorkina, E., Ivanov, M., & Valyavskiy, A. Y. (2018). Students' Research Competence Formation of the Quality of Open and Distance Learning. In V. Mkrttchian & L. Belyanina (Eds.), *Handbook of Research on Students' Research Competence in Modern Educational Contexts* (pp. 364–384). Hershey, PA: IGI Global. doi:10.4018/978-1-5225-3485-3.ch019

Ekren, G., Karataş, S., & Demiray, U. (2017). Understanding of Leadership in Distance Education Management. In I. Management Association (Ed.), Educational Leadership and Administration: Concepts, Methodologies, Tools, and Applications (pp. 34-50). Hershey, PA: IGI Global. doi:10.4018/978-1-5225-1624-8.ch003

Elmore, W. M., Young, J. K., Harris, S., & Mason, D. (2017). The Relationship between Individual Student Attributes and Online Course Completion. In K. Shelton & K. Pedersen (Eds.), *Handbook of Research on Building, Growing, and Sustaining Quality E-Learning Programs* (pp. 151–173). Hershey, PA: IGI Global. doi:10.4018/978-1-5225-0877-9.ch008

Ercegovac, I. R., Alfirević, N., & Koludrović, M. (2017). School Principals' Communication and Co-Operation Assessment: The Croatian Experience. In I. Management Association (Ed.), Educational Leadership and Administration: Concepts, Methodologies, Tools, and Applications (pp. 1568-1589). Hershey, PA: IGI Global. doi:10.4018/978-1-5225-1624-8.ch072

Everhart, D., & Seymour, D. M. (2017). Challenges and Opportunities in the Currency of Higher Education. In K. Rasmussen, P. Northrup, & R. Colson (Eds.), *Handbook of Research on Competency-Based Education in University Settings* (pp. 41–65). Hershey, PA: IGI Global. doi:10.4018/978-1-5225-0932-5.ch003

Farmer, L. S. (2017). Managing Portable Technologies for Special Education. In V. Wang (Ed.), *Encyclopedia of Strategic Leadership and Management* (pp. 977–987). Hershey, PA: IGI Global. doi:10.4018/978-1-5225-1049-9.ch068

Farmer, L. S. (2018). Optimizing OERs for Optimal ICT Literacy in Higher Education. In J. Keengwe (Ed.), *Handbook of Research on Mobile Technology, Constructivism, and Meaningful Learning* (pp. 366–390). Hershey, PA: IGI Global. doi:10.4018/978-1-5225-3949-0.ch020

Fındık, L. Y. (2017). Self-Assessment of Principals Based on Leadership in Complexity. In I. Management Association (Ed.), Educational Leadership and Administration: Concepts, Methodologies, Tools, and Applications (pp. 978-991). Hershey, PA: IGI Global. doi:10.4018/978-1-5225-1624-8.ch047

Flor, A. G., & Gonzalez-Flor, B. (2018). Dysfunctional Digital Demeanors: Tales From (and Policy Implications of) eLearning's Dark Side. In I. Management Association (Ed.), The Dark Web: Breakthroughs in Research and Practice (pp. 37-50). Hershey, PA: IGI Global. doi:10.4018/978-1-5225-3163-0.ch003

Floyd, K. K., & Shambaugh, N. (2017). Instructional Design for Simulations in Special Education Virtual Learning Spaces. In T. Kidd & L. Morris Jr., (Eds.), *Handbook of Research on Instructional Systems and Educational Technology* (pp. 202–215). Hershey, PA: IGI Global. doi:10.4018/978-1-5225-2399-4.ch018

Giovannini, J. M. (2017). Technology Integration in Preservice Teacher Education Programs: Research-based Recommendations. In M. Grassetti & S. Brookby (Eds.), *Advancing Next-Generation Teacher Education through Digital Tools and Applications* (pp. 82–102). Hershey, PA: IGI Global. doi:10.4018/978-1-5225-0965-3.ch005

Good, S., & Clarke, V. B. (2017). An Integral Analysis of One Urban School System's Efforts to Support Student-Centered Teaching. In J. Keengwe & G. Onchwari (Eds.), *Handbook of Research on Learner-Centered Pedagogy in Teacher Education and Professional Development* (pp. 45–68). Hershey, PA: IGI Global. doi:10.4018/978-1-5225-0892-2.ch003

Grobler, B. (2015). The Relationship between Emotional Competence and Instructional Leadership and Their Association with Learner Achievement. In K. Beycioglu & P. Pashiardis (Eds.), *Multidimensional Perspectives on Principal Leadership Effectiveness* (pp. 373–407). Hershey, PA: IGI Global. doi:10.4018/978-1-4666-6591-0.ch017

Hamidi, F., Owuor, P. M., Hynie, M., Baljko, M., & McGrath, S. (2017). Potentials of Digital Assistive Technology and Special Education in Kenya. In C. Ayo & V. Mbarika (Eds.), *Sustainable ICT Adoption and Integration for Socio-Economic Development* (pp. 125–151). Hershey, PA: IGI Global. doi:10.4018/978-1-5225-2565-3.ch006

Heavin, C., & Neville, K. (2015). Addressing the Learning Needs of Future IS Security Professionals through Social Media Technology. In M. Khosrow-Pour (Ed.), *Encyclopedia of Information Science and Technology* (3rd ed.; pp. 4766–4775). Hershey, PA: IGI Global. doi:10.4018/978-1-4666-5888-2.ch468

Henderson, L. K. (2017). Meltdown at Fukushima: Global Catastrophic Events, Visual Literacy, and Art Education. In R. Shin (Ed.), *Convergence of Contemporary Art, Visual Culture, and Global Civic Engagement* (pp. 80–99). Hershey, PA: IGI Global. doi:10.4018/978-1-5225-1665-1.ch005

Hismanoglu, M. (2012). Important Issues in Online Education: E-Pedagogy and Marketing. In I. Management Association (Ed.), E-Marketing: Concepts, Methodologies, Tools, and Applications (pp. 676-701). Hershey, PA: IGI Global. doi:10.4018/978-1-4666-1598-4.ch041

Howard, B. C. (2008). Common Features and Design Principles Found in Exemplary Educational Technologies. *International Journal of Information and Communication Technology Education*, *4*(4), 31–52. doi:10.4018/jicte.2008100104

Howard, B. C., & Tomei, L. A. (2008). The Classroom of the Future and Emerging Educational Technologies: Introduction to the Special Issue. *International Journal of Information and Communication Technology Education*, *4*(4), 1–8. doi:10.4018/jicte.2008100101

Hudgins, T., & Holland, J. L. (2018). Digital Badges: Tracking Knowledge Acquisition Within an Innovation Framework. In I. Management Association (Ed.), Wearable Technologies: Concepts, Methodologies, Tools, and Applications (pp. 1118-1132). Hershey, PA: IGI Global. doi:10.4018/978-1-5225-5484-4.ch051

Ion, G., Tomàs, M., Castro, D., & Salat, E. (2015). Analysis of the Tasks of School Principals in Secondary Education in Catalonia: Case Study. In K. Beycioglu & P. Pashiardis (Eds.), *Multidimensional Perspectives on Principal Leadership Effectiveness* (pp. 39–58). Hershey, PA: IGI Global. doi:10.4018/978-1-4666-6591-0.ch003

Janus, M., & Siddiqua, A. (2018). Challenges for Children With Special Health Needs at the Time of Transition to School. In I. Management Association (Ed.), Autism Spectrum Disorders: Breakthroughs in Research and Practice (pp. 339-371). Hershey, PA: IGI Global. doi:10.4018/978-1-5225-3827-1.ch018

Jesus, R. A. (2018). Screencasts and Learning Styles. In M. Khosrow-Pour, D.B.A. (Ed.), Encyclopedia of Information Science and Technology, Fourth Edition (pp. 1548-1558). Hershey, PA: IGI Global. doi:10.4018/978-1-5225-2255-3.ch134

Kaplan-Rakowski, R., & Rakowski, D. (2011). Educational Technologies for the Neomillennial Generation. In E. Dunkels, G. Franberg, & C. Hallgren (Eds.), *Interactive Media Use and Youth: Learning, Knowledge Exchange and Behavior* (pp. 12–31). Hershey, PA: IGI Global. doi:10.4018/978-1-60960-206-2.ch002

Karpinski, A. C., D'Agostino, J. V., Williams, A. K., Highland, S. A., & Mellott, J. A. (2018). The Relationship Between Online Formative Assessment and State Test Scores Using Multilevel Modeling. In M. Khosrow-Pour, D.B.A. (Ed.), Encyclopedia of Information Science and Technology, Fourth Edition (pp. 5183-5192). Hershey, PA: IGI Global. doi:10.4018/978-1-5225-2255-3.ch450

Kats, Y. (2017). Educational Leadership and Integrated Support for Students with Autism Spectrum Disorders. In I. Management Association (Ed.), *Educational Leadership and Administration: Concepts, Methodologies, Tools, and Applications* (pp. 101-114). Hershey, PA: IGI Global. doi:10.4018/978-1-5225-1624-8.ch007

Kaya, G., & Altun, A. (2018). Educational Ontology Development. In M. Khosrow-Pour, D.B.A. (Ed.), *Encyclopedia of Information Science and Technology, Fourth Edition* (pp. 1441-1450). Hershey, PA: IGI Global. doi:10.4018/978-1-5225-2255-3.ch124

Keough, P. D., & Pacis, D. (2017). Best Practices Implementing Special Education Curriculum and Common Core State Standards using UDL. In P. Dickenson, P. Keough, & J. Courduff (Eds.), *Preparing Pre-Service Teachers for the Inclusive Classroom* (pp. 107–123). Hershey, PA: IGI Global. doi:10.4018/978-1-5225-1753-5.ch006

Kilburn, M., Henckell, M., & Starrett, D. (2018). Factors Contributing to the Effectiveness of Online Students and Instructors. In M. Khosrow-Pour, D.B.A. (Ed.), *Encyclopedia of Information Science and Technology, Fourth Edition* (pp. 1451-1462). Hershey, PA: IGI Global. doi:10.4018/978-1-5225-2255-3.ch125

Konecny, L. T. (2017). Hybrid, Online, and Flipped Classrooms in Health Science: Enhanced Learning Environments. In I. Management Association (Ed.), *Flipped Instruction: Breakthroughs in Research and Practice* (pp. 355-370). Hershey, PA: IGI Global. doi:10.4018/978-1-5225-1803-7.ch020

Kowch, E. G. (2013). Towards Leading Diverse, Smarter and More Adaptable Organizations that Learn. In J. Lewis, A. Green, & D. Surry (Eds.), *Technology as a Tool for Diversity Leadership: Implementation and Future Implications* (pp. 11–34). Hershey, PA: IGI Global. doi:10.4018/978-1-4666-2668-3.ch002

Krezmien, M., Powell, W., Bosch, C., Hall, T., & Nieswandt, M. (2017). The Use of Tablet Technology to Support Inquiry Science for Students Incarcerated in Juvenile Justice Settings. In I. Levin & D. Tsybulsky (Eds.), *Optimizing STEM Education With Advanced ICTs and Simulations* (pp. 267–295). Hershey, PA: IGI Global. doi:10.4018/978-1-5225-2528-8.ch011

Leach, L. F., Winn, P., Erwin, S., & Benedict, L. P. (2015). What 21st Century Students Want: Factors that Influence Student Selection of Educational Leadership Graduate Programs. *International Journal of Technology and Educational Marketing*, *5*(1), 15–28. doi:10.4018/ijtem.2015010102

Leng, H. K. (2014). An Update on the Use of Facebook as a Marketing Tool by Private Educational Institutions in Singapore. In I. Lee (Ed.), *Trends in E-Business, E-Services, and E-Commerce: Impact of Technology on Goods, Services, and Business Transactions* (pp. 191–205). Hershey, PA: IGI Global. doi:10.4018/978-1-4666-4510-3.ch011

Leone, S. (2018). An Open Learning Format for Lifelong Learners' Empowerment. In M. Khosrow-Pour, D.B.A. (Ed.), *Encyclopedia of Information Science and Technology, Fourth Edition* (pp. 1517-1528). Hershey, PA: IGI Global. doi:10.4018/978-1-5225-2255-3.ch131

Ley, K., & Gannon-Cook, R. (2010). Marketing a Blended University Program: An Action Research Case Study. In S. Mukerji & P. Tripathi (Eds.), *Cases on Technology Enhanced Learning through Collaborative Opportunities* (pp. 73–90). Hershey, PA: IGI Global. doi:10.4018/978-1-61520-751-0.ch005

Loose, W., & Marcos, T. (2016). Instructional Design for Millennials: Instructor Efficiency in Streamlining Content, Assignments, and Assessments. In P. Dickenson & J. Jaurez (Eds.), *Increasing Productivity and Efficiency in Online Teaching* (pp. 1–25). Hershey, PA: IGI Global. doi:10.4018/978-1-5225-0347-7.ch001

Lovell, K. L. (2017). Development and Evaluation of Neuroscience Computer-Based Modules for Medical Students: Instructional Design Principles and Effectiveness. In J. Stefaniak (Ed.), *Advancing Medical Education Through Strategic Instructional Design* (pp. 262–276). Hershey, PA: IGI Global. doi:10.4018/978-1-5225-2098-6.ch013

Manuel, N. N. (2016). Angolan Higher Education, Policy, and Leadership: Towards Transformative Leadership for Social Justice. In N. Ololube (Ed.), *Handbook of Research on Organizational Justice and Culture in Higher Education Institutions* (pp. 164–188). Hershey, PA: IGI Global. doi:10.4018/978-1-4666-9850-5.ch007

Marouchou, D. V. (2015). The Impact of Academic Beliefs on Student Learning. In M. Khosrow-Pour (Ed.), *Encyclopedia of Information Science and Technology* (3rd ed.; pp. 4796–4804). Hershey, PA: IGI Global. doi:10.4018/978-1-4666-5888-2.ch471

McCormack, V. F., Stauffer, M., Fishley, K., Hohenbrink, J., Mascazine, J. R., & Zigler, T. (2018). Designing a Dual Licensure Path for Middle Childhood and Special Education Teacher Candidates. In D. Polly, M. Putman, T. Petty, & A. Good (Eds.), *Innovative Practices in Teacher Preparation and Graduate-Level Teacher Education Programs* (pp. 21–36). Hershey, PA: IGI Global. doi:10.4018/978-1-5225-3068-8.ch002

McDaniel, R. (2017). Strategic Leadership in Instructional Design: Applying the Principles of Instructional Design through the Lens of Strategic Leadership to Distance Education. In V. Wang (Ed.), *Encyclopedia of Strategic Leadership and Management* (pp. 1570–1584). Hershey, PA: IGI Global. doi:10.4018/978-1-5225-1049-9.ch109

Memon, R. N., Ahmad, R., & Salim, S. S. (2018). Critical Issues in Requirements Engineering Education. In I. Management Association (Ed.), Computer Systems and Software Engineering: Concepts, Methodologies, Tools, and Applications (pp. 1953-1976). Hershey, PA: IGI Global. doi:10.4018/978-1-5225-3923-0.ch081

Mendenhall, R. (2017). Western Governors University: CBE Innovator and National Model. In K. Rasmussen, P. Northrup, & R. Colson (Eds.), *Handbook of Research on Competency-Based Education in University Settings* (pp. 379–400). Hershey, PA: IGI Global. doi:10.4018/978-1-5225-0932-5.ch019

Mense, E. G., Griggs, D. M., & Shanks, J. N. (2018). School Leaders in a Time of Accountability and Data Use: Preparing Our Future School Leaders in Leadership Preparation Programs. In E. Mense & M. Crain-Dorough (Eds.), *Data Leadership for K-12 Schools in a Time of Accountability* (pp. 235–259). Hershey, PA: IGI Global. doi:10.4018/978-1-5225-3188-3.ch012

Mense, E. G., Griggs, D. M., & Shanks, J. N. (2018). School Leaders in a Time of Accountability and Data Use: Preparing Our Future School Leaders in Leadership Preparation Programs. In E. Mense & M. Crain-Dorough (Eds.), *Data Leadership for K-12 Schools in a Time of Accountability* (pp. 235–259). Hershey, PA: IGI Global. doi:10.4018/978-1-5225-3188-3.ch012

Mestry, R., & Naicker, S. R. (2017). Exploring Distributive Leadership in South African Public Primary Schools in the Soweto Region. In I. Management Association (Ed.), Educational Leadership and Administration: Concepts, Methodologies, Tools, and Applications (pp. 1041-1064). Hershey, PA: IGI Global. doi:10.4018/978-1-5225-1624-8.ch050

Monaghan, C. H., & Boboc, M. (2017). (Re)Defining Leadership in Higher Education in the U.S. In V. Wang (Ed.), *Encyclopedia of Strategic Leadership and Management* (pp. 567–579). Hershey, PA: IGI Global. doi:10.4018/978-1-5225-1049-9.ch040

Muthee, J. M., & Murungi, C. G. (2018). Relationship Among Intelligence, Achievement Motivation, Type of School, and Academic Performance of Kenyan Urban Primary School Pupils. In M. Khosrow-Pour, D.B.A. (Ed.), Encyclopedia of Information Science and Technology, Fourth Edition (pp. 1540-1547). Hershey, PA: IGI Global. doi:10.4018/978-1-5225-2255-3.ch133

Naranjo, J. (2018). Meeting the Need for Inclusive Educators Online: Teacher Education in Inclusive Special Education and Dual-Certification. In D. Polly, M. Putman, T. Petty, & A. Good (Eds.), *Innovative Practices in Teacher Preparation and Graduate-Level Teacher Education Programs* (pp. 106–122). Hershey, PA: IGI Global. doi:10.4018/978-1-5225-3068-8.ch007

Nkabinde, Z. P. (2017). Multiculturalism in Special Education: Perspectives of Minority Children in Urban Schools. In J. Keengwe (Ed.), *Handbook of Research on Promoting Cross-Cultural Competence and Social Justice in Teacher Education* (pp. 382–397). Hershey, PA: IGI Global. doi:10.4018/978-1-5225-0897-7.ch020

Nkabinde, Z. P. (2018). Online Instruction: Is the Quality the Same as Face-to-Face Instruction? In J. Keengwe (Ed.), *Handbook of Research on Digital Content, Mobile Learning, and Technology Integration Models in Teacher Education* (pp. 300–314). Hershey, PA: IGI Global. doi:10.4018/978-1-5225-2953-8.ch016

O'Connor, J. R. Jr, & Jackson, K. N. (2017). The Use of iPad® Devices and "Apps" for ASD Students in Special Education and Speech Therapy. In Y. Kats (Ed.), *Supporting the Education of Children with Autism Spectrum Disorders* (pp. 267–283). Hershey, PA: IGI Global. doi:10.4018/978-1-5225-0816-8.ch014

Okolie, U. C., & Yasin, A. M. (2017). TVET in Developing Nations and Human Development. In U. Okolie & A. Yasin (Eds.), *Technical Education and Vocational Training in Developing Nations* (pp. 1–25). Hershey, PA: IGI Global. doi:10.4018/978-1-5225-1811-2.ch001

Paciga, K. A., & Hoffman, J. L. (2015). Realizing the Potential of e-Books in Early Education. In M. Khosrow-Pour (Ed.), *Encyclopedia of Information Science and Technology* (3rd ed.; pp. 4787–4795). Hershey, PA: IGI Global. doi:10.4018/978-1-4666-5888-2.ch470

Paulson, E. N. (2017). Adapting and Advocating for an Online EdD Program in Changing Times and "Sacred" Cultures. In I. Management Association (Ed.), *Educational Leadership and Administration: Concepts, Methodologies, Tools, and Applications* (pp. 1849-1876). Hershey, PA: IGI Global. doi:10.4018/978-1-5225-1624-8.ch085

Petersen, A. J., Elser, C. F., Al Nassir, M. N., Stakey, J., & Everson, K. (2017). The Year of Teaching Inclusively: Building an Elementary Classroom for All Students. In C. Curran & A. Petersen (Eds.), *Handbook of Research on Classroom Diversity and Inclusive Education Practice* (pp. 332–348). Hershey, PA: IGI Global. doi:10.4018/978-1-5225-2520-2.ch014

Pfannenstiel, K. H., & Sanders, J. (2017). Characteristics and Instructional Strategies for Students With Mathematical Difficulties: In the Inclusive Classroom. In C. Curran & A. Petersen (Eds.), *Handbook of Research on Classroom Diversity and Inclusive Education Practice* (pp. 250–281). Hershey, PA: IGI Global. doi:10.4018/978-1-5225-2520-2.ch011

Preast, J. L., Bowman, N., & Rose, C. A. (2017). Creating Inclusive Classroom Communities Through Social and Emotional Learning to Reduce Social Marginalization Among Students. In C. Curran & A. Petersen (Eds.), *Handbook of Research on Classroom Diversity and Inclusive Education Practice* (pp. 183–200). Hershey, PA: IGI Global. doi:10.4018/978-1-5225-2520-2.ch008

Randolph, K. M., & Brady, M. P. (2018). Evolution of Covert Coaching as an Evidence-Based Practice in Professional Development and Preparation of Teachers. In V. Bryan, A. Musgrove, & J. Powers (Eds.), *Handbook of Research on Human Development in the Digital Age* (pp. 281–299). Hershey, PA: IGI Global. doi:10.4018/978-1-5225-2838-8.ch013

Rawlins, P., & Kehrwald, B. (2010). Education Technology in Teacher Education: Overcoming Challenges, Realizing Opportunities. In R. Luppicini & A. Haghi (Eds.), *Cases on Digital Technologies in Higher Education: Issues and Challenges* (pp. 50–63). Hershey, PA: IGI Global. doi:10.4018/978-1-61520-869-2.ch004

Rell, A. B., Puig, R. A., Roll, F., Valles, V., Espinoza, M., & Duque, A. L. (2017). Addressing Cultural Diversity and Global Competence: The Dual Language Framework. In L. Leavitt, S. Wisdom, & K. Leavitt (Eds.), *Cultural Awareness and Competency Development in Higher Education* (pp. 111–131). Hershey, PA: IGI Global. doi:10.4018/978-1-5225-2145-7.ch007

Riel, J., Lawless, K. A., & Brown, S. W. (2017). Defining and Designing Responsive Online Professional Development (ROPD): A Framework to Support Curriculum Implementation. In T. Kidd & L. Morris Jr., (Eds.), *Handbook of Research on Instructional Systems and Educational Technology* (pp. 104–115). Hershey, PA: IGI Global. doi:10.4018/978-1-5225-2399-4.ch010

Roberts, C. (2017). Advancing Women Leaders in Academe: Creating a Culture of Inclusion. In S. Mukerji & P. Tripathi (Eds.), *Handbook of Research on Administration, Policy, and Leadership in Higher Education* (pp. 256–273). Hershey, PA: IGI Global. doi:10.4018/978-1-5225-0672-0.ch012

Rodgers, W. J., Kennedy, M. J., Alves, K. D., & Romig, J. E. (2017). A Multimedia Tool for Teacher Education and Professional Development. In C. Martin & D. Polly (Eds.), *Handbook of Research on Teacher Education and Professional Development* (pp. 285–296). Hershey, PA: IGI Global. doi:10.4018/978-1-5225-1067-3.ch015

Romanowski, M. H. (2017). Qatar's Educational Reform: Critical Issues Facing Principals. In I. Management Association (Ed.), Educational Leadership and Administration: Concepts, Methodologies, Tools, and Applications (pp. 1758-1773). Hershey, PA: IGI Global. doi:10.4018/978-1-5225-1624-8.ch080

Ruffin, T. R., Hawkins, D. P., & Lee, D. I. (2018). Increasing Student Engagement and Participation Through Course Methodology. In M. Khosrow-Pour, D.B.A. (Ed.), Encyclopedia of Information Science and Technology, Fourth Edition (pp. 1463-1473). Hershey, PA: IGI Global. doi:10.4018/978-1-5225-2255-3.ch126

Rutaisire, J. (2011). Innovations in Technology for Educational Marketing: Stakeholder Perceptions and Implications for Examinations System in Rwanda. In P. Tripathi & S. Mukerji (Eds.), *Cases on Innovations in Educational Marketing: Transnational and Technological Strategies* (pp. 214–233). Hershey, PA: IGI Global. doi:10.4018/978-1-60960-599-5.ch013

Sabina, L. L., Curry, K. A., Harris, E. L., Krumm, B. L., & Vencill, V. (2017). Assessing the Performance of a Cohort-Based Model Using Domestic and International Practices. In I. Management Association (Ed.), Educational Leadership and Administration: Concepts, Methodologies, Tools, and Applications(pp. 913-929). Hershey, PA: IGI Global. doi:10.4018/978-1-5225-1624-8.ch044

Santamaría, A. P., Webber, M., & Santamaría, L. J. (2017). Effective School Leadership for Māori Achievement: Building Capacity through Indigenous, National, and International Cross-Cultural Collaboration. In I. Management Association (Ed.), Educational Leadership and Administration: Concepts, Methodologies, Tools, and Applications (pp. 1547-1567). Hershey, PA: IGI Global. doi:10.4018/978-1-5225-1624-8.ch071

Santamaría, L. J. (2017). Culturally Responsive Educational Leadership in Cross-Cultural International Contexts. In I. Management Association (Ed.), Educational Leadership and Administration: Concepts, Methodologies, Tools, and Applications (pp. 1380-1400). Hershey, PA: IGI Global. doi:10.4018/978-1-5225-1624-8.ch064

Sarafidou, J., & Xafakos, E. (2015). Transformational Leadership and Principals' Innovativeness: Are They the "Keys" for the Research and Innovation Oriented School? In K. Beycioglu & P. Pashiardis (Eds.), *Multidimensional Perspectives on Principal Leadership Effectiveness* (pp. 324–348). Hershey, PA: IGI Global. doi:10.4018/978-1-4666-6591-0.ch015

Segredo, M. R., Cistone, P. J., & Reio, T. G. (2017). Relationships Between Emotional Intelligence, Leadership Style, and School Culture. *International Journal of Adult Vocational Education and Technology*, 8(3), 25–43. doi:10.4018/IJAVET.2017070103

Shaik, N., & Ritter, S. (2012). Social Media Based Relationship Marketing. In I. Management Association (Ed.), E-Marketing: Concepts, Methodologies, Tools, and Applications (pp. 88-110). Hershey, PA: IGI Global. doi:10.4018/978-1-4666-1598-4.ch006

Shalev, N. (2017). Empathy and Leadership From the Organizational Perspective. In Z. Nedelko & M. Brzozowski (Eds.), *Exploring the Influence of Personal Values and Cultures in the Workplace* (pp. 348–363). Hershey, PA: IGI Global. doi:10.4018/978-1-5225-2480-9.ch018

Siamak, M., Fathi, S., & Isfandyari-Moghaddam, A. (2018). Assessment and Measurement of Education Programs of Information Literacy. In R. Bhardwaj (Ed.), *Digitizing the Modern Library and the Transition From Print to Electronic* (pp. 164–192). Hershey, PA: IGI Global. doi:10.4018/978-1-5225-2119-8.ch007

Siozos, P. D., & Palaigeorgiou, G. E. (2008). Educational Technologies and the Emergence of E-Learning 2.0. In D. Politis (Ed.), *E-Learning Methodologies and Computer Applications in Archaeology* (pp. 1–17). Hershey, PA: IGI Global. doi:10.4018/978-1-59904-759-1.ch001

Siu, K. W., & García, G. J. (2017). Disruptive Technologies and Education: Is There Any Disruption After All? In I. Management Association (Ed.), Educational Leadership and Administration: Concepts, Methodologies, Tools, and Applications (pp. 757-778). Hershey, PA: IGI Global. doi:10.4018/978-1-5225-1624-8.ch037

Skibba, K., Moore, D., & Herman, J. H. (2013). Pedagogical and Technological Considerations Designing Collaborative Learning Using Educational Technologies. In J. Keengwe (Ed.), *Research Perspectives and Best Practices in Educational Technology Integration* (pp. 1–27). Hershey, PA: IGI Global. doi:10.4018/978-1-4666-2988-2.ch001

Slagter van Tryon, P. J. (2017). The Nurse Educator's Role in Designing Instruction and Instructional Strategies for Academic and Clinical Settings. In J. Stefaniak (Ed.), *Advancing Medical Education Through Strategic Instructional Design* (pp. 133–149). Hershey, PA: IGI Global. doi:10.4018/978-1-5225-2098-6.ch006

Slattery, C. A. (2018). Literacy Intervention and the Differentiated Plan of Instruction. In *Developing Effective Literacy Intervention Strategies: Emerging Research and Opportunities* (pp. 41–62). Hershey, PA: IGI Global. doi:10.4018/978-1-5225-5007-5.ch003

Smith, A. R. (2017). Ensuring Quality: The Faculty Role in Online Higher Education. In K. Shelton & K. Pedersen (Eds.), *Handbook of Research on Building, Growing, and Sustaining Quality E-Learning Programs* (pp. 210–231). Hershey, PA: IGI Global. doi:10.4018/978-1-5225-0877-9.ch011

Souders, T. M. (2017). Understanding Your Learner: Conducting a Learner Analysis. In J. Stefaniak (Ed.), *Advancing Medical Education Through Strategic Instructional Design* (pp. 1–29). Hershey, PA: IGI Global. doi:10.4018/978-1-5225-2098-6.ch001

Spring, K. J., Graham, C. R., & Ikahihifo, T. B. (2018). Learner Engagement in Blended Learning. In M. Khosrow-Pour, D.B.A. (Ed.), Encyclopedia of Information Science and Technology, Fourth Edition (pp. 1487-1498). Hershey, PA: IGI Global. doi:10.4018/978-1-5225-2255-3.ch128

Stocklin, S. (2015). Building Capacity by Managing a Mission. In J. Feng, S. Stocklin, & W. Wang (Eds.), *Educational Strategies for the Next Generation Leaders in Hotel Management* (pp. 115–139). Hershey, PA: IGI Global. doi:10.4018/978-1-4666-8565-9.ch005

Storey, V. A., Anthony, A. K., & Wahid, P. (2017). Gender-Based Leadership Barriers: Advancement of Female Faculty to Leadership Positions in Higher Education. In V. Wang (Ed.), *Encyclopedia of Strategic Leadership and Management* (pp. 244–258). Hershey, PA: IGI Global. doi:10.4018/978-1-5225-1049-9.ch018

Stottlemyer, D. (2018). Develop a Teaching Model Plan for a Differentiated Learning Approach. In *Differentiated Instructional Design for Multicultural Environments: Emerging Research and Opportunities* (pp. 106–130). Hershey, PA: IGI Global. doi:10.4018/978-1-5225-5106-5.ch005

Stottlemyer, D. (2018). Developing a Multicultural Environment. In *Differentiated Instructional Design for Multicultural Environments: Emerging Research and Opportunities* (pp. 1–27). Hershey, PA: IGI Global. doi:10.4018/978-1-5225-5106-5.ch001

Swami, B. N., Gobona, T., & Tsimako, J. J. (2017). Academic Leadership: A Case Study of the University of Botswana. In N. Baporikar (Ed.), *Innovation and Shifting Perspectives in Management Education* (pp. 1–32). Hershey, PA: IGI Global. doi:10.4018/978-1-5225-1019-2.ch001

Swanson, K. W., & Collins, G. (2018). Designing Engaging Instruction for the Adult Learners. In M. Khosrow-Pour, D.B.A. (Ed.), Encyclopedia of Information Science and Technology, Fourth Edition (pp. 1432-1440). Hershey, PA: IGI Global. doi:10.4018/978-1-5225-2255-3.ch123

Swartz, B. A., Lynch, J. M., & Lynch, S. D. (2018). Embedding Elementary Teacher Education Coursework in Local Classrooms: Examples in Mathematics and Special Education. In D. Polly, M. Putman, T. Petty, & A. Good (Eds.), *Innovative Practices in Teacher Preparation and Graduate-Level Teacher Education Programs* (pp. 262–292). Hershey, PA: IGI Global. doi:10.4018/978-1-5225-3068-8.ch015

Taliadorou, N., & Pashiardis, P. (2015). Emotional Intelligence and Political Skill Really Matter in Educational Leadership. In K. Beycioglu & P. Pashiardis (Eds.), *Multidimensional Perspectives on Principal Leadership Effectiveness* (pp. 228–256). Hershey, PA: IGI Global. doi:10.4018/978-1-4666-6591-0.ch011

Taliadorou, N., & Pashiardis, P. (2017). Emotional Intelligence and Political Skill Really Matter in Educational Leadership. In I. Management Association (Ed.), Educational Leadership and Administration: Concepts, Methodologies, Tools, and Applications (pp. 1274-1303). Hershey, PA: IGI Global. doi:10.4018/978-1-5225-1624-8.ch060

Tam, F. W., & Kwan, P. Y. (2011). School Images, School Identity, and How Parents Select Schools for Their Children: The Case of Hong Kong. In P. Tripathi & S. Mukerji (Eds.), *Cases on Innovations in Educational Marketing: Transnational and Technological Strategies* (pp. 87–103). Hershey, PA: IGI Global. doi:10.4018/978-1-60960-599-5.ch005

Tandoh, K. A., & Ebe-Arthur, J. E. (2018). Effective Educational Leadership in the Digital Age: An Examination of Professional Qualities and Best Practices. In J. Keengwe (Ed.), *Handbook of Research on Digital Content, Mobile Learning, and Technology Integration Models in Teacher Education* (pp. 244–265). Hershey, PA: IGI Global. doi:10.4018/978-1-5225-2953-8.ch013

Tinoca, L., Pereira, A., & Oliveira, I. (2014). A Conceptual Framework for E-Assessment in Higher Education: Authenticity, Consistency, Transparency, and Practicability. In S. Mukerji & P. Tripathi (Eds.), *Handbook of Research on Transnational Higher Education* (pp. 652–673). Hershey, PA: IGI Global. doi:10.4018/978-1-4666-4458-8.ch033

Tobin, M. T. (2018). Multimodal Literacy. In M. Khosrow-Pour, D.B.A. (Ed.), Encyclopedia of Information Science and Technology, Fourth Edition (pp. 1508-1516). Hershey, PA: IGI Global. doi:10.4018/978-1-5225-2255-3.ch130

Torres, M. L., & Ramos, V. J. (2018). Music Therapy: A Pedagogical Alternative for ASD and ID Students in Regular Classrooms. In P. Epler (Ed.), *Instructional Strategies in General Education and Putting the Individuals With Disabilities Act (IDEA) Into Practice* (pp. 222–244). Hershey, PA: IGI Global. doi:10.4018/978-1-5225-3111-1.ch008

Toulassi, B. (2017). Educational Administration and Leadership in Francophone Africa: 5 Dynamics to Change Education. In S. Mukerji & P. Tripathi (Eds.), *Handbook of Research on Administration, Policy, and Leadership in Higher Education* (pp. 20–45). Hershey, PA: IGI Global. doi:10.4018/978-1-5225-0672-0.ch002

Umair, S., & Sharif, M. M. (2018). Predicting Students Grades Using Artificial Neural Networks and Support Vector Machine. In M. Khosrow-Pour, D.B.A. (Ed.), Encyclopedia of Information Science and Technology, Fourth Edition (pp. 5169-5182). Hershey, PA: IGI Global. doi:10.4018/978-1-5225-2255-3.ch449

Usman, L. M. (2011). Adult Education and Sustainable Learning Outcome of Rural Widows of Central Northern Nigeria. *International Journal of Adult Vocational Education and Technology*, 2(2), 25–41. doi:10.4018/javet.2011040103

Vettraino, L., Castello, V., Guspini, M., & Guglielman, E. (2018). Self-Awareness and Motivation Contrasting ESL and NEET Using the SAVE System. In M. Khosrow-Pour, D.B.A. (Ed.), Encyclopedia of Information Science and Technology, Fourth Edition (pp. 1559-1568). Hershey, PA: IGI Global. doi:10.4018/978-1-5225-2255-3.ch135

Wang, V. C. (2013). Marketing Educational Programs through Technology and the Right Philosophies. In P. Tripathi & S. Mukerji (Eds.), *Marketing Strategies for Higher Education Institutions: Technological Considerations and Practices* (pp. 15–24). Hershey, PA: IGI Global. doi:10.4018/978-1-4666-4014-6.ch002

Wiemelt, J. (2017). Critical Bilingual Leadership for Emergent Bilingual Students. In I. Management Association (Ed.), Educational Leadership and Administration: Concepts, Methodologies, Tools, and Applications (pp. 1606-1631). Hershey, PA: IGI Global. doi:10.4018/978-1-5225-1624-8.ch074

Williams, D. D. (2006). Measurement and Assessment Supporting Evaluation in Online Settings. In D. Williams, M. Hricko, & S. Howell (Eds.), *Online Assessment, Measurement and Evaluation: Emerging Practices* (pp. 1–9). Hershey, PA: IGI Global. doi:10.4018/978-1-59140-747-8.ch001

Wolf, F., Seyfarth, F. C., & Pflaum, E. (2018). Scalable Capacity-Building for Geographically Dispersed Learners: Designing the MOOC "Sustainable Energy in Small Island Developing States (SIDS)". In U. Pandey & V. Indrakanti (Eds.), *Open and Distance Learning Initiatives for Sustainable Development* (pp. 58–83). Hershey, PA: IGI Global. doi:10.4018/978-1-5225-2621-6.ch003

Woodley, X. M., Mucundanyi, G., & Lockard, M. (2017). Designing Counter-Narratives: Constructing Culturally Responsive Curriculum Online. *International Journal of Online Pedagogy and Course Design*, 7(1), 43–56. doi:10.4018/IJOPCD.2017010104

Woods, P. A., & Woods, G. J. (2011). Lighting the Fires of Entrepreneurialism?: Constructions of Meaning in an English Inner City Academy. *International Journal of Technology and Educational Marketing*, 1(1), 1–24. doi:10.4018/ijtem.2011010101

Yell, M. L., & Christle, C. A. (2017). The Foundation of Inclusion in Federal Legislation and Litigation. In C. Curran & A. Petersen (Eds.), *Handbook of Research on Classroom Diversity and Inclusive Education Practice* (pp. 27–52). Hershey, PA: IGI Global. doi:10.4018/978-1-5225-2520-2.ch002

Zhao, J. (2011). China Special Education: The Perspective of Information Technologies. In P. Ordóñez de Pablos, J. Zhao, & R. Tennyson (Eds.), *Technology Enhanced Learning for People with Disabilities: Approaches and Applications* (pp. 34–43). Hershey, PA: IGI Global. doi:10.4018/978-1-61520-923-1.ch003

Zinger, D. (2016). Developing Instructional Leadership and Communication Skills through Online Professional Development: Focusing on Rural and Urban Principals. In A. Normore, L. Long, & M. Javidi (Eds.), *Handbook of Research on Effective Communication, Leadership, and Conflict Resolution* (pp. 354–370). Hershey, PA: IGI Global. doi:10.4018/978-1-4666-9970-0.ch019

Zutshi, A., Pogrebnaya, M., & Fermelis, J. (2014). Wellness Programs in Higher Education: An Australian Case. In N. Baporikar (Ed.), *Handbook of Research on Higher Education in the MENA Region: Policy and Practice* (pp. 391–419). Hershey, PA: IGI Global. doi:10.4018/978-1-4666-6198-1.ch017

About the Contributors

Jean-Eric Pelet holds a PhD in Marketing, an MBA in Information Systems and a BA (Hns) in Advertising. As an assistant professor in management, he works on problems concerning consumer behaviour when using a website or other information system (e-learning, knowledge management, e-commerce platforms), and how the interface can change that behavior. His main interest lies in the variables that enhance navigation in order to help people to be more efficient with these systems. He works as a visiting professor both in France and abroad (England, Switzerland) teaching e-marketing, ergonomics, usability, and consumer behaviour at Design Schools (Nantes), Business Schools (Paris, Reims), and Universities (Paris Dauphine – Nantes). Dr. Pelet has also actively participated in a number of European Community and National research projects. His current research interests focus on, social networks, interface design, and usability.

* * *

Francois Acquatella holds a PhD in Management Science at Télécom ParisTech. His research focuses on analysis of online training market, and specially on digital training platforms. His current research interests focus on the impact of artificial intelligence on platforms strategies. He published several articles on e-learning strategic management. He also teaches digital strategies.

Neeta Baporikar is currently Director/Professor (Business Management) at Harold Pupkewitz Graduate School of Business (HP-GSB), Namibia University of Science and Technology, Namibia. Prior to this she was Head-Scientific Research, with Ministry of Higher Education CAS-Salalah, Sultanate of Oman, Professor (Strategic Management and Entrepreneurship) at IIIT Pune and BITS India. With more than a decade of experience in industry, consultancy and training, she made a lateral switch to research and academics in 1995. Dr. Baporikar holds D.Sc. (Management Studies) USA, PhD in Management, University of Pune INDIA with MBA (Distinction) and Law (Hons.) degrees. Apart from this, she is also an External Reviewer, Oman Academic Accreditation Authority, Accredited Management Teacher, Qualified Trainer, Doctoral Guide and Board Member of Academics and Advisory Committee in accredited B-Schools. Reviewer for international journals, she has to her credit several conferred doctorates, several refereed research papers, and authored books in the area of Entrepreneurship, Strategy, Management and Higher Education.

Anna Liza Daunert is working as a research associate since April 2017 at the University of Mainz, Germany while writing her dissertation on „Measuring Teachers' Critical Thinking and Fostering it in their Work-Related Decision-Making and in Professional Learning". She also worked as a research associate with teaching load at the University of Paderborn, Germany from April 2011 until March 2017. Prior to that, she was a pre-school teacher, a private tutor, and a full-time instructor in both F2F and online sessions in the AMA Computer University in the Philippines. She earned her Bachelor's degree in Philosophy and Psychology and a Master's degree in Educational Foundations under the Division of Curriculum and Instruction from the University of the Philippines as well as a Master's degree in Educational Science in Instructional Design from the University of Freiburg, Germany.

Silvia Fat, PhD Degree in Education Sciences, thesis title: "Building professional identity of teachers. An ethno methodological perspective"; research experiences in developing educational studies and evaluative research in eLearning projects; participation in virtual community iTeach (http://iteach.ro/) and eLearning Romania (www.elearning.ro) by developing specialized articles and dissemination of project results; curriculum design competences, teaching strategies for implementing student-centered educational context; expert in education within several national and international projects; publications in ISI and BDI quoted journals.

Valérie Fernandez is a Professor in Management Science and Head of the Economic and Social Sciences department at Télécom ParisTech. In collaboration with industrial partners and international researchers, she examines companies' organizational transformations linked to digital technology. Her most recent work focused on managerial innovations regarding several crucial new forms of organization: open innovation, mobile work, virtualized professional worlds, and information system governance.

Thomas Houy is an Associate Professor in Management Science at Télécom ParisTech, where he teaches business strategy and entrepreneurship. His research investigates some generally accepted ideas surrounding digital start-ups. His books and articles offer results that are directly applicable by the entrepreneur community. He teaches at Paris-Dauphine University and at the École Nationale de la Statistique et de l'Administration Économique (ENSAE). He has founded several businesses and now offers coaching and mentoring to start-ups.

Xavier Inghilterra graduated from the University of Toulon as a Ph.D. in Information and Communication Sciences. Qualified as a senior lecturer in the 71th section of the National Council of Universities (CNU) in 2017, he currently teaches at the University of Lorraine (France) and has a researcher activity at the CREM (EA 3476). His research is focused on the effects of social sharing digital devices on the practices of collaboration, communication and mediation of students in context of distance learning.

Pedro Isaias is an Associate Professor at the Institute for Teaching and Learning Innovation (ITaLI), and an affiliated associate professor at the Business School, The University of Queensland, Australia. He teaches topics in Management Information Systems (MIS). He has a background in MIS. Currently he researches in learning technologies and also in e-Business.

Iulia Lazar Science and Environmental Engineering Habilitation Diploma; graduate of the University of Bucharest, Romania; fields of research of interest: natural science, use of new teaching technologies in teaching science; responsible and/or member of 11 research projects, won by international or national competition; publications in ISI and BDI quoted journals that have accumulated more than 300 citations, with a Hirsch index h = 6 (http://www.researcherid.com/rid/B-5974-2011).

Liliana Mâţă is Ph.D. in Educational Sciences and Associate Professor at Teacher Training Department of "Vasile Alecsandri" University of Bacău, Romania. She has published books, book chapters and articles in international journals on current issues in the domain of Educational Sciences: teacher training, curricular innovations, educational use of information technology. She also worked as a research expert, member and director in national and international research projects on current educational themes.

Paula Miranda holds a Ph.D. in Information Science and Technology from the ISCTE – University Institute of Lisbon. She is Auxiliary Professor in the Department of Informatics and Systems Engineering of the Setubal School of Technology, Polytechnic Institute of Setubal. Her areas of interest include Information Systems in general, Social Media, eLearning, more specifically the use of Web 2.0 and Web 3.0 technologies in learning environments and the integration of technology in education.

Georgeta Panisoara Science Education Habilitation Diploma; graduate of the University of Bucharest, Romania; fields of research of interest: educational psychology, psychology of learning, organizational and economic psychology, managerial psychology, applied organizational behavior, motivation and reward at work, recruitment and selection of personnel, psycho-emotional development of child and adolescent (in the past psychology of ages, education psychology), responsible in many research projects; publications in ISI and BDI quoted journals that have accumulated more than 250 citations, with a Hirsch index h = 8 calculated using data from Google Scholar.

Ion-Ovidiu Panisoara is Professor, director of the Department of Teacher Education from Faculty of Psychology and Educational Sciences. He coordinates PhDs in Education Sciences Domain at University of Bucharest, Romania. He participated as an expert at international and national seminars and conferences (as moderator, key-speaker and president). Also he is involved in research programs (as director, trainer and evaluator). He actively participates with written contributions and interviews to the academic press.

Sara Pífano is a Researcher at the Information Society Research Lab (ISRLab) where she conducts research on the broad field of the Information Society. She holds a PhD in Information Management from the Universidade Aberta (Portuguese Open University), a MA in Refugee Studies from City University (London, United Kingdom) and a Bachelor degree in International Relations from the University of Minho (Braga, Portugal). At the ISRLab, she is responsible for conducting and fostering scientific research, including the design, implementation and evaluation of research initiatives addressing the use of Web 2.0 in several domains of the information society, particularly education and business, the application of social media in the context of e-Learning, learning technologies, digital literacy, and online communities.

Linda Price is the Director of Academic and Organisational Development in the University of Bedfordshire. She is also a visiting Professor in Lund University in Sweden and in Kingston University, London. She previously worked at the Open University in various strategic leadership roles developing higher education agendas. Linda has over 28 years of experience in higher education in a range of national and international contexts. Her research investigates how organisations can holistically advance strategic university agendas through sustainable and appropriate uses of educational technology. Her research is distinguished by its strong synergistic and strategic approach to research and practice, traversing the fields of education and educational technology, research and scholarship. She has advised the Danish government on the future of higher education and has given numerous international keynotes on how to improve the quality of learning and teaching, supported by technology.

Miguel Sánchez-Acevedo is a professor at the Universidad de la Cañada where he is a faculty member since 2015. He is the Director of the businness incubator and Head of the Computing Degree. His areas of interest are: Collective Intelligence, 3D Modeling, Sensor Networks, Augmented Reality, Machine Learning, Distributed Computing, Big Data Analysis and Technology in Education.

Zdzisław Sroczyński is a graduate at the Faculty of Automatic Control, Electronics and Computer Science. He received Ph.D. degree in computer science in 2011 from Silesian University of Technology, Gliwice, Poland. Currently an assistant professor at the Faculty of Applied Mathematics of Silesian University of Technology. His scientific interest include image and natural language processing, human-computer interaction, multimedia systems, assistive technologies, e-learning, programming of mobile devices.

Joanna Zukowska is an Assistant Professor at the Institute Enterprise at Warsaw School of Economics. She holds International Coach Certificate in the scope of coaching, learning and development, issued by Edexcel and BTEC Professional Qualifications. She was conferred the CoachWise Certificate accredited with the International Coach Federation. The founder and tutor of Coaching Scientific Society. Head of Post-Graduation Studies of Academy of Professional Coach at Warsaw School of Economics. She specializes at HR management, marketing communication, coaching, creation of relationships with clients. She makes her core research in HRM area. She is specially interested in employees' evaluation theories and methods. She took part in scholarship at the University of Bologna in Italy and at Fordham University of New York City. She was the visiting professor in Toulouse Business School, ISCAP Porto, Vilnius Business School, Turku School of Economics, ISCTE Lisbon, Budapest Business School. The authoress of numerous scientific publications and researches on the above topics, lecturer at conferences and seminars.

Index

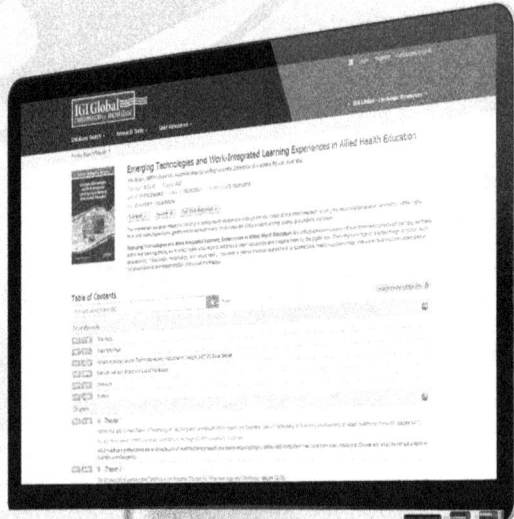

CPSIA information can be obtained
at www.ICGtesting.com
Printed in the USA
BVHW011700070219
539734BV00008B/152/P